IN SEARCH OF THE CRADLE OF CIVILIZATION

Praise for

IN SEARCH OF THE CRADLE OF CIVILIZATION

"This reinterpretation of humankind's early history has the most profound implications for our understanding of modern society and its problematic future. The issue of the true 'cradle of civilization' is of far more than academic importance; it is at the heart of our collective understanding of our roots and our apparent destiny. This is a tremendously important book—and 'a good read' as well. Feuerstein, Kak, and Frawley have performed a magnificent service toward our understanding of ourselves. I have unqualified praise for this important scholarly contribution."

—Willis Harman, President, Institute of Noetic Sciences

"In Search of the Cradle of Civilization *is obsessively readable and of tremendous importance, redating as it does the age of civilization by four thousand years."*

—Colin Wilson, author of *The Outsider, Religion and the Rebel*, and *The Mind Parasites*

"The authors have successfully unfolded the mystery of Indian cultural traditions to the eyes of Westerners and particularly the Indians who continue to see India through Western eyes."

—Dr. S. P. Gupta, chairman of the Indian Archaeological Society, New Delhi

"With ease and economy, this small volume pulls together a wide spectrum of research to dramatically redraw the contours of academic convention..."

—Robert Lawlor, author of *Voices of the First Day* and *Sacred Geometry*

"In Search of the Cradle of Civilization *dispenses with several jaded and time-worn academic myths about ancient India.... Moreover, this book is straightforward but nonetheless challenging in its careful presentation, long overdue, of the significance of ancient Indian civilization and culture for the study of world history."*

—Dr. Guy L. Beck, Department of Religious Studies, Loyola University of New Orleans, author of *Sonic Theology*

RUSSIA
AFGHANISTAN
IRAN
ARABIA
ARABIAN SEA
RICA

CHINA
TIBET
INDIA
BAY OF
BENGAL
INDIAN
OCEAN

IN SEARCH OF THE CRADLE OF CIVILIZATION

New Light on Ancient India

GEORG FEUERSTEIN,
SUBHASH KAK AND DAVID FRAWLEY

MOTILAL BANARSIDASS PUBLISHERS
PRIVATE LIMITED • DELHI

Reprint: Delhi, 2008
Second Revised Edition: Delhi, 2005
(The Edition reproduced from Quest Books, 2001 Edition)
First Edition: USA, 1995

ISBN: 978-81-208-1626-8 (Cloth)
ISBN: 978-81-208-2037-1 (Paper)

MOTILAL BANARSIDASS
41 U.A. Bungalow Road, Jawahar Nagar, Delhi 110 007
8 Mahalaxmi Chamber, 22 Bhulabhai Desai Road, Mumbai 400 026
203 Royapettah High Road, Mylapore, Chennai 600 004
236, 9th Main III Block, Jayanagar, Bangalore 560 011
Sanas Plaza, 1302 Baji Rao Road, Pune 411 002
8 Camac Street, Kolkata 700 017
Ashok Rajpath, Patna 800 004
Chowk, Varanasi 221 001

PRINTED IN INDIA
BY JAINENDRA PRAKASH JAIN AT SHRI JAINENDRA PRESS,
A-45 NARAINA, PHASE-I, NEW DELHI 110 028
AND PUBLISHED BY NARENDRA PRAKASH JAIN FOR
MOTILAL BANARSIDASS PUBLISHERS PRIVATE LIMITED,
BUNGALOW ROAD, DELHI 110 007

CONTENTS

PART ONE

Journeying Back in Time: An Eight-Thousand-Year Adventure

PART TWO

The Splendor of Ancient India: Its Cultural and Spiritual Legacy

ILLUSTRATIONS

Maps

Tables

Illustrations

INTRODUCTION TO THE SECOND EDITION

IN THE IMAGINATION OF THE WEST, INDIA IS THE LAND of magic and mystery, wisdom and religiosity, tradition and ritual. India has long held exotic appeal; its arts, literature, music are distinct. But, at the same time, there are aspects of Indic culture that speak straight to the heart of the West, which should not surprise us because India and the West have had a shared history going back many thousands of years.

Sanskrit is the oldest of any of the Indo-European languages. The ancient Vedic culture of India resembles the ancient European, particularly the Celtic, which had similar orders of priests and bards. The question of whether the Indic peoples and the Europeans shared the same homeland in remote antiquity has been the grist of ceaseless speculation. Today many Indians are still connected to the glorious past of their country, keeping alive an ancient stream of knowledge and wisdom. We may ask: Is India also a doorway to the long-forgotten past of the West?

Columbus set out to find a new sea route to India and ended up discovering America. Since then, the West and India have met in the realm of the mind. Thus, in the last century, Mohandas Gandhi's ideas influenced the human rights movement. Most recently, Hindu wisdom about Yoga, mind-body connection, and self-knowledge has swept the Western hemisphere. It appears that, by understanding the heart of India's great civilization, we are nearing the time when the quest of Columbus will be taken to its logical conclusion. Indic spirituality, which goes back to a distant past in unbroken sequence, holds a special fascination for Westerners. It is a spirituality that is universal and addresses the deepest questions of meaning and knowledge, and thus also speaks to humanity's innermost concerns in the present Age of Science.

The sages, philosophers, and mystics of India have held out a shining vision that has inspired the world in many ways. Some 2300 years ago, Alexander the Great brought yogis back to Greece with him, and Athens is said to have been visited by impressive *gymnosophistes*, naked wise men, from the Indian subcontinent. Indic elements have been detected in early Greek art. The influence of Eastern, notably Indic, teachings was so pervasive in ancient Greece that Diogenes Laërtius (3rd century A.D.) felt it necessary to determine whether Greek philosophy was of foreign origin or a product of native efforts. What is more, he was only one in a long line of discussants. Pythagoras (6th century B.C.), an early luminary of Mediterranean philosophizing, is increasingly acknowledged to have been a transmitter of knowledge and wisdom received from the East. This was already the view of his younger contemporary Philostratus. Hellenism is precisely the product of indigenous Greek thought and Eastern influences. Neoplatonism, which rose out of Hellenism, dominated the European worldview between the second and sixth centuries A.D., before the Christian scholastics ushered in an era of Aristotelian dominance that lasted until the sixteenth century and paved the way for modern science.

Long before the Greeks, however, we find Indic peoples in West Asia in the second millennium B.C., in the Kassite kingdom of Babylon and the Mitannis of Syria. The father of the famous Queen Nefertiti of Egypt was the Mitanni king Tushratha. It is quite conceivable that the religious traditions of West Asia preserve a remembrance of their Indic past.

Thus Indic thought transformed not only China and Southeast Asia through the export of Hindu and Buddhist teachings, but it also provided key impulses to Western thought. In this connection, let us also not forget that the modern mind was shaped after the West adopted two powerful ideas, which are integral to the Indic civilization: the idea of living in harmony with nature and the idea that reality has a scientific basis. In the past couple of centuries, these ideas and other India-derived notions have inspired many great scholars, scientists, and literary figures: Hegel, Fichte, Schlegel, Goethe, Nietzsche, Schopenhauer, Shelley, Wordsworth, Carlyle, Thoreau, Emerson, Tennyson, Yeats, A. E. Russell, Edwin Arnold, E. M. Forster, Blavatsky, Romain Rolland, Aldous Huxley, Christopher Isherwood, C. F. von Weizsäcker, Robert Oppenheimer, David Bohm, and others.

Possibly the most remarkable intellectual achievement of the twentieth century is quantum theory, which is at the basis of our understanding of chemistry, biology, and physics and consequently is at the basis of the astonishing technological advances witnessed during the past century. One of the two creators of this theory was Erwin Schrödinger. In an autobiographical essay, he explains that his discovery of quantum mechanics was an attempt to give form to the central notions of the nondualist philosophy of Vedanta. Thus, in this indirect sense, India has played a role in the birthing of quantum theory as well.

Quantum mechanics has led to an effective understanding of the world, leading to the creation of new machines and tools. Today humanity is facing the last frontier, namely the human mind. It is here that Indic ideas will possibly prove even more valuable and decisive.

Clearly, there are a number of reasons why we should be interested in India. Some relate to the origins of science and religion, others concern our yearning for knowledge of self and humanity's future destiny. The Indic culture area provides us with extensive material, across a very broad time span, that can help us understand the earliest history of ideas. The ancient Indic texts are layered in such a fashion that we can see the gradual development of mathematical, physical, linguistic, and psychological concepts. We find that their authors were deeply interested in cognitive science, in which they were so advanced that their insights may yet prove useful to modern science.

The scholarly understanding of the chronological framework of the Indic civilization has changed greatly in the last few years due to truly revolutionary discoveries in archaeology. The main archaeological periods are:

Rock Art Period	—	40,000 B.C. onwards to historical times
Indus-Sarasvati Tradition	—	8000 B.C. to 1300 B.C.
Early Harappan Period	—	3300 B.C. to 2600 B.C.
Mature Harappan Period	—	2600 B.C. to 1900 B.C.
Late Harappan Period	—	1900 B.C. to 1300 B.C.
Regionalization Period	—	1300 B.C. to 800 B.C.
Northern Black Polished Ware	—	800 B.C. to 500 B.C.

The earliest Indic art is preserved on rocks and dates from the Paleolithic, Mesolithic, and Neolithic periods. The beginnings of the rock art have been traced back to the decorated ostrich eggshells from Rajasthan, dated to around 40,000 B.C. by means of radiocarbon techniques. Subsequent phases have been determined on the basis of stylistic considerations and comparative radiocarbon dates.

For the Mesolithic period (12000-6000 B.C.), the rock sites are found distributed all over the country, although the most impressive sites are to be found in Madhya Pradesh. The earliest drawings of this tradition are characterized by dynamic action, vitality in form, and an acute insight into abstraction and visual perception.

A striking aspect of the early rock art is its drawing of tessellations, which show infinite repetition. This repetition may occur specific to a basic pattern or, more abstractly, the lines extend spatially in such a manner that a basic pattern is repeated in two directions. An understanding of this abstract concept must have been a part of the thought system of these early artists. This motif can be seen as being continuous with the central notion of infinity in later Indic thought. Also, a significant continuity of motif between the rock art and the art of the Indus-Sarasvati civilization (8000-1900 B.C.) has been found, indicating an unbroken link between this great urban culture and the Paleolithic and Mesolithic cultures of India.

According to the archaeological record, there is an unbroken tradition going back to about 8000 B.C. The earliest textual source is the *Rig-Veda,* which is a compilation of very ancient material. Astronomical references in this and other Vedic works recall events in the third to fifth millennium B.C. and earlier. The recent geological discovery that the Sarasvati, the preeminent river of Rig-Vedic times, went dry around 1900 B.C. as a result of tectonic upheavals implies that the *Rig-Veda* must be dated prior to this date. According to tradition, which scholars are finally beginning to take more seriously, the *Rig-Veda* is the creation of a period preceding 3100 B.C.

The Puranic genealogies start with mythical events, and the early Saptarshi calendar begins with the year 6676 B.C., which is understood to be the starting point of the royal genealogies; a later Saptarshi calendar, still in use in different parts of the India, begins with 3076 B.C. Other old calendars are Kaliyuga (3102 B.C.), Vikrama (58 B.C.), and Shaka (78 A.D.). The Bharata War marks an epochal crisis in ancient Indic society. Later astronomers assigned it to 3137 B.C., 2449 B.C., or 1924 B.C. The main actors of this War belong to generation number 94 in a list that is supposed to commence with 6676 B.C. If a generation is reckoned as spanning 25 years, we arrive at 3326 B.C. Underwater archaeology has found evidence of a submerged city identified as Dvaraka, the hometown of Krishna, one of the main actors in the Bharata War. The city has been dated back to about 1500 B.C., thus offering yet another date for the war. In any case, native Indic historical traditions, which once seemed fantastic, have become more plausible, and Western scholars are beginning to revise their historical reconstructions.

Since the first edition of the present book, considerable new evidence has come in that further supports our original conclusions. Scholars now trace the antecedents of writing in India to 3300 B.C., that is, as early as in Sumer and Egypt. Significant new sites relating to Indian antiquity have been discovered, such as the great city of Dholavira in Gujarat, one of the largest ports in the ancient world. Excavation has started in Rakhigarhi west of Delhi, a city that was considerably larger than Mohenjodaro and Harappa and at least as old. Ancient sites have recently been found in the east of India as far as Lucknow. Geologists in India have done numerous studies verifying the course of the Sarasvati River and the civilization along it and have produced an entire tome on it. New biological evidence suggests that the Indian population has lived in the peninsula for at least 50,000 years. The analysis of the genetic evidence suggests that the splitting up of the Indic and the European people took place as long as 9000 years ago. Meanwhile no solid evidence of any migration, much less invasion of populations from Central Asia into India, has yet to be found.

India has emerged as the oldest continuous civilization on Earth, which continues to fertilize the West with its profound spirituality. Today an estimated 20 million Americans are practicing Yoga. Even though most of them are interested in Yoga only as a system of health and fitness, they are indirectly exposed also to its deeper aspects. The old adage *ex oriente lux* still applies.

The Authors

NOTE

See T. Kivisild et. al., "Deep common ancestry of Indian western-Eurasian mitochondrial DNA lineages," *Current Biology* 9:22 (1999): 1331-1334.

REFERENCES

Feuerstein, G. *The Yoga Tradition*. Prescott, AZ: Hohm Press, 1998.

Frawley, D. *Yoga and Ayurveda: Self-healing and Self-realization*. Twin Lakes, WI: Lotus Press, 1999.

Kenoyer, J. M. *Ancient Cities of the Indus Valley Civilization*. Oxford: Oxford University Press, 1988.

Lal, B. B. *The Earliest Civilization of South Asia*. New Delhi: Aryan Books International, 1997.

Lorblanchet, M., ed. *Rock Art in the Old World*. New Delhi: Indira Gandhi National Centre for the Arts, 1992.

Napier, A. *Foreign Bodies: Performance, Art, and Symbolic Anthropology*. Berkeley, CA: University of California Press, 1992.

Rao, T. R. N., and S. Kak. *Computing Science in Ancient India*. Lafayette, LA: USL Press, 1998; Delhi: Munshiram Manoharlal, 2000.

PREFACE

THIS IS A BOOK ABOUT HISTORY—NOT THE KIND OF dull chronology of dynasties and battles to which we were exposed in our school days but *meaningful* history that is deeply relevant to our lives today. It is about the human spirit struggling for self-expression and self-understanding, which is a struggle that continues to this day, perhaps more so than ever.

We live in an age of unprecedented challenges and opportunities. On the one hand, we face the grim reality of overpopulation, hunger, ecological disasters, and new devastating diseases, as well as the ever-present possibility of a nuclear holocaust. On the other hand, science constantly expands our intellectual horizon and helps create new technological wonders that, we hope, will solve some of our problems. Biologists are "engineering" genes to increase the productivity of vegetables and fruit trees; chemists are unlocking enzymes to make them usable for nonbiological purposes, such as waste disposal, or to repair DNA in order to enhance and prolong life; and physicists are working on superconductivity and the use of lasers in computers. Scientists are also exploring the possibility of bionic organs, the application of electromagnetic fields in the healing process, and artificial intelligence. The list could easily be extended to fill the remaining pages of this book.

Every day science adds a profusion of knowledge to our data banks. Yet only a fraction of this knowledge finds its way into our brains, and only a small proportion of that fraction is truly assimilated by us. Indeed, the knowledge explosion is one of the problems we are facing. Like any explosion, it leaves us with fragments. Even specialists are no longer able to keep abreast of the developments in their own discipline. They know less and less about more and more. With around 7,000 scientific papers written every day in the English language alone, how could any one person be expected to follow, never mind catch up with, the ever-receding horizon of scientific exploration?

The lay public is even less able to keep up with, or make sense of, scientific knowledge. There is a significant time lag of approximately twenty-five years between a scientific discovery and its assimilation by the public at large. In other words, what scientists are investigating today will not be common knowledge until our children are young adults and perhaps have children of their own. Our school books are outdated, and even university textbooks tend to reflect only "well-established" knowledge. Facts and hypotheses that do not readily fit into the current way of thinking—the reigning paradigm—are generally ignored, if not suppressed. When it comes to pet theories and cherished opinions, scientists are as human as anyone else. This is true whether we are considering physics, chemistry, astronomy, archaeology, or historiography (the description of history).

The alarming truth is that we have no firm grasp on what all the information produced by science means. We are unable to understand the interconnection between the amassed facts and figures. Our so-called Information Age is rich in data but sadly lacking in understanding. Generalists—scientists or scholars who attempt to see the larger picture—are few and far between, because they are generally not encouraged by the academic establishment. Hence we are left with bits and pieces that seldom fit together, giving rise to anxiety rather than understanding.

And yet, in order to live meaningful and happy lives, we must be whole not only in our bodies but also in our hearts and minds. This means we must have a viable vision to live by. Yet science, which for many people has replaced religion and to which all of us to one degree or another look for guidance, offers us no overarching synthesis of knowledge. Therefore, our modern civilization as a whole is comparable to a rudderless ship. We have no shared vision, and, as the biblical proverb says, "Where there is no vision, the people perish."

As many clear-sighted observers of the human drama have noted, our era is short in vision and wisdom. It is therefore not surprising that many of us are wondering about bygone ages and past civilizations. How did they meet life's challenges? How did they view Nature? What trials and tribulations shaped their experience of the world? How did they meet the great natural catastrophes—earthquakes and volcanic eruptions—that we know afflicted humankind throughout its civilized history? How did they use their knowledge? Did they have true wisdom? For what reasons did civilizations like Sumer, Babylonia, Assyria, Dilmun, Elam and, not least, pharaonic Egypt become extinct? What errors of judgment did our distant ancestors commit? How did they fail to adapt successfully to the changing conditions in the world? To be sure, many ancient cultures looked nostalgically back at a Golden Age when peace and harmony reigned in the world, while their own times were frequently marked by political turbulence and cultural upheaval. Was there such a Golden Age? Has any of its wisdom survived? How has the torch of human understanding been passed from one age to the next? What has been lost in the process of spanning millennia? Can we learn any lessons from the thin strands of tradition that withstood the attrition of time?

Questions like these, which concern the value of what may have been lost, are not asked by mainstream historians because, like their colleagues in physics or chemistry, they chase the mirage of a value-free science. In real life, however, facts and values are inextricably interlinked. By ignoring this circumstance, scientists merely squeeze the lifeblood out of reality, making it into an abstraction that cannot give us meaningful guidance.

In this book we are trying to answer some of these questions in regard to a civilization that has a very special place in the story of human cultural evolution and that nonetheless is barely known. Ever since Napoleon's days, we in the West have been dazzled by the splendor of pharaonic Egypt—with its impressive pyramids, the mysterious Sphinx, and the magnificent treasures of Tutankhamen. We also have been impressed with the intellectual achievements of the learned elite of Sumer, which, according to our schoolbooks, was responsible for the invention of writing, the potter's wheel, wheeled carts, cylinder seals, cosmology, formal law, and bicameral political congress.

Most of the "first time ever" claims made for the Sumerians have in recent years been exposed as exaggerated or absurd. There is mounting evidence that neither Sumer nor Egypt quite deserve the pride of place among the ancient civilizations. Rather the cradle of civilization appears to lie beyond the fertile valleys of the Nile, Tigris, and Euphrates Rivers. We invite the reader to join us in a journey of discovery, which in its implications, seems far more thrilling to us than the discoveries of Troy, the Elamite civilization in Iran, the "lost" civilization of Dilmun on the island of Bahrain in the Arabian/Persian Gulf or, most recently, the discovery of what may have been the kingdom of Sheba in the extreme south of the Arabian peninsula.

As we will show, India is the giant that looms behind these early urban cultures. This astonishing finding completely revolutionizes our understanding of ancient history. It challenges us anew to look for the cradle of human civilization. We do not claim to have solved the riddle of the Big Bang of our civilized universe, merely that we are possibly closer to it than ever before. In this book we introduce exciting new evidence that sheds light on a hitherto obscure phase of ancient history. We believe the recent findings are significantly narrowing the gap between the early Neolithic civilizations and the end of the Ice Age and its Paleolithic cultures.

This is the first time that these amazing developments in archaeology and history are reviewed in a comprehensive and comprehensible fashion. Why has it taken so long to recognize the significance of ancient India in the saga of human civilization? In his book *Looking for Dilmun*, Geoffrey Bibby rightly remarked that the "Indus Valley civilization is the Cinderella of the ancient world."[1] Indeed, for a variety of reasons, ancient India has been sorely neglected by archaeologists and historians. Prevailing misconceptions and biases have long hampered the study of ancient India's civilization. Fortunately this regrettable situation is beginning to change, and the new attitude in scholarly circles has already proven enormously productive. Quite likely, the recent successes in reinterpreting ancient India's civilization will further speed up this promising process of revisioning ancient history that a handful of daring historians and archaeologists have begun.

As we have indicated, we believe that all this is not merely of theoretical interest. Our understanding of history can prove crucial to how we interpret life in the present. Of course, cynics hold that we

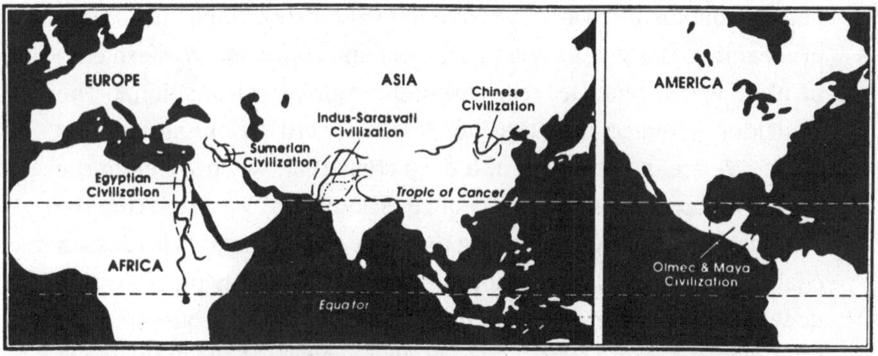

MAP 1. ***All the early civilizations arose close to the Tropic of Cancer.***

can learn only one lesson from history: that humanity so far has learned nothing from it. Sadly enough, there is some substance to this claim. But this pessimistic view does not penetrate deep enough. For we must not overlook the fact that it is precisely our awareness of the past, especially our errors, that has guaranteed humanity's continued existence to date. Our species would have become extinct long ago if we had not learned anything at all from our mistakes.

We know that entire civilizations have perished, but there always have been survivors to tell the story and to resume the human experiment. But this time around we are facing the unbelievable danger of there not being a single survivor on this planet. Unlike past civilizations, which were relatively local societies, our own civilization has spread itself across the entire planet. The ecological imbalance triggered by our unwise way of life affects not only one region or continent, but every living organism on Earth. A nuclear holocaust or global ecological catastrophe could bring modern civilization perilously close to extinction. This makes it all the more pressing to understand our species' past and benefit from the experience and hard-won knowledge of our ancestors. While the present-day challenge is unique in its magnitude, it involves fundamental matters of living—particularly in the moral and spiritual realm—that may well have been better understood by earlier civilizations and cultures.

Clearly we moderns are in a quandary. We have effectively departed from the old ways but have not yet created viable new forms of meaning. Many of us feel utterly lost and confused. Western civilization, whose tentacles reach around the globe, is transitional. The transition is radical and decisive. Another word for our situation is *crisis*. We are in the throes of a deep crisis that, when we go to the root of our problems, is a crisis of consciousness. We are facing the considerable challenge of having to evolve into planetary citizens—a challenge that calls for conscious choice and commitment. We would do well to ponder the wisdom of the ancients, who had to pass through their own crises and formulate their own answers to the problems of existence. We must not expect that all their answers or solutions will apply to our present-day situation. However, we can expect that some of our ancestors' more important answers—their wisdom distilled in the crucible of life—will have a bearing on our own dilemma.

Ancient India, we feel, has much to teach us.

ACKNOWLEDGMENTS

MANY INDIVIDUALS HAVE HELPED IN THE COURSE OF OUR respective investigations both during the preparation of the manuscript and leading up to it—from friends and colleagues to librarians. Our gratitude goes out to all of them. We would, however, like to single out several persons who have contributed significantly to our project: Prof. Seshagiri Rao for his warm moral support of our work; Dr. S. P. Gupta for providing most of the photographs of the artifacts of the Indus-Sarasvati civilization; Jan Fairservis for willingly giving us permission to reproduce her captivating drawings of Indus seals; Shri Palaniswami, Shri Kathirswami, and the rest of the staff of *Hinduism Today* for generously retrieving illustrations from their archives and going beyond the call of duty; Matthew Greenblatt, editor of *Inner Directions* magazine, for kindly sharing with us his photographs of yogis and Indian temples; Rosemary Clark for rushing her photo of the Sphinx to us; Harry Hicks, of the Foundation for Cultural Preservation, for permission to reproduce his photograph of the Vasishtha Head; Ray Grasse, for his unfailing practical help; Trisha Lamb Feuerstein for her editorial magic in getting the manuscript to the publisher in the best possible shape and also for compiling the index; Mary Holden for her fine copyediting work; Beth Hansen for creating the book's beautiful design and responding patiently to the authors' wishes; and not least Brenda Rosen, Quest Books' dynamic executive editor, for her farsighted initiative in proposing a comprehensive restructuring of the contents of the book, which has led to a far more viable and readable version, and also for giving us the greatest possible latitude in collaborating on the book's design and production.

Existence or nonexistence was not then. The bright region was not, nor the space (vyoman) that is beyond. What encompassed? Where? Under whose protection? What water was there—deep, unfathomable?

Death or immortality was not then. There was no distinction between night and day. That One breathed, windless, by itself. Other than that there was nothing beyond.

In the beginning there was darkness concealed by darkness. All this was water without distinction. The One that was covered by voidness emerged through the might of the heat-of-austerity.

In the beginning, desire, the first seed of mind, arose in That. Poet-seers, searching in their heart with wisdom, found the bond of existence in nonexistence.

Their [visions'] ray stretched across [existence and nonexistence]. Perhaps there was a below; perhaps there was an above. There were givers of seed; there were powers: effort below, self-giving above.

Who knows the truth? Who here will pronounce it whence this birth, whence this creation? The Gods appeared afterward, with the creation of this [world]. Who then knows whence it arose?

Whence this creation arose, whether it created itself or whether it did not? He who looks upon it from the highest space, he surely knows. Or maybe He knows not.

Rig-Veda *X.129.1-7*

PART ONE

Journeying Back in Time: A Ten-Thousand-Year Adventure

CHAPTER 1

Revisioning the Past, Envisioning the Future

Lifting the Veil of the Past

WHAT WE CALL HISTORY IS A PALE RECONSTRUCTION of the actual events of the past. We make models of what we think happened, and frequently we confuse our models with reality. The fact is that our models, particularly those concerning the remote past, are no more accurate than a papier-mâché model of a jet engine. We have the rough outlines but lack insight into the essentials. This statement becomes truer the farther back we go in time.

The trouble is that the less we really know, the more we want certainty, and so historians have been busily constructing their own versions of history. Since most historians are employed by academic institutions, they must ensure that their particular version does not stray too far from the accepted norm, lest they find themselves under attack or out of a job. Often this felt need to safeguard their reputation obliges professional historians and archaeologists to ignore evidence and offhandedly dismiss theories that do not fit readily into the prevailing framework of explanations. Existing paradigms are generally rocked only when this ill-fitting evidence becomes so mountainous that it can no longer be swept under the carpet of complacency.

In his widely acclaimed book *The Structure of Scientific Revolutions*, philosopher Thomas S. Kuhn has described some of the ways in which reigning scientific paradigms collapse and make room for new paradigms, seldom without fierce struggle within the scientific community.[1] A paradigm shift, as Kuhn recognized, demands a shift of vision. This amounts to a cognitive revolution that radically alters one's point of view. This is seldom an easy task because scientists, like anyone else, have a lot at stake in adopting or abandoning a particular point of view.

To lift the veil of the past, we must first lift the veil of our own minds. Our preconceptions tend to cloud our perceptions. We can see clearly only when we are willing to suspend our judgment and, as much as humanly possible, allow the evidence to speak for itself. Above all, we must be prepared to reexamine our theories when we encounter a sufficient number of anomalous or ill-fitting facts.

The Lesson of the Sphinx

We believe that the anomalous evidence for ancient India has reached such a critical mass and that we are on the threshold of a new understanding of the early Indic civilization. Significantly enough, the new understanding chronicled in the present book is paralleled by similar revisions in the study of other Neolithic civilizations, notably the Egyptian and the Mayan, which can serve as useful comparisons.

In his widely read book *Serpent in the Sky*, John Anthony West seriously challenges Egyptologists when he invokes a single, if extraordinary, piece of geological evidence to call into question the conventional date for the Sphinx.[2] This mysterious sculpture, carved out of living rock, has long fascinated and puzzled pilgrims and travelers to Egypt and numerous others who have seen it captured in drawings, paintings, photographs, or films.

In his influential memoirs entitled *Description of Egypt*, Benoît de Maillet, who was the French consul-general in Egypt under Louis XIV, described the Sphinx as "a woman's head grafted on to a lion's body."[3] He speculated that it might represent a three-dimensional combination of the astrological signs of Virgo and Leo. Since astrology/astronomy was one of the most important crafts or sciences of antiquity and is among the oldest intellectual preoccupations, his speculation may not be too far off the mark.

However, the face of the Sphinx is so badly mutilated that it is difficult to tell whether it represents a woman or a man. The archaeological establishment considers the Sphinx to be a likeness of its creator, or sponsor, the fourth-dynasty pharaoh Chephren (Khaufre). He is thought to have lived around 2700 B.C. and is also held responsible for the building of the second pyramid at Giza.

FIG. 1. ***The Sphinx's timeless gaze is in the direction of the rising sun.***

Today the Sphinx is severely damaged from weather and the barbaric habit of the eighteenth-century Mamelukes of using this time-honored work of art as an artillery target. Nevertheless, standing sixty-six feet tall, the Sphinx—half human, half lion—still commands our respect and admiration, and we can only guess at the awe pious pilgrims of bygone ages must have felt in front of this towering sacred image.

West got the clue for his book on the Sphinx from the Alsatian scholar R. A. Schwaller de Lubicz, whose symbological or "symbolist" studies we will have occasion to mention shortly. He was the first to notice that the erosion damage on the body of the Sphinx was due not to the action of wind and sand, as commonly believed, but to water. The difficulty surrounding this finding is that the last severe flooding of the Giza Plateau is thought to have occurred around 10,000 B.C. when the huge Sahara Desert was still fertile land.

In 1991, a small team consisting of three geologists, a geophysicist, and an oceanographer organized by West studied this problem on location. The investigators concluded that the erosion damage to the Sphinx was indeed from water, but from precipitation and running water rather than from a huge flood. The geological report favors a construction date for the Sphinx between 5000 B.C. and 7000 B.C. West, however, has continued to champion an earlier date, connecting the damage to the Sphinx with the melting of the glaciers at the end of the last Ice Age. Even the more conservative date of 5000 B.C. makes the Sphinx over two thousand years older than mainstream archaeology assumes.

We must note here that there are considerable problems with pharaonic chronology in general. The dates given by Egyptologists for Menes, who unified the upper and the lower kingdoms and thereby inaugurated the first dynasty, range from 5867 B.C. (Jean F. Champollion, who deciphered the famous Rosetta Stone) to 2224 B.C. (Edward H. Palmer)—a difference of 2,500 years. Sir Flinders Petrie, who almost single-handedly invented Egyptology, proposed 5546 B.C. as the date of Egypt's political unification. The well-known Egyptologist James Henry Breasted placed Menes at around 3400 B.C., whereas the consensus of recent scholarly opinion favors 2900 B.C.

The chronology of predynastic Egypt is similarly bedeviled with difficulties. It is now generally thought to extend from around 5000 B.C. to 3000 B.C. As the British archaeologist Michael Rice has shown in his fine book *Egypt's Making*, the predynastic Egyptians may have had contact with, and even have been greatly inspired by, the Sumerians.[4] There certainly are many fascinating similarities in symbolism and artistic expression between these two peoples. However, this is an area still awaiting thorough exploration. The question of who built the Sphinx remains unanswered, as does the related question of what it symbolizes.

In seeking to refute current archaeological thinking about the Sphinx, West relies on a single geological feature. Understandably, most Egyptologists have been less than accepting of his redating of this monument, hoping that some other explanation can be found for the strange marks of erosion.

By contrast, in our own case, we are not dealing with merely a single piece of evidence; rather the facts have been piling up to such an extent that the old theory about ancient India has simply collapsed. The only problem is that few scholars are aware of all the new evidence. We hope that our book—though written for a nonspecialist audience—will fall into their hands as well and entice them to look at the available evidence anew. So often Indologists (specialists on India's culture) simply reiterate the consensus understanding, without themselves checking the primary material or at least secondary sources. Paul W. Lapp, who is an archaeologist and Old Testament specialist, made these pertinent comments about historical sources:

> *The dreary days of plodding are punctuated by new discoveries, fresh insights. The sources prove true to their name. They are sources of new ideas; without them the past would be lost and a depth dimension of life missing. They may seem an arid desert, and the historian is often wearied by the journey. At the end is an oasis, a spring, a source—refreshment for the human spirit as it presses forward on the endless path toward self-understanding.*[5]

Lapp further remarked that in addition to primary and secondary sources, there is a third essential source in the creation of history, which is the historian himself or herself. He or she must have a fertile mind and the ability for disciplined and lucid thinking (and writing). More than that, however, the historian must be willing to live with ambiguity and mystery, for the past can never be completely known. Therefore, we must approach it not only with a high measure of openness (to take in as much as we can) but also an equal measure of modesty and self-honesty (to accept that our understanding is bound to remain incomplete and subject to correction in the future). In practice, historians tend to present their historical reconstructions as final solutions. As Lapp observed:

> *This belief of the historian that he can construct a historical framework and write a historical work borders on the paradoxical or the absurd.*[6]

But the historian's task is an activity, as Lapp rightly pointed out, by which we enhance our own humanity, for writing history asserts our faith in ourselves and in the meaningfulness of our existence. In reading history, we affirm the same faith.

A Lesson from Mesoamerica

To give another example of recent efforts at revisioning ancient history, we can refer to the enigmatic Maya civilization. But first some background. Orthodox theory has it that the New World was first populated toward the end of the Ice Age, when roving bands of Asiatic peoples crossed over the Bering Straits land bridge, which now is under 140 feet of water. These nomads then spread fairly rapidly across North America and, by around 9000 B.C., had reached the windswept southern tip of South America.

This official version of history, which is still repeated in many publications, has in recent decades been challenged by a number of important archaeological finds that show the presence of early humanity in the New World long before the melting of the glaciers around 10,000 B.C. Migrants from Asia could have arrived 30,000 and even 40,000 years ago, when sea levels also were low enough to free up the narrow strip of land that connects North America to Siberia. Some researchers, including the world-renowned paleontologist Louis Leakey, believe they have found traces of a much earlier occupation, though the evidence is considered highly controversial. At any rate, archaeological dates have been systematically pushed back in recent years for a variety of cultures.

This also applies to the people known as the Maya, who occupied—and still occupy—the large area of what are now Mexico, Honduras, Belize, Guatemala, and El Salvador. Not too long ago the Maya were thought to have emerged from sheer barbarism as late as the first or second century A.D. Then the Olmec civilization, best known for its creation of colossal basalt heads six to nine feet high in the Mexican states of Tabasco and Veracruz at the Gulf of Mexico, was discovered. As Jacques Soustelle, a professor of anthropology, prehistory, and ethnology at the prestigious French Centre National du Recherche Scientifique, wrote:

Their sudden appearance on the scene in Mesoamerican antiquity had the same effect as one of those devastating hurricanes that their region sometimes undergoes: the accepted schemas suddenly collapsed, and it was necessary to revise them, to think them through again from the ground up—not without reluctance. The entire familiar panorama, with every detail seemingly in its proper place, was thrown into chaos. It is not surprising that many controversies shook the scholarly world before the facts compelled recognition. Today no one doubts that Olmec civilization reaches far back into antiquity.[7]

FIG. 2. ***The Temple of the Magician at Uxmal, Yucatan, the only ovoid Mayan pyramid.***

The beginnings of the Olmec civilization, which belongs to the Mayan world, have been dated back to at least 1500 B.C. Today, archaeologists very confidently affirm the presence of human beings in Mesoamerica by at least 20,000 B.C., and they also assign the beginnings of Mayan culture to the third millennium B.C.. The earliest Maya tribes, who made pottery and cultivated maize, are thought to have arrived in the highlands of Guatemala around 2500 B.C., though it is not known from where. During the classical period (now reckoned between 200 A.D. and 900 A.D.), the Maya became the only other civilization apart from the Egyptians to construct true pyramids.

Speculations about the origin and reason for these temple pyramids abound. Particularly the so-called Sun and Moon pyramids of Teotihuacan near Mexico City have stirred the imagination of professionals and would-be professionals alike. A readable historical review of the more controversial speculations and historical reconstructions was provided by Peter Tompkins in his popular book *Mysteries of the Mexican Pyramids*.[8] Specialists are slowly beginning to take a new look at some of the evidence that has been discarded or suppressed by mainstream archaeology and Mayan studies.

The Recovery of Symbolism

It appears that both paleontology and archaeology are consistently pushing back their chronologies, revealing earlier and earlier beginnings for specific cultural features or whole civilizations. There is also a slow but significant change in the way we think about our ancestors. We are beginning to appreciate that they were no mere primitives but had a sophisticated understanding of the world that, in some respects, exceeds our own. In particular, their knowledge of the symbolic (analogical rather than logical) connection between things—including both mathematics and astronomy/astrology—was superior to our own. As we are gradually discovering, such knowledge is important to our survival, because it discloses to us the deeper harmony of existence, the geometry of the sacred. Without it, we are spiritually and morally adrift.

In suggesting water as the cause of the Sphinx's worst erosion, De Lubicz demonstrated acute perception, which effectively corrected two hundred years of scholarly myopia. De Lubicz's overwhelming originality emanates from every page of his monumental work *Le Temple de l'Homme*, which was first published in 1957. He showed, among other things, that the striking asymmetry of the Temple of Luxor in Upper Egypt encodes the ancient Egyptians' notion of the Cosmic Man, the Macranthropos. It contains significant symbolic ratios, which include the fundamental mathematical coefficients *pi* (the ratio of a circle to its diameter) and *phi* (the Golden Section, the ratio 1.6180339. . . , arrived at by dividing a line in such a way that the smaller portion is to the larger as the larger is to the whole).

The Temple of Luxor was erected during the New Kingdom, more specifically the eighteenth dynasty, comprising fourteen pharaohs, including Tutankhamen. However, the symbolic knowledge encapsulated in the temple's design is unquestionably much older. "In Egypt," writes West, "symbolism was a precise science." He also noted that symbolism was "perhaps the single most pervasive and striking feature of its civilisation."[9] What holds true of Egypt also holds true of the other ancient civilizations, including India.

Symbological research on ancient civilizations, which were very sensitive to the correspondences between "above" (divine order) and "below" (human order), has found adherents in disciplines other than Egyptology. In her work *The Hindu Temple*, published in 1946, the renowned American scholar Stella Kramrisch explored the symbolic dimension of temple building in India.[10] She too found a strong correlation between architectural proportions, mathematics, and cosmology.

In the field of Mayan studies, the ground-breaking works of Linda Schele, David Freidel, Joy Parker, and Mary Ellen Miller are particularly characteristic of the new approach.[11] These and other studies bear witness to the ingenuity of the ancients and their passion for preserving the sacred order in their cultural creations. Whether we are probing into the civilization of the Maya, the Egyptians, the Sumerians, the Chinese, or the Indians, we encounter a worldview and ethos that is suffused with a deep symbolism in which Heaven and Earth are connected through multiple correlations.

In this book, we will focus on the symbolic dimension of the Indic civilization, with occasional side glances at the other great civilizations of antiquity. Our principal sources will be of two kinds, archaeological and literary. Each source sheds its own light on the past, throwing into relief different features. We need both sources to obtain a fuller view and understanding.

India has no imposing pyramids, no mysterious Sphinx, no massive four-thousand-year-old stone temples, and no prolific inscriptions on temple walls complete with colorful illustrations. Its artifacts may be less spectacular than those of Egypt or the Maya kingdoms, but they are no less important. Moreover, its potential for yielding many more significant artifacts is great. For, as we will show, archaeologists have dug perhaps not in the wrong places but outside the heartland of the ancient Indic civilization. We cannot know what treasures lie buried beneath the numerous mounds of the vast Thar Desert until archaeologists start to dig there.

What is certain is that the Indic civilization is incredibly complex, while our historical models are necessarily simple, if not simplistic. As the great British historian Arnold Toynbee observed, "India is a whole world in herself: she is a society of the same magnitude as our Western society."[12] We must begin to appreciate this fact. What is more, India antedates European (or Western) civilization by thousands of years and is in fact the oldest known continuous civilization on Earth. Pharaonic Egypt and Sumer are long gone, and the modern Maya know almost nothing about their ancient heritage, having been forcibly converted to Christianity by the Spaniards in the sixteenth century. Even China, once praised as the oldest civilization on Earth, started little before 2500 B.C.

In our quest for the cradle of civilization, we must properly grasp India's place in the scheme of things. This is the challenge tackled by this book.

CHAPTER 2

The Vedas: *Pyramids of the Spirit*

The Buried Treasure of the Sacred Canon of the Hindus

IN THE PREVIOUS CHAPTER, WE INTRODUCED THE IDEA of historical sources and indicated that in our presentation we would be resorting to both archaeological and literary sources. We begin with the latter because they were the first to strike Western scholars in their endeavor to understand the Indic civilization. Ever since the British Raj, India's past has preoccupied a small group of specialists eager to trace modern Hinduism—the main cultural tradition of India—back to its roots.

The beginnings of Indology—the study of India's culture—are rather prosaic. In order to govern their Hindu subjects successfully, the British overlords were eager to become acquainted with the indigenous worldview and so they encouraged the study of Sanskrit and Sanskrit literature. As Sir Monier Monier-Williams, one of the pioneers of Indological research, put it toward the end of the nineteenth century:

> *To know the Hindus, to understand their past and present condition, to reach their very heart and soul, we must study Sanskrit literature. It is, in truth, even more to India than classical and patristic literature was to Europe at the time of the Reformation. It gives a deeper impress to the Hindu mind,*

so that every Hindu, however unlettered, is unconsciously affected by it.[1]

Sanskrit was and still is the lingua franca of the educated priestly elite, the brahmins, and the great sacred scriptures of Hinduism are written in this ancient language. The very first Sanskrit text to be translated into English—in 1785—was the *Bhagavad-Gita* ("Lord's Song"), which has been compared to the New Testament. Although it does not officially belong to the sacred canon of Hinduism, this scripture is held in high esteem and is widely regarded as an honorary member of the sacred corpus.[2] It is a didactic poem in which the God-man Krishna instructs his royal disciple Prince Arjuna in spiritual matters on the eve of the greatest war fought on Indian soil in antiquity.

Scholars recognized right away that this immensely popular work, which is frequently cited and recited by brahmins and educated Hindus, belongs to an early phase in the evolution of Hinduism. Significantly, the *Bhagavad-Gita* itself refers back to a still more ancient period, which produced the source scriptures of the sacred canon, the four Vedic hymnodies. Scholars were understandably eager to procure a copy of this canonical quartet. However, for a period the brahmin custodians of the sacred Sanskrit literature refused to share the four *Vedas* with inquisitive Western researchers. When they finally did, it turned out that, although they could faultlessly recite the Vedic hymns, they were rather ignorant of the meaning of the thousands of verses flowing smoothly from their tongues. In fact, it was Western scholarship in partnership with India's pundits that opened up the *Vedas* not only for Westerners but for the Indians themselves. Today Vedic research is an important, if still curiously neglected branch, of Indology.

Being the fountainhead of Hinduism and Indian culture in general, the four *Vedas* are, as can be expected, of the utmost importance to historians. Yet, surprisingly, their significance as historical documents has generally been underplayed.[3] Scholars have chosen to see in them literary creations of little more than mythological and theological relevance. This attitude parallels the attitude displayed toward the Bible prior to the revolutionary archaeological discoveries in the Middle East during the latter part of the nineteenth century. Excavations in Mesopotamia, Palestine, and Egypt gave substance to many of the people, places, and events chronicled in the Bible that had until then been dismissed as merely legendary. As the German writer Werner Keller noted in *The Bible As History*, which has sold more than ten million copies and been translated into twenty-four languages:

> *Often the results of investigation correspond in detail with the Biblical narratives. They do not only confirm them, but also illumine the historical situations out of which the Old Testament and the Gospels grew.*[4]

While not everything in the biblical narratives has been confirmed by archaeology, the correlation between scriptural testimony and artifactual evidence has been astounding. Today biblical archaeology is a scientific discipline in its own right, continuing to shed light on the Bible as a historical document.

Unlike the Bible, the *Vedas* are poor in the kind of information that could be translated into a historical context, such as the migration of tribes, succession of rulers, or wars. Their wealth lies in the domain of theology and mythology. In this respect, the *Vedas* are similar to the Homeric epics, which nevertheless led Heinrich Schliemann to the discovery of Agamemnon's Troy. The *Vedas* are likewise not entirely mute when it comes to historically relevant data. We will show in later chapters how the names of rivers, geographical descriptions, and especially astronomical information in the Vedic hymns contain very important clues for historians. Clearly, behind the sacred utterances of the *Vedas* was a real world. The reluctance among scholars to make proper use of the *Vedas*, in our view, is connected with a prevailing prejudice that regards these texts as unhistorical sacred tradition.

In the face of the archaeological surprises during the past 150 years or so, which have brought to light the worlds behind such great literary creations as the Bible, the *Iliad* and the *Odyssey*, as well as the Arthurian legends and the *Popol Vuh* ("Communal Book") of the Quiché Maya of Guatemala, we should not be too pessimistic about the historical basis and value of the *Vedas* either. On the contrary, the information in the *Vedas* allows us to make sense of some of the archaeological spadework already done in northern India, providing we place it in its proper perspective.

Before delving into the controversial question of the age of the *Vedas*, we will furnish a rough outline of the sacred literature of Hinduism. This will provide the reader with useful basic definitions on which the rest of our discussion is built.

The Four *Vedas*: The Transmission of Heard Wisdom

The Sanskrit word *veda* means literally "knowledge" or "wisdom." The term is applied to the four ancient collections of hymns—the *Rig-Veda*, *Yajur-Veda*, *Sama-Veda*, and *Atharva-Veda*. These hymnodies, about which we will say more shortly, are deemed to be records of revealed wisdom. They are in fact the largest body of sacred literature surviving from the ancient world. For literally thousands of years they have been passed down faithfully by special families within the brahmin communities of India.

FIG. 3. ***South Indian priest performing a fire ceremony (*****puja*****).***

The transmission of this sacred knowledge appears to have been primarily by word of mouth, usually from father to son, generation after generation. The Vedic lore, thought of as divine revelation, was kept in such high regard that every word was painstakingly memorized. Even when the original meaning of many of the words had been lost, the brahmins vigorously adhered to the ideal of remembering and reciting the hymns with utmost fidelity. After the passage of several thousand years, only one uncertain reading of a single word can be found in the entire *Rig-Veda* (VII.44.3), the oldest of the four Vedic hymnodies.

The brahmins ascribed special potency to the very sound of the Vedic utterances. They regarded the *Vedas* as a manifestation of the eternal Sound or what the Gnostics much later called the *logos*. The brahmins felt a special responsibility for representing this epiphany of the divine Reality as faithfully as possible. One scholar even suggested that perhaps because the *Rig-Veda* "was so imperfectly understood [this] helped to preserve the purity of its transmission."[5]

While it is by no means certain that the *Vedas* were not written down early on, as most Indologists assume, the emphasis was clearly on accurate oral transmission. The Vedic knowledge was considered so precious that no perishable writing materials—birch bark and palm leaves—could be solely trusted for its preservation. Paper does not appear to have been introduced into India until the Muslims made their political presence felt in the period after 1000 A.D.

There can be little question that the *Vedas* are the most impressive literary achievement of antiquity. In extent, they far surpass the Bible, and they dwarf Homer's epics as they do the sacred canon of the ancient Chinese civilization. The four *Vedas* consist of 20,358 verses, amounting to approximately two thousand printed pages. These served as the foundation for the later revealed literature comprising the *Brahmanas* (ritual texts), the *Aranyakas* (ritual and meditational texts for forest-dwelling ascetics), and the *Upanishads* (esoteric texts). This derivative literature within the category of revealed knowledge, or *shruti* ("what is heard"), is vast and diversified. The *Upanishads* alone comprise over two hundred separate works, though a traditional figure of 108 is frequently mentioned: The numeral 108 suggests sacred completeness or wholeness.

In addition, there are the numerous works belonging to the category of remembered or traditional knowledge, or what is called *smriti*. This secondary literature includes *Sutras* (telegram-style explanatory treatises) dealing with ritual, law, and morality, as well as India's two great epics—the *Mahabharata* and the *Ramayana*—and dozens of *Puranas* (sacred encyclopedia-type histories). The *Mahabharata* itself runs to around 100,000 stanzas, and thus is probably the longest book in the world. The nucleus of this gargantuan epic goes back to around 1500 B.C. or perhaps even 3100 B.C., both of which have been suggested as possible dates for the great civil war of the Bharata nation. However, the religious and moral teachings of the *Mahabharata* are unthinkable without the much older Vedic revelation. All these scriptures contain scores of ideas and practices derived directly from the four *Vedas*, which are acknowledged as the sacred fountainhead of Hinduism.

Thus, in the realm of the human spirit, the *Vedas* are like the pyramids that still tower enigmatically above us—a lasting tribute to the ingenuity and lofty aspiration of the ancients. Through the centuries, India's mystics and sages have held the *Vedas* in great veneration, if not awe. This alone should cause us to look at this body of work with high expectation.

In modification of Sir Monier-Williams's statement quoted above, we could say that in order to understand India, we must study especially the archaic literature of the *Vedas*. More than any other literary genre produced on the Indian subcontinent, they allow us to feel the pulse of Indic humanity. After a lifelong study of Eastern spiritual traditions, Thomas Berry, a historian of culture, felt called to make the following remark about the Vedic heritage:

> *In quality, in quantity, in significance for man's intellectual, cultural, and spiritual life, this literature in its totality is unsurpassed among all other literary traditions of the world.*[6]

The ability to preserve this comprehensive literature against the ravages of time is itself an incredible achievement. India, like the rest of the world, suffered repeated foreign invasions—at the hands of the Yueh-chi nomads from China, the Shaka (Sakai) nomads from the northwest, the Greeks (under Alexander the Great), and the Huns. They all wreaked havoc to varying degrees. Particularly during the devastating Muslim invasions in the long period from 1000 A.D. to 1700 A.D., many schools, monasteries, temples, and not least libraries were erased.

Equally, if not more, destructive was the British Raj. When, in the eighteenth century, imperialist politics and profiteering led to the formation of the British rule in India, an all-out attempt was made to Christianize and modernize the country by discrediting Hindu culture. In the words of Lord Macaulay, one of the architects of the British Raj, the goal was to create a new breed of Anglo-Indians, who were "Indian in blood and colour but English in taste, in morals and in intellect." Nevertheless, the encounter with the West also spurred a spiritual and cultural renaissance in India, and Western scholarship has played no small role in India's rediscovery of its own splendid past marked by cultural and spiritual greatness.

Apart from the destructive impact of the various invasions, India's heritage had to contend with another foe—the inclement weather. The subcontinent possesses a tropical climate that is hostile to the preservation of books, whether printed on paper or written on palm leaves. That India nonetheless succeeded in maintaining its ancient literature with a completeness and accuracy unparalleled in the world attests to the utmost reverence in which that tradition has been held by the Hindus.

Pathways of Interpretation

While the actual Vedic texts, as mentioned above, have been preserved with extraordinary fidelity, their meaning has in many instances become a matter of interpretation. This should not surprise us given the passage of time and the numerous cultural changes through the millennia. But it is a source of dogmatic quibbling among the Hindus themselves and of scholarly controversy among Westerners looking in upon the Hindu tradition from the outside.

There exist several Sanskrit commentaries on the *Rig-Veda*, some of which are quite old and all of which are fragmentary or incomplete. The most famous and only complete commentary was authored rather late, in the fourteenth century, by Sayana, who was a great scholar and mentor of King Bukka I of Vijayanagar in South India. Although one or two pioneers of Vedic research thought that Sayana's explanations would suffice to unlock the secrets of the *Rig-Veda*, most researchers quickly arrived at a different and more correct opinion. They realized that Sayana's commentary did not deal with the inner meaning of the *Vedas* but only provided elucidations of the outer or ritualist significance of the *Rig-Veda* and the three other Vedic hymnodies. In his explanations, Sayana relied greatly on such early works as the *Brahmanas* and *Aranyakas*. However, unlike modern ritualistic commentators, he did not deny the deeper level of meaning in the *Vedas*.

Like most ancient documents, the *Vedas* are a composite of symbol, metaphor, allegory, myth, and story, as well as paradox and riddle. Additionally, much of the communicated wisdom seems to be in a secret code that was intelligible only to initiates. Not surprisingly, modern historians and archaeologists, who come from an entirely different intellectual and cultural background in which esotericism is frowned on, by and large have been unable to make any sense of the Vedic hymns. Ever since the first German renderings of the *Sama-Veda* by Theodor Benfey in 1848 and of the *Rig-Veda* by Hermann Grassmann and Alfred Ludwig in the last quarter of the nineteenth century, Western scholars have tackled this difficult text from various angles. Despite more than a century of scholarly labor, however, we have yet to reach the essence of the Vedic corpus and unlock its spiritual secrets. In this respect, the *Vedas* are like the Cheops pyramid, which has been pried into by various means—from primitive iron tools used by treasure hunters long ago to sophisticated electronic equipment—but which has not yet yielded its secret.

The underlying reasons for this inability to comprehend the deeper meaning of the *Vedas* are the same as those that have made it difficult to interpret the archaeological evidence for the ancient Indic civilization: an ideological bias arising from Eurocentric ideas, Western religious preconceptions, and a certain disregard for spiritual perception, esotericism, or mysticism. We must recall that, in the eighteenth and nineteenth centuries when Europeans rediscovered the *Vedas*, Europe was in ascendancy and held much of the world under its military and economic domination. Asia and Africa were considered cultural backwaters and were subjected to various degrees of slavery and exploitation. India was without question the most important colony of the British empire, bringing to Britain's treasury an abundance of much-needed revenue.

Western countries have also had a persistent and strong missionary and reformist motivation toward Asian cultures, attempting to both modernize and Christianize them. Hindu culture proved a great obstacle to these efforts, and in the early days the study and interpretation of the Vedic literature by Western scholars was often tainted with a hidden motive to discredit the *Vedas* and undermine native religious and social traditions. Western thinkers found Hinduism to be a bewildering motley of numerous deities and strange mystic cults. As a rule, they had little appreciation for the religious and spiritual traditions of India, ancient or modern.

Even those few who were impressed with the nondualist logic of Vedanta philosophy generally displayed little interest in, or understanding of, the ritual, symbolic, or mythological aspects of the vast Hindu tradition. The great majority of scholars dismissed India's great mystics, saints, and sages as beggars, magicians, madmen, or charlatans. Out of touch with spiritual or yogic practice and ignorant of meditation and higher states of awareness, European scholars typically denied the *Vedas* any deeper meaning. Instead they viewed them as unintelligible mumbo-jumbo or, at best, primitive poetry. They believed to have discovered in the Vedic hymns an archaic ritualism intent on propitiating the forces of Nature in an attempt to secure sustenance and shelter or the timely arrival of the rains. The attitude of regarding the *Vedas* as relics of a primitive mentality has effectively prevented us from understanding the core of the Vedic message. The charge of primitivism, literary or otherwise, has been refuted by historian Thomas Berry, who made the following appreciative statement about the *Vedas*:

> *This hymnal literature is not "primitive." It is highly developed in its literary form, in its intellectual insight, and in its questioning attitude. The glory of this literature, however, is its imaginative and emotional qualities. There is a deeply religious mood in the longer hymns to [God] Varuna, an awareness of divine might in the hymns to [God] Indra, a*

> *special radiance and loveliness in the hymns to [Goddess] Ushas.*[7]

Twentieth-century Western scholars have seldom shown such sensitivity. They have tended to read the *Vedas* in the light of modern psychology, sociology, or anthropology. With few exceptions, they have failed to explore the texts from a spiritual standpoint, which is at the heart of the Vedic heritage. Nor have they looked into the mathematical and astronomical code of Vedic symbolism, which was an important part of that tradition. Their readings of the *Vedas* often tell more about twentieth-century trends and problems than they do about the Vedic era.

This is particularly true in the case of Marxist historians, who still dominate the institutes of higher learning in India itself. They consider the *Vedas* as documents of class struggle, in which the elitist priesthood of invading Aryan tribes exploited the native population. In fact, this theory reflects not what actually occurred at the time of the *Vedas* but what happened during the British Raj thousands of years later.

The charge of Eurocentrism is not new. It was leveled against Western scholarship more than half a century ago by the French savant René Guénon. In his book *Introduction to the Study of the Hindu Doctrines*, he referred to this bias as the "classical prejudice," explaining it as "the predisposition to attribute the origin of all civilization to the Greeks and Romans."[8] Guénon observed:

> *It seems scarcely possible to account for this attitude except by means of the following explanation: because their own civilization hardly goes any further back than the Graeco-Roman period and derives for the most part from it, Westerners are led to believe that it must have been the same in every other case and they have difficulty in conceiving of the existence of entirely different and far more ancient civilizations; it might be said that they are mentally incapable of crossing the Mediterranean.*[9]

Guénon's criticism of scholarly myopia still applies in many instances. We must also not forget that Eurocentrism is undermined by the testimony of the classical writers themselves, who made it clear that many of the Greeks' most precious ideas were inspired, if not borrowed, from the Egyptians. As Plato records in his *Timaeus*, the Egyptians looked upon the Greeks as mere children in the evolution of human civilization. Thales, Solon, and Pythagoras sat at the feet of Egyptian philosophers.

But where did the Egyptians themselves get their wisdom? We know that they owed a great debt to the learned men and sages of India. There was a colony of Indic people in Memphis as long ago as 500 B.C. But Egypt's connection with India may go back much farther in time. Indeed, there are many curious parallels between Egyptian and Indic mythology and symbolism, which deserve careful investigation.

Moreover, learned men and ascetics from India are known to have visited Greece, and some of the greatest Greek thinkers are said to have traveled in India. The impact of Indic traditions on the influential religions of Orphism and Manicheanism and also on the spiritual movement of Neoplatonism has been acknowledged by many experts. Also, the Essenes of Palestine and the Therapeutae of Alexandria appear to have incorporated philosophical and other elements from India's rich philosophical heritage. We say more about the Western world's indebtedness to India in Chapter 13.

In any case, modern scholars all too often make pronouncements about the *Vedas* on the basis of a few select Vedic passages and the doubtful comments of an earlier generation of Vedic specialists. The fact is that there are only a handful of Indologists who have thorough firsthand knowledge of the *Vedas*, which are composed in a difficult archaic form of Sanskrit that intimidates all but the most intrepid researchers. But even such researchers may never have studied the Vedic ritual or philosophy, which alone makes the hymns intelligible. Thus, there is a tendency to take hymns out of context in order to substantiate favored theories without providing a consistent or comprehensive interpretation of the Vedic tradition as a whole.

Nevertheless, it must be said that even traditional Hindu interpretations of the *Vedas* generally fail to do justice to their deeper meaning and significance. The *Vedas* were already archaic and obscure texts by the time of the Buddha, so much so that even early Sanskrit commentators—like their modern counterparts—complained that the *Vedas* made no sense. A similar complaint can be brought against other ancient works of spiritual import, such as the so-called Pyramid Texts of the fifth and sixth dynasties, the *Egyptian Book of the Dead*, or the Chinese *I Ching*, which demand a great deal of knowledge and a particular kind of sensitivity on the part of the translator in order to yield at least some of their hidden meanings.

Even at its best, interpretation is a task beset with difficulties. In her 1981 book *The Rig Veda*, which contains renderings of 108 hymns, Wendy Doniger O'Flaherty made the point that translators are "painters rather than photographers, and painters make mistakes." Of course, even photography is interpretive and thus liable to distortion. At any rate, Doniger O'Flaherty was right when she said that "translations made ten years from now would probably be . . . different."[10] However, the degree of difference can be expected to be slight in those scholarly renderings that continue to project the Eurocentric bias on their object of study. Real progress in the translation of the ancient Vedic corpus will be made only when that bias is recognized and removed and when the *Vedas* are seen for the profoundly spiritual literature that they are.[11] Voicing a kindred view, the British Vedicist Jeanine Miller, who fully appreciates the spiritual dimension of the *Vedas*, remarks:

> *Vedic thought, especially with regard to meditation and eschatology, reveals an unexampled depth of insight into the intricacies of the human mind, the background philosophy of which was the root of all subsequent speculations. The hymns do not mark the start of the Vedic cult, they rather embody the culmination of a culture whose beginnings were already remote in the eyes of its promoters and to which they constantly looked back. The layers of thought that may be distinguished—mythological and philosophical—are steeped in an age-old tradition going back to a distant past ever present in the* rishis' *[sages'] mind as the time of their*

ancestors, the beneficent patriarchs whose heirloom was their treasure and the foundation of their civilization.[12]

In order to give the *Vedas* a fuller hearing, Miller also had to distance herself from the popular understanding of mythology. As she explains, myth is not merely an entertaining made-up story but a pictograph of great evocative power that is intended to connect us to the reality which it purports to image. It is a representation of the living truth of the sacred reality or realities. Vedic myth, as Miller affirms, "depicts in dramatic terms certain insights realised in deep absorption such as characterises every mystic."[13] In other words, the *Vedas* are the product of a mature introspective culture, which, unlike our own postmodern civilization, was firmly grounded in the direct perception and interaction with the unseen world of numinous beings and forces.

The idea of a spiritual or symbolic interpretation of the *Vedas* is clearly articulated in the *Brahmanas* and *Upanishads*, which speak of the meaning of the sacred Vedic utterances (*mantra*) on the level of the innermost self (*adhyatma*). The same idea is mentioned by the oldest Vedic commentators, such as Yaska (sixth century B.C.) and the slightly later Shaunaka. In his *Nirukta* ("Explanation"), Yaska explains a number of Vedic hymns from a spiritual (*adhyatmika*) perspective, but he offers samples rather than a complete examination. No extensive texts about the esoteric significance of the Vedic hymns have survived from ancient times. Vast as the available Vedic literature is, it represents a fraction of what was once available. Many of the extant works refer to no longer available scriptures and to authorities about whom nothing but the name is known. This loss is not surprising from another point of view: It would appear that in the course of their development, all spiritual and religious traditions tend to move from living spirituality, which is mystical in its core, toward external ritualism and formalism.

In contrast to much of Western scholarship, several modern Hindu scholars have championed an interpretation of the *Vedas* in terms of a deeper spiritual meaning. Here we must single out Sri Aurobindo, Swami Dayananda Sarasvati, Sri Anirvan, and Ganapati Muni. Other lesser known Vedic teachers in India, who did not write in English, entertained similar views. Sri Aurobindo, one of modern India's greatest mystics and sages, saw the *Vedas* as expressing a spiritual vision of the highest order. In fact, he detected in them the antecedents of his own supramental or integral world-transforming Yoga. Aurobindo criticized Western scholarship as follows:

> *Is there at all or is there still a secret of the* Veda*? According to current conceptions the heart of that ancient mystery has been plucked out and revealed to the gaze of all, or rather no real secret ever existed.*[14]

Aurobindo continued:

> *The ritual system recognised by Sayana may, in its externalities, stand; the naturalistic sense discovered by European scholarship may, in its general conceptions, be accepted; but behind them there is always the true and still hidden secret of the* Veda,*—the secret words . . . which were spoken for the purified in soul and the awakened in knowledge.*[15]

Swami Dayananda Sarasvati, the famous nineteenth-century social reformer and founder of the Arya Samaj, looked upon the *Vedas* as a source for his own message of monotheism, emancipation of women, and the removal of caste prejudices. Maharishi Mahesh Yogi, who brought Transcendental Meditation to the West, similarly regards the *Vedas* as containing fundamental insights into all levels of existence—from gross matter to pure consciousness. While we need not uncritically endorse every interpretation that these traditional authorities have put forward, we would clearly benefit from considering their views in an unprejudiced manner.

A somewhat kinder climate of opinion exists in certain progressive circles of psychology—notably transpersonal psychology—which take cognizance of the fact that, as we change our state of consciousness, we begin to encounter the world differently, or different levels of the world. This promising new attitude is summed up well by psychiatrist Roger Walsh, one of the leading figures of transpersonal psychology:

> *The observer who is not adequate to the higher levels of significance will not know that they are being missed . . . Western-trained scientists must recognize that without specific preparation there may be epistemological and paradigmatic limits to one's ability to comprehend and assess these disciplines, that scientific objectivity may need to be balanced (in at least some researchers) by personal experience and training, and that cautious open-mindedness to yogic claims may be a more skillful stance than automatic rejection of anything not immediately logical and comprehensible.*[16]

The kind of epistemological openness proposed by Walsh is essential if we want to comprehend nonmodern, traditional ways of thought and their ritual expressions. Walsh himself has shown the advantages of such a relaxed stance relative to Shamanism. In his book *The Spirit of Shamanism*, he observes how psychiatrists and psychoanalytically minded anthropologists have typically misdiagnosed certain shamanic experiences and behavior patterns as "hysteria" or "schizophrenia." They have done so, in his view, despite "considerable evidence to the contrary."[17] As a consequence, they have failed to appreciate the deeper and quite positive aspects of Shamanism. A similar tragic misdiagnosis has barred us from understanding the spiritual message of the *Vedas*. We, sadly, may add the Vedic seers to Walsh's to-the-point remark that "Yogis, saints, shamans, and sages have thus all been chopped down to neurotic size."[18]

The Scope of Vedic Literature

We have, then, in the *Vedas* a formidable body of literature that not only allows us to glimpse into the culture and mind of a people who were intensely committed to a spiritual view of the world but that, indirectly, also offers a valuable commentary on our problem-ridden contemporary world. Having hopefully set the stage for a more discerning attitude toward the *Vedas*, we will next provide a thumbnail sketch of the four Vedic "collections" (*samhitas*) that to this day inspire Hindus with sacred awe.

The Rig-Veda

The principal and, taken in its totality, the oldest of the four Vedic hymnodies is the *Rig-Veda*. The Sanskrit word *ric*, which for euphonic reasons is changed to *rig*, means literally "praise." It refers to a "chant" or "hymn" in praise of the Divine. Each hymn is also called a *mantra* or sacred "utterance" charged with numinous power.

The composers of the hymns were inspired or illumined seers because they saw or envisioned the truths which they so eloquently communicated in their verse compositions. According to Jeanine Miller, the Vedic seers proceeded by means of what she calls "visioning" and contemplation. As she explains:

> *Visioning may mean receiving knowledge as in a flash and thereby intuitively knowing, or it may mean "seeing" certain realities beyond the world of the senses, both means implying direct apprehension of certain truths that do not fall within the field of ordinary human sensuous experience. Contemplating implies meditation, the steady focusing of the inner insight upon a particular object, or idea, or vision. Intellectual inferences and logical deductions do play their parts, but they are secondary and only means of explaining and expanding upon what has been seen or discovered in a supramental state of consciousness.*[19]

In the *Rig-Veda* itself, the seers are called "poets." However, the Sanskrit equivalent, *kavi*, implies much more than what we mean by a poet. More than gifted wordsmiths, the kavis were golden-tongued visionaries, who, in their spiritual illumination, gave expression to divine truths. They were recipients and revealers of the invisible order of the cosmos. Their ideas were not just clever thoughts but inspired insights or illumined visions. The Vedic Sanskrit term for this higher awareness is *dhi*—a word related to the later term *dhyana*, meaning "meditation" or "contemplation."

Because the hymns were seen or envisioned by wise folk, the *Vedas* as a whole are considered sacred revelation (*shruti*). If we see less in them, it is because of our own cultural lens, which is cut in

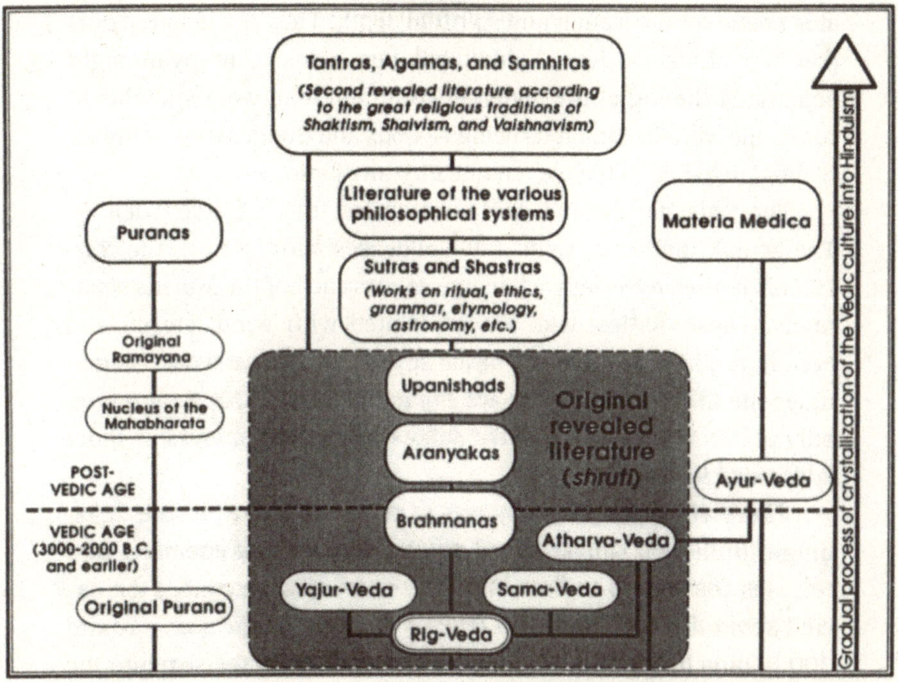

FIG. 4. *The major categories of Vedic and Hindu literature and their interconnection.*

such a way as to reflect to us a purely secularized world, lacking in awe as well as in wonders and miracles.

There are a total of 1,028 hymns (including eleven supplementary hymns) comprising 10,589 verses in the *Rig-Veda*, which are distributed over ten chapters, called *mandalas* ("circles" or "cycles"). The hymns were composed in various periods and by many individuals. The *Rig-Veda* is the oldest book in the Sanskrit language, indeed in any Indo-European language. More than that, if we are correct, it is the oldest book in the world, and for this reason alone deserves our attention. As noted earlier, it is a special kind of book, because for countless generations it was carried in the memory of a few select individuals capable of remembering every last syllable of this sacred corpus.

Generally speaking, the hymns of the *Rig-Veda* show considerable poetic sophistication and spiritual depth. They are inspired outpourings of visionaries, or illumined ones, whose clairvoyant sight penetrated the fog of the material world and who were still able to commune with the luminous beings—Gods and Goddesses—of higher realms, invisible to the eye unaided by meditation.

The Vedic pantheon is said to comprise "thrice eleven" deities. The actual number of Gods and Goddesses addressed in the *Rig-Veda* is higher, especially when one counts each of the Maruts separately. These deities, who are associated with wind, storm, and breath, are said to number "thrice seven" or "thrice sixty." Sometimes the thirty-three deities are expanded into 3,339. At any rate, only about twenty of the Vedic deities have three hymns or more addressed to them.

There are around 250 hymns in praise of Indra, whose lightning thunderbolt causes havoc among demons and enemies, who releases the waters to flow into the ocean, who recovered the sacred *soma* draught, and who reveals the light of the sun. Around 200 hymns invoke God Agni, who descends from the sun into the sacred sacrificial fire and teaches human beings the secret of the births of the deities. Over 100 hymns are dedicated to God Soma, whose mystery is embodied in the immortal nectar (also called *soma*) that is consumed by the illumined sages to stimulate their visionary experiences. Fewer but no less edifying hymns are addressed to other deities like God Varuna, the guardian of the cosmic order; the Ashvins, or heavenly twins, who are supreme healers and teach the secret knowledge; Goddess Ushas (Aurora in Latin), who makes her presence felt in the golden splendor of dawn; Goddess Aditi, the embodiment of primordial boundlessness; Goddess Sarasvati, who is embodied in the once mighty river named after her and who can be considered the patron deity of the ancient Vedic civilization as a whole.

Some scholars believe to have detected different strata of thought in this hymnody, ranging from naturalistic polytheism to monotheism and monism.[20] Max Müller even coined a new term—*henotheism*—in order to explain the tendency in the *Vedas* to ascribe supremacy now to one deity and later to another, as if they all were perfectly interchangeable. He saw this as a form of religiosity hovering between polytheism and monotheism. However, the teaching of many deities who are simultaneously one is the same idea found in later Hinduism, where deities like Brahma, Vishnu, Shiva, and their consorts are all deemed aspects of the same supreme Reality, the Godhead. The various attempts to read an evolution of thought into the *Vedas* remain unconvincing and in this case also unverifiable, because we have no dates for particular hymns or chapters.

Contrary to the opinion of one widely respected Western scholar, the Vedic hymns were *not* meant "to puzzle, to surprise, to trouble the mind."[21] No such purpose would have occurred to the Vedic sages, whose intent, if anything, was to alleviate confusion and suffering. What seems far more likely, those few hymns that are in the form of riddles served the purpose of awakening higher intuition. Like Zen koans, some of the Vedic riddles may well have no logical solution, but the creative tension in them is resolved at a higher level, when the perplexed mind is transcended and beholds the truth. In the case of other Vedic riddles, the answers were undoubtedly known to initiates who were the main audience for which the *Vedas* were originally intended. In this connection, we also must remind ourselves that the hymns were not intended to be merely edifying or entertaining, but they played an essential role in the context of Vedic ritualism. We will say more about this shortly.

The Vedic hymns were composed in an older type of linguistic framework wherein the abstract and the concrete, the spiritual and the material, are not so rigidly differentiated as in modern tongues. It is therefore inappropriate and unproductive to judge the hymns by means of the materialistic languages of modern times. Like any mystic poetry, they require the right angle of vision for a fuller appreciation.

The Sama-Veda

The *Sama-Veda* can be looked upon as a liturgical manual for the chanting or singing of the Vedic hymns. Most of its 1.875 stanzas were incorporated from the *Rig-Veda*, and only seventy-five verses are original to the *Sama-Veda*. The Sanskrit word *saman*, which is pronounced with a long first *a*, means "song" or "melody." A related word is *sama* (with two short *a* sounds), meaning "evenness" or "equanimity." This second connotation also applies to the Vedic chants, which are songs of propitiation, by which the deities are invoked in their gentle and pleasing nature. To reach the deities with his chants, the priest first had to become calm. That is because communication with the higher realms was known to depend on the laws of resonance: Only a tranquil mind can hope to contact the divine beings who are established in harmony.

The text of the *Sama-Veda* contains no clues about the melodies to which the verses were to be sung. These were taught by direct transmission, through hearing the songs. A few *Sama-Veda* singers can still be found in India today, who learned their craft from a teacher who knew how to chant the hymns. However, at a later time, song books were created that, in addition to the musical notation, indicated which syllables had to be prolonged or repeated during singing. There were also syllables—like *hun, hin, hai, hau, hoyi, huva*—that had to be interpolated at certain points of the song, similar to the medieval European plain song of the ninth and tenth centuries. A large number of melodies were known, which those studying the *Sama-Veda* had to master thoroughly. In his outline of the religious literature of India, J. N. Farquhar commented on the rigors of a traditional pupilage in the schools of *Sama-Veda* as follows:

> *He had to learn to sing, readily and accurately, all the tunes that were used in the many distinct Soma-sacrifices, and he had also to know which strophes were required for each sacrifice and in what order they were sung. Therefore, that the young priest might master all the tunes thoroughly and have any one at command at any moment, each was connected with a single stanza of the right metre, and the teacher made his pupils sing it over and over again, until tune and stanza were firmly imprinted, in indissoluble association, in the memory.*[22]

The Yajur-Veda

The third venerated collection of hymns is the *Yajur-Veda*. The word *yajus* (which, for grammatical reasons, is changed to *yajur*) is derived from the root *yaj*, meaning "to sacrifice." Thus the *Yajur-Veda* consists of hymns that are in the form of sacrificial formulas or prayers. About a third of its 1,975 verses, distributed over forty chapters, are taken from the *Rig-Veda*; the rest is original and in prose. The text is arranged in the order in which it was and still is used in the ceremonies. Unlike the *Sama-Veda*, which exclusively contains hymns that are relevant to the soma sacrifice, the *Yajur-Veda* includes formulas for all sacrifices, including those of a purely internal and spiritual nature.

FIG. 5. ***South Indian Shaiva priests and young acolytes performing a rain-making ceremony around a fire altar.***

The *Yajur-Veda* was compiled toward the end of the Vedic era. This is evident, among other things, from the many versions or recensions of it that have survived. The core of the home territory of the *Yajur-Veda* is known as the "field of the Kuru tribe" (*kuru-kshetra*), where the great war of the Bharatas was fought. In his *Oxford History of India*, Vincent A. Smith rightly stated that the *Yajur-Veda* helps to bridge the gap between the *Rig-Veda* and what we now know as Hinduism.[23]

The religion reflected in the *Yajur-Veda*, though remaining true to the principles of the earlier *Rig-Veda*, shows many new developments. Certain deities, such as Prajapati ("Father of Creatures"), Vishnu, and Rudra-Shiva attained greater prominence. But, above all, the sacerdotal ritualism assumed vast and complicated proportions. The brahmins had become highly specialized religious experts, and many scholars have seen in their religious practice a degree of mechanicalness that contrasts to the earlier spontaneity of the *Rig-Veda*. Indian philosopher and statesman Sarvepalli Radhakrishnan made this observation:

> *In the history of thought creative and critical epochs succeed each other. Periods of rich and glowing faith are followed by those of aridity and artificiality. When we pass from the* Rig-Veda *to the* Yajur *and the* Sama-Vedas *and the* Brahmanas, *we feel a change in the atmosphere. The freshness and simplicity of the former give place to the coldness and artificiality of the latter. The spirit of religion is in the background, while its forms assume great importance. The need for prayer-books is felt. Liturgy is developed. The hymns are taken out of the* Rig-Veda *and arranged to suit sacrificial necessities. The priest becomes the lord . . . The religion of the* Yajur-Veda *is a mechanical sacerdotalism.*[24]

While there is truth to Radhakrishnan's comments, they also reflect exposure to Western scholarly stereotypes. Proliferation of sacrificial concerns and a tendency toward formalism, overspecialization, as well as speculative elaboration, were certainly aspects of the late Vedic religion at the time of the *Yajur-Veda* and the *Brahmanas*. Yet we must not lose sight of the fact that underlying these developments was a profound sacrificial spirituality. Thus, like the other Vedic collections, the *Yajur-Veda* can be understood as promoting an inward, spiritual attitude within the framework of the Vedic sacrificial religion. Offering the mind and the senses to the Divine was as important as the elaborate external ritual.

The Atharva-Veda

The fourth and final hymnody is the *Atharva-Veda*, which received its name from the seer Atharvan who belonged to one of the greatest seer families in Vedic times. This collection contains 731 hymns comprising 5,977 verses distributed over twenty chapters. About one-fifth of the hymns are drawn from the *Rig-Veda*. As a collection, the *Atharva-Veda* is generally thought to have been composed in an era considerably more recent than the *Rig-Veda*. However, it is quite possible, as some experts have suggested, that individual hymns of this hymnody may be as old as the oldest hymns of the *Rig-Veda*. Still, the language of Atharvan's collection of hymns is younger than that of the *Rig-Veda*.

The status of the *Atharva-Veda* as part of the sacred Vedic revelation has from the beginning been rather controversial. An apparently late hymn of the *Rig-Veda* (X.90.9) refers only to the three *Vedas*, omitting the *Atharva-Veda*. A similar custom was maintained by some later Sanskrit authorities, while others acknowledged the existence of four *Vedas*. In part, the reason for highlighting the three *Vedas* was symbolic: They were regarded as corresponding to the threefold hierarchy of the world. When a fourfold cosmological schema was used, the authorities did not hesitate to make reference to four *Vedas*.

Yet it is true that many Vedic thinkers have had an ambivalent attitude toward the *Atharva-Veda*, largely because this hymnody contains many spells and incantations that are not used in the orthodox ritual ceremonies. At the same time, however, it also includes many hymns with a medical or healing intent, such as prayers for health and the commonweal. In many ways, the *Atharva-Veda* foreshadows the syncretism of medieval Tantrism, where spiritual practice, sorcery, and medicine are often closely intertwined. Here we must note that sorcery and medicine are also found in the hymns of the *Rig-Veda*, though they are not given the same prominence as in the *Atharva-Veda*.

The *Atharva-Veda* describes itself as part of the Vedic literature and as a creation of the same seer families that also produced the other Vedic hymnodies. It nowhere criticizes the other *Vedas*, but on the contrary glorifies them as voicing the same great metaphysical understanding. Moreover, it contains many hymns from the *Rig-Veda* and the *Yajur-Veda*, which clearly evinces its legitimate status as a part of the Vedic canon.

The Ritual Dimension of the Vedas

In the traditional scheme of the three *Vedas*, the *Rig-Veda* can be said to represent the sacred utterance, the *Sama-Veda* stands for the sacred song or the inner meaning of the hymns, while the *Yajur-Veda* embodies the dimension of ritual action. Viewed from this perspective, the three *Vedas* are not separate texts but distinct and related aspects of the same teaching: the word, its meaning, and the action arising from it. The *Atharva-Veda* is sometimes said to represent the word as power. Hindu traditionalists have drawn up the following correspondences:

Rig-Veda : divine speech : earth : fire : waking
Yajur-Veda : divine mind : atmosphere : wind : dream
Sama-Veda : divine breath : heaven : sun : deep sleep

According to another schema found in the *Manu-Samhita* (IV.123), an ancient Sanskrit work on moral conduct, the *Rig-Veda* relates to the deities, the *Yajur-Veda* to human concerns, and the *Sama-Veda* to the ancestral spirits. Such traditionalist models are helpful in understanding the native worldview with its wealth of unsuspected correlations.

Generation after generation, there have been those who follow and preserve the teachings of the *Rig-Veda*; those who memorize and chant the *Sama-Veda*; those who preserve and employ the sacrificial prayers of the *Yajur-Veda*; and those who are faithful custodians of the tradition of the *Atharva-Veda*. The daily chanting and performance of Vedic rituals continues in India to this day in an unbroken tradition that spans several millennia.

At this point, an important fact needs to be stated. The performers of Vedic worship cannot be regarded as priests in the ordinary sense. Vedic religion was in principle a private affair. The home was the temple, though we need not rule out the existence of temples as special places of worship during that early period. The oldest surviving temples stem from the Gupta period (fourth century A.D.), but there is no reason to assume that temples fashioned from wood, brick, and clay did not have a long history by then. Greek travelers in the pre-Christian era, for example, reported seeing numerous temples in India.

Yet, Vedic religion revolved around the daily worship at the domestic fire altar. Both men and women were empowered to establish their own personal connection to the Divine through the age-old institution of ritual worship. The brahmins were simply available as officiants who could assist the individual worshiper. They specialized in performing the more complex rituals on behalf of an entire community or the king.

The Vedic tradition distinguishes between two comprehensive categories of sacrifice—*griha-yajnas* (domestic sacrifices) and *shrauta-yajnas* (public sacrificial ceremonies). The former category comprises the various simple domestic sacrifices undertaken in the privacy of the home. The ritual performers were husband and wife, who were sometimes, though not necessarily, aided by a brahmin (who, in those days, could also be a woman). In Vedic times, every householder was permitted and expected to keep a daily schedule of prayers and sacrificial rituals, which were performed at the hearth. These domestic ceremonies included the daily morning and evening offerings and special sacrifices on the occasion of a birth, childhood initiation, marriage, and death.

The *shrauta* ("heard") category comprises various public sacrifices, which tended to be complicated and long, drawn-out affairs, calling for an assembly of priests, each of whom had a distinct function.[25] There were four principal priests—the *hotri*, *adhvaryu*, *udgatri*, and *brahmana* (brahmin). Some ceremonies, however, called for seven or eight and, toward the end of the Vedic era, even sixteen priests. The *hotri* recited the hymns of the *Rig-Veda*. The *adhvaryu* was the chief officiant, who constructed the fire altar, tended the fire, handled the utensils, and prepared the oblations. The *udgatri* recited the hymns addressed to God Soma and chanted the songs relating to the deities of the hymns recited by the *hotri*. The brahmin silently oversaw the ceremony, ensuring that the rituals were accurately performed. In case of error, he quickly performed the prescribed rituals of expiation. More than the other three main priests, he was the holder of the sacred power (*brahman*).

The Ritual Literature: The *Brahmanas* and *Aranyakas*

Associated with each *Veda* are various explanatory or subsidiary scriptures, which also are deemed to be revealed knowledge. These fall into the genres of *Brahmanas* (or ritual texts), *Aranyakas* (texts for forest dwellers), and *Upanishads* (esoteric scriptures). There are more than a dozen *Brahmanas*, which consist primarily of explications of the Vedic hymns and practical instructions for the priests. Over the millennia, the Vedic ritual grew more and more complex, calling for specialists who had the specific task of memorizing not only the numerous hymns but also their melodies and accompanying ritual gestures and the obligation to acquire and keep alive the astronomical and calendrical knowledge necessary for the Vedic sacrificial ceremonies.

The brahmins arose as a priestly class as a result of the ever more comprehensive and exacting sacrificial ritualism, with its intricate cosmology, psychology, and metaphysics. Thus, step by step, the home-based Vedic religious practice was replaced by a professional class of hereditary priests, who made the sacrifice ever more elaborate. As can be expected, this sacerdotal professionalism led to a certain haughty exclusiveness as well as exploitation of the religious community. Rather than being a means to an end, as in early Vedic times, the sacrifice almost became an end in itself, and the original piety often became replaced by ostentation. This situation finally provoked the kind of criticism found in the *Upanishads* and the early Buddhist scriptures. They spoke out against excessive and barren ritualism, lacking in wisdom and mystical experience. The *Chandogya-Upanishad* (I.12.1-4), for instance, contains a satire on priestly chanting. Here a certain Baka Dalbhya, who had gone forth to study the *Vedas*, is portrayed as instructing a band of hungry dogs in chanting "*Om*. May we eat! *Om*. May we drink . . . O Lord of Food, bring food here! Bring it! *Om*."

The *Brahmana* scriptures are perhaps even less understood and appreciated by modern scholars than the *Vedas* themselves. Last century, Max Müller said of them that they "deserve to be studied as the physician studies the twaddle of idiots, and the raving of madmen."[26]

One modern scholar compared them in obscurity only to the Gnostic texts.[27] Though intended as a slur, this comparison is valid. For the *Brahmanas*, like the Gnostic scriptures, are mystical treatises. Fortunately, there has been a movement in scholarly circles toward a reappraisal of these works. It is now recognized that the *Brahmanas* contain teachings of considerable psychological sophistication. Some recent works of modern Western scholarship have opened the door for a deeper appreciation of the *Brahmanas*, and these mark an important new approach to them, radically different from the nineteenth-century view.[28]

The *Aranyakas* are scriptures similar to the *Brahmanas*, but intended for those "twice-born" (or duly initiated) men and women who, having fulfilled their householder duties, live in solitude in the forest (*aranya*). Their ritual obligations are somewhat different from those of householders. The focus is on certain particularly powerful and hence potentially dangerous rites that lead to ritual purity followed by the awakening of mystical powers. The element of danger in them is that they can ruin the life of an individual who prematurely abandons his or her householder existence. Much like the *Upanishads*, the *Aranyakas* also contain a number of meditational and devotional teachings, and they stand midway between the *Brahmanas* and the *Upanishads*.

The Esoteric Literature: The *Upanishads*

The *Upanishads*, which are magnificent Gnostic treatises in the broad sense, form the capstone of the Vedic edifice. They are the best known aspect of Vedic literature and have been lauded by great thinkers throughout the world. The German philosopher Arthur Schopenhauer said of them that they were a comfort to him in his life and his death. He also remarked:

> *How every line is of such strong, determined, and consistent meaning! And on every page we encounter deep, original, lofty thoughts, while the whole is suffused with a high and holy seriousness.*[29]

In his survey of philosophical systems and approaches, the American professor of philosophy Abraham Kaplan commented that the *Upanishads* are "remarkable in literary quality as well as in content."[30] Max Müller, who was critical of many aspects of the Vedic heritage, confessed toward the end of his life:

> *The conception of the world as deduced from the* Veda, *and chiefly from the* Upanishads, *is indeed astounding.*[31]

Müller not only edited and translated the *Rig-Veda* but also offered translations of the major *Upanishads*, and his introduction to Vedanta philosophy is still useful today. Robert Ernest Hume, whose renderings of thirteen principal *Upanishads* published in 1921 are still widely read, wrote:

> *In the long history of man's endeavor to grasp the fundamental truths of being, the metaphysical treatises known as the* Upanishads *hold an honored place . . . they are replete with sublime conceptions and with intuitions of universal truth.*[32]

Sarvepalli Radhakrishnan, a former president of India and translator of eighteen of more than two hundred *Upanishads*, noted:

> *If the* Upaniṣads *help us to rise above the glamour of the fleshly life, it is because their authors, pure of soul, ever striving towards the divine, reveal to us their pictures of the splendours of the unseen. The* Upaniṣads *are respected not because they are a part of* Śruti *or revealed literature and so hold a reserved position but because they have inspired generations of Indians with vision and strength by their inexhaustible significance and spiritual power. Indian thought has constantly turned to these scriptures for fresh illumination and spiritual recovery or recommencement, and not in vain. The fire still burns bright on their altars. Their light is for the seeing eye and their message is for the seeker after truth.*[33]

Already in the oldest *Upanishads*, which have been dated back to about 900 B.C., but by our reckoning belong to a still earlier period, one can perceive all the cardinal philosophical tenets of Hinduism: karma, rebirth, Self-realization through wisdom or gnosis (*jnana*), the ultimate unity of existence, and introspection and meditation as means to spiritual liberation. These ideas have generally been described as innovations of the Upanishadic sages. However, in many ways they are faithful to the early Vedic heritage, though giving it new expression. They are the building blocks of the metaphysical tradition of Vedanta—a word that means literally "Veda's end."

Although the *Upanishads*, having been composed over a huge span of time, give expression to many schools of thought, the general thrust of their teachings is toward nondualism (*advaita*). This philosophical orientation is based on the fundamental assumption that, ultimately, all things are one, that the innermost essence of the human being is the very same essence that underlies the universe at large.

Without this fundamental unity, spiritual liberation would be impossible. For such liberation is the realization of that unity, beyond the constantly changing human world and beyond even the heavenly realms of the Gods and Goddesses. That ultimate unity is called *brahman* (when viewed objectively) and *atman* (when viewed subjectively, as the Self). Self-realization brings an end to finitude and suffering. The Self is complete in itself, immortal, and blissful. In the words of Yajnavalkya, perhaps the greatest sage whose voice is recorded in the *Brihadaranyaka-Upanishad* (IV.5.15), which may be the earliest work of this genre:

> *The Self (*atman*) is not this, not that (*neti neti*). It is ungraspable because it cannot be grasped. It is indestructible because it cannot be destroyed. It is unattached because it does not attach itself [to anything]. Being unfettered, it does not suffer; it cannot be injured.*

Such nondualist teachings have often been blamed by Western outsiders for India's supposed failure to create a successful material civilization. Nothing could be farther from the truth. Just as the Vedic seers and sages have given rise in subsequent centuries to an unparalleled profusion of metaphysical ideas and lofty spiritual ideals in the wisdom schools, they also have provided the impetus for ingenious and diversified scientific and other secular knowledge. This knowledge can be found embedded in the rich secondary literature on astronomy, mathematics, medicine, architecture, grammar, phonetics, etymology, art, music, dance, sexology, statecraft, weaponry, and ethics in general.

Timing the Timeless Wisdom

So far we have deliberately said nothing of the age of the *Vedas*, and we still do not wish to anticipate too much of our subsequent findings, which vigorously call into question current thinking. Let us simply note at this stage that it was the eminent German-born scholar Max Müller, a professor at Oxford, who arbitrarily fixed the lower limit to between 1200 B.C. and 1000 B.C. The sheer weight of his formidable authority silenced other opinions. Yet, in his work *The Six Systems of Indian Philosophy*, published shortly before his death in 1900, Müller made this significant admission:

> *Whatever the* Vedas *may be called, they are to us unique and priceless guides in opening before our eyes tombs of thought richer in relics than the royal tombs of Egypt, and more ancient and primitive in thought than the oldest hymns of Babylonian or Accadian poets. If we grant that they belonged to the second millennium before our era, we are probably on safe ground, though we should not forget that this is a constructive date only, and that such a date does not become positive by mere repetition.*[34]

A few paragraphs later the aged Müller, seemingly having wearied of the whole chronological debate, observed:

> *Whatever may be the date of the Vedic hymns, whether 1500 or 15,000 B.C., they have their own unique place and stand by themselves in the literature of the world.*[35]

These telling remarks notwithstanding, and even in the face of all the counterevidence available today, Müller's earlier dating of the *Vedas* has proven incredibly tenacious. However, most scholars today concede that the bulk of the *Rig-Veda* was written several centuries earlier than Müller would have it. The consensus of scholarly opinion hovers around the fictitious date of 1500 B.C. Thus in the posthumously published book *The Origins and Development of Classical Hinduism*, the renowned Indologist A. L. Basham expresses the orthodox view when he assigns the four *Vedas* to the period between 1500 B.C. and 900 B.C.[36] Our own view, which we will unfold in the following chapters, is that there are stringent reasons for accepting a much earlier date for the *Rig-Veda* and also for the three other Vedic hymnodies.

FIG. 6. ***Max Müller (1823-1900), founder of comparative mythology and a great Sanskrit scholar, was one of the principal architects of the now refuted Aryan invasion theory.***

In the next chapter, we will revisit one of the greatest follies of Indology—the Aryan invasion theory—by which Müller and many other scholars sought—and to some extent still seek to justify their comparatively recent dating of the *Rig-Veda*.

CHAPTER 3

The Aryans: Exploding a Scientific Myth

The Ignoble Origins of the Aryan Myth

WHEN ADOLF HITLER CAME TO POWER IN POST-Bismarck Germany, he coupled his nationalistic goals with a powerful ideology that had a peculiar racial twist. After World War I he joined the German Workers Party, which had been founded specifically to promote nationalism, anti-Communism, anti-Semitism, and the supremacy of the Aryan race. The Party was funded by the Thule Gesellschaft (Thule Society), a secret organization founded in Munich in 1918 dedicated to occultism and the establishment of a pan-German state.[1]

The Thule Gesellschaft derived its name from the legendary island in the North Sea that occultists believe to have been a part of the lost continent of Atlantis. Thule was thought to have served as a refuge for the fleeing Atlantean Aryans and as a point of origin for all higher culture—an imaginative tale for which there is no material evidence.

Among the Thulists were several high-placed politicians. After taking over the leadership of the German Workers Party, Hitler used Thulist ethnocentrism to create a mass political movement that would give the German "master race" absolute supremacy in the world.

Occultism continued to play an important role in the Nazi party to the end. Hitler seems to have believed that the Aryans originated in Atlantis and that he was destined to restore the race to its original purity and greatness. He wanted to breed a race of supermen. Heinrich

Himmler, the leader of the SS elite corps, especially dedicated himself to this political ideal, primarily by seeking the extermination of "inferior" races, thus venting Hitler's long-standing resentment against the Jews.

Nazi racism was the ill-begotten child of philosopher Friedrich Nietzsche's ideal of the superman (*Übermensch*) and occult doctrines of adepts who supposedly inherited their secret knowledge from the survivors of Atlantis, some of whom had found refuge in the remote areas of Mongolia and Tibet. German racist anthropologists described the typical Aryan as blond and blue-eyed, with a robust physique—the Nordic type found in the Scandinavian countries rather than in Bavaria where Nazism originated. This racist notion of "Aryan" represents a complete perversion of the original meaning of this word.

Aryan: Language or Race?

Whence did the Nazi occultists get their dangerous notion of an Aryan race? We know that one of their intellectual sources was Alfred Rosenberg's *Der Mythus des 20. Jahrhunderts* (The Myth of the Twentieth Century), which was something like a manifesto for the Nazi ideologues. Another source was the journal *Ostara*, which was the official organ of the Ariosophic movement. Rosenberg and the Ariosophist writers, in turn, derived their racist and political doctrines from more reputable scholars who were nonetheless wrong in their historical appraisal of the Aryans of India. We will shortly explain just how wrong they were.

First, however, we must note that the word "Aryan" stems from the Sanskrit language and is the anglicized version of *arya*, meaning "noble" or "cultured." This is how the people who transmitted the sacred heritage of the *Vedas* described themselves. Thus originally the Sanskrit word *arya* did not refer to a particular race or language but to a moral quality or mental disposition—that of nobility—uniting those of like mind into a felt kinship with one another. Manu, the mythical progenitor of humankind in the present world cycle, is said in the Vedic texts to have given the area between the Himalayas and the Vindhya Mountains the name *arya-varta*, meaning "abode of the noble folk."

However, later the word *arya* seems to have taken on secondary meanings in India and also in ancient Persia—there being a close connection between Vedic Sanskrit and the Iranian language. Thus, in a cuneiform inscription from Old Persia, dating to 520 B.C., emperor Darius declared: "I have made the writing of a different sort in Aryan, which did not exist before." An entire book could be written on how, from these simple original meanings, "Aryan" became what J. P. Mallory called the "most loaded of Indo-European words."[2] But this is not our purpose here.

The word "Aryan" is thought to be cognate with "Iran" and also with "Eire" (the old name of Ireland). What the Aryans of India, the Iranians of Persia, and the Celts of Ireland have in common, first and foremost, is their Indo-European language. That the languages spoken by these peoples are related was not known until the late eighteenth century. In 1786 Sir William Jones, a British judge at the High Court in Calcutta and one of the pioneer Sanskritists, noticed to his great surprise that there are striking similarities in the vocabulary and grammar of Sanskrit, Persian, Greek, Latin, Celtic, and Gothic. The following table shows the striking resemblance between key words in these languages.

TABLE 1. *The first ten numbers in various languages of the Indo-European family.*

ENGLISH	SANSKRIT	PERSIAN	GREEK	LATIN	LITHUANIAN	CELTIC	GOTHIC	GERMAN
one	eka	yak	eis	unus	vienas	oen	ains	eins
two	dva	du	duo	duo	dvy	dau	twai	zwei
three	tri	sih	treis	tres	trys	tri	threis	drei
four	catur	chahar	tessares	quattuor	keturi	cethir	fidwor	vier
five	panca	panj	pente	quinque	penki	coic	fimf	fünf
six	shat	shash	ez	sex	szezi	se	saihs	sechs
seven	sapta	haft	epta	septem	septyni	secht	sibun	sieben
eight	ashtau	hasht	okto	octo	asztuoni	ocht	ahtau	acht
nine	nava	nuh	ennea	novem	devyni	noi	niun	neun
ten	dasha	dah	deka	decem	deszimt	deich	taihun	zehn

A particularly striking example of family resemblance between the various Indo-European languages is afforded by the word "mother," which has the following cognates: *mata* (Sanskrit), *matér*, *mata* (Latin), *mathair* (Irish Celtic), *mathir* (Persian), *Mutter* (German), *módir* (Icelandic), *moder* (Swedish), *mor* (Danish and Norwegian), *moeder* (Dutch and Flemish), *mère* (French), *madre* (Spanish), *mãe* (Portuguese), *mama* (Rumanian), *matko* (Czech and Polish), *matj* (Russian), *maika* (Bulgarian), *motina* (Lithuanian), *māte* (Latvian), and *mair* (Armenian).

ENGLISH	SANSKRIT	GREEK	LATIN	CELTIC	GOTHIC
(I) am	asmi	eimi	sum	am	im
(You) are	asi	ei, essi	es	at	is
(He) is	asti	esti	est	is	ist

TABLE 2. ***Grammatical comparison reveals the close relationship between Sanskrit and various European languages.***

Jones's discovery led to the creation of a whole new scholarly discipline—comparative linguistics. This innovative discipline represented a major departure from the orthodox understanding of the Judeo-Christian heritage, which regarded Hebrew as the matrix of all languages. According to the Bible, the human race began with Adam and Eve, who were created by Yahweh shortly after He had fashioned the world. Following Bishop Ussher, the Christian authorities favored a date of 4004 B.C. for the moment of creation. Because human beings were created on the sixth day of God's creative endeavor, humanity is practically as old as the Earth. Since the most direct descendants of Adam and Eve were Semitic tribes, Hebrew was hailed as the oldest language in the world.

This belief was undermined by the discoveries of comparative linguistics. Jones and his school did for language what seventy-two years later Charles Darwin did for biology when, together with Alfred Russel Wallace, he presented his famous paper at the Linnaean Society on July 1, 1858. Both Jones's and Darwin's efforts freed important aspects of human life from religious dogma. Yet the tremendous implications of Darwin's and Wallace's joint paper seem to have completely escaped their peers—a common experience for scientific pioneers. It took another generation, after the publication of Darwin's *The Descent of Man* (1872), before it was grasped that Darwin's work attacked and effectively demolished the traditionalist notion that all animal species had been created simultaneously and were immutable. The human species, too, was portrayed as having undergone many mutations, as a result of natural selection.

Jones's earlier discovery never achieved the popularity of Darwinian evolutionism, but it too contributed to the growing gap between religious dogma and scientific theory. Notably the German linguists Friedrich von Schlegel and Franz Bopp were instrumental in developing this newly fledged branch of scholarship. For a long time, prior to the emergence of prehistoric archaeology, the historical explanations proffered for the similarities between the various Indo-European languages were rather unsophisticated and highly speculative. By the middle of the nineteenth century, the idea that all Indo-European languages derive from a much older Proto-Indo-European language gained momentum. Scholars endeavored to reconstruct not only that protolanguage but also the culture associated with it. Most importantly, they became preoccupied with identifying the original homeland of that hypothetical culture.

In the late nineteenth century, these linguistic-cultural considerations began to be marred by racial overtones. The ubiquitous Max Müller, who equated linguistic communities with ethnic groups, was among those who naively succumbed to this scholarly racialism, unsuspecting of its explosive potential. He wrote:

> *The Aryan nations, who pursued a northwesterly direction, stand before us in history as the principal nations of northwestern Asia and Europe. They have been the prominent actors in the great drama of history, and have carried to their fullest growth all the elements of active life with which our nature is endowed. They have perfected society and morals; and we learn from their literature and works of art the*

elements of science, the laws of art, and the principles of philosophy. In continual struggle with each other and with Semitic and Turanian races, these Aryan nations have become the rulers of history, and it seems to be their mission to link all parts of the world together by the chains of civilisation, commerce and religion.[3]

In later years, when anti-Semitists were using arguments like Müller's to bolster their virulent racism, the aged scholar, horrified at the political developments, was anxious to revoke some of his earlier careless pronouncements. In particular he debunked the concept of an Aryan race, emphasizing that "Aryan" and "Semitic" were linguistic and not ethnic labels.

Even such a remarkable scholar as Gordon Childe fell under the spell of this widespread racialism. In his classic work *The Aryans*, he sought to trace the expansion of the Aryan people from their supposed homeland throughout Europe and India. He avoided speaking of an Aryan race but postulated a unified Aryan culture. He commented:

To whatever physical race or races they [the Aryans] belonged, they must have possessed a certain spiritual unity reflected in and conditioned by their community of speech. To their linguistic heirs they bequeathed, if not skull-types and bodily characteristics, at least something of this more subtle and more precious spiritual identity. . . . [T]he Aryans must have been gifted with exceptional mental endowments, if not in enjoyment of a high material culture.[4]

Yet, to his own regret and lasting embarrassment, Childe allowed himself, at the end of his book, to speak of the Aryans' "superiority in physique" which "fitted them to be the vehicles of a superior language" and of their "superior strength to conquer even more advanced peoples and so to impose their language on areas from which their bodily type has almost completely vanished." Here we are clearly presented not merely with the idea of a unified Aryan culture but, as in Müller's case, its supposed racial characteristics.

Thus, sadly, scholarly racialism paved the way for fascist racism. Once one believes that there is a culturally or even genetically superior race, the inevitable next step will be to promote that race politically to the detriment of other races.

Apart from this serious flaw in Childe's book, it represented a first major synthesis of Aryan research, bringing the weight of both linguistics and archaeology to bear on the subject. Childe was well qualified for this task because he had been trained both as a philologist and an archaeologist.

Over the years, the linguistic models of the Indo-European language community have been refined and new archaeological evidence has come to light. Today the work of archaeologist Marija Gimbutas, building on Childe's efforts, is widely respected.[5] In her books and articles, she has tried to reconstruct what she calls "the pre-Indo-European culture of Europe" or "the civilization of Old Europe," preceding the invasions of the Proto-Indo-European communities from outside Europe, between 4500 B.C. and 2500 B.C. At any rate, Gimbutas avoids the word "Aryan" and pays little attention to linguistic issues, confining herself strictly to the archaeological evidence.

Not so the British archaeologist Colin Renfrew. In his controversial but fascinating study *Archaeology and Language*, he specifically tackles, as the book's subtitle states, "the puzzle of Indo-European origins."[6] He boldly challenges the reticence felt by most post–World War II archaeologists to address linguistic problems. He argues—rather convincingly—that a proper appraisal of both linguistic and archaeological data actually yields an intriguing synthesis, giving us a whole new picture of the Indo-Europeans.

Renfrew reiterates that "Aryan" or "Indo-European" refers to a language, not a culture. Understandably, he rejects the still more erroneous equation of language with race. Yet, when he and others look for a homeland for the Indo-European-speaking tribes, this separation between language and culture begins to break down again. But, perhaps, if scholars persist in associating Indo-European language with cultural characteristics, it is because language is an instrument of culture. Thus, while we must not assume a one-on-one relationship between language and culture, we must also not make the opposite error of denying any relationship between them. Language and culture *may* coincide, and so *may* language and race. For instance, the !Kung bushmen of the Kalahari Desert in southern Africa speak a unique language, have a unique culture, and represent a specific racial group. But we must not a priori assume a one-on-one linkage between language, culture, and race. Historical actuality tends to be more complex than our theories permit, and in our theoretical constructs we must allow for the fact that simplification may and usually does lead to distortion. What definitely needs to be kept carefully uncoupled is language/culture/race on the one hand and the presumption of racial superiority or inferiority on the other.

The Indo-European Migrations and the Quest for the Original Homeland

Ever since the discovery of the kinship between the various Indo-European languages, scholars have puzzled over the original homeland of the Indo-European speakers. The similarities in their various languages pointed to a common ancestral language, and divergences were explained as the result of migrations from a shared place of origin.

MAP 2. *Recently proposed homelands for the original Indo-Europeans.*

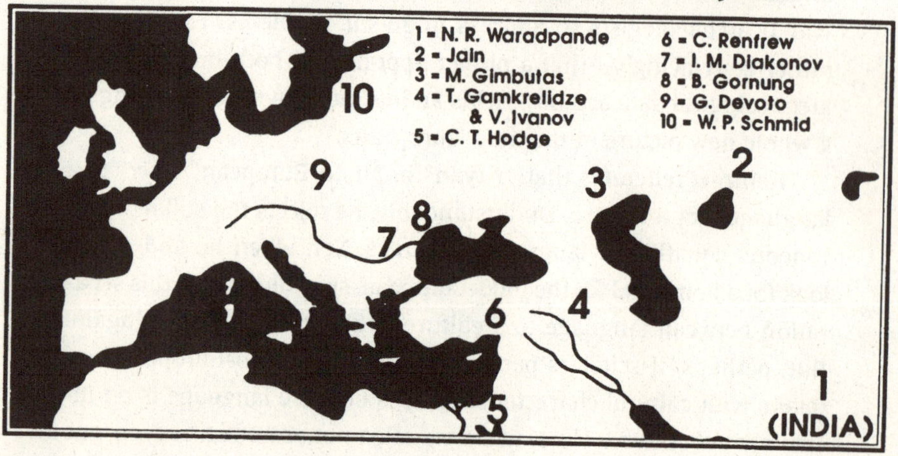

Northern Europe (the Nazis' favorite), even the North Pole, Central Asia, southern Russia, India and lately Anatolia (modern Turkey) have been proposed as likely candidates for that ancestral language. Most contemporary scholars believe that the original Indo-European speakers—or Proto-Indo-European speakers—were located somewhere in the steppes of southern Russia near the Caspian Sea. From there they supposedly spread to Europe, the Middle East (notably Iran), and India.

More recently, an excellent case has been made in favor of eastern Anatolia, which reverses the presumed migratory route: Now the Indo-Europeans are thought to have spread out from the East to the West. With this the myth of the blond Aryan superman has been safely put to rest, for the physical types of Anatolia are more like the Mediterranean type.

With regard to India, which is our present focus, the mainstream model argues that the Vedic Aryans entered India from the northwest through the mountain passes of Afghanistan. The picture painted is of barbaric seminomadic tribes in search of new grazing land for their precious cattle. In their pursuit of wealth, so the story goes, the blond and blue-eyed Aryans were as ruthless and merciless as the later Huns, conquering and subduing the native population of the Indian peninsula by the sword. Bloodthirsty and wild-eyed, they maimed and killed their opponents, ransacked the villages and towns, burned the fields, and devastated the gardens. In the process they destroyed the existing political and economic order. In successive waves over several centuries, they came pouring down from the mountains on fast horses or, according to some far-fetched accounts, in horse-drawn war chariots, surprising their enemies with showers of arrows. Hardened by their long travel across the steppes of southern Russia and over the difficult mountain passes, the fierce, illiterate Aryans arrived in India lusting for war. The Aryans' innate aggressiveness, combined with a superior military technology of iron weapons and chariots, ensured their total victory over a population that was unprepared for this onslaught. More than anything, the Vedic Aryans coveted the cattle of the native Indians, for personal wealth was measured in the size of the herd a man owned.

Haughtily the Aryans looked down on the conquered enemy, sneering at the snubnosed features and dark skin of the native population. They also ridiculed and rejected the speech of the conquered as barbaric, forcing them to learn their own Vedic Sanskrit. They replaced the existing priesthood and its divine pantheon with their own shamanic specialists and deities. The conquered were forced to occupy the lowest rung—that of the shudras—in the Vedic social hierarchy. They were reduced to performing those tasks that the Aryans deemed too demeaning for themselves.

So goes the Aryan invasion theory. Our succinct portrayal of it is actually a composite of the many versions of this theory. Although its defendants include many distinguished academics, the fact is that this theory is little more than a scholarly myth—and a myth that has proven incredibly hypnotic. Fortunately, scholars are beginning to extricate themselves from its spell, largely because the evidence demands it.

The Aryan invasion is supposed to have occurred in the period between 1500 B.C. and 1200 B.C. This date was proposed because of certain epigraphic data from Asia Minor. Cuneiform clay tablets were found in the Hittite capital of Boghazköy that record a treaty between the Hittite king Subiluliuma and the Mitanni ruler Mattiwaza. Whereas Hittite has been recognized as an Indo-European language, Hurrian (the language spoken in the Mitanni kingdom) is neither Indo-European nor Semitic. The treaty mentions the names Mi-it-tra-as-si-il, U-ru-w-na-as-si-il, In-da-ra, and Na-sa-at-ti-ia-an-na. These have been identified as Mitanni versions of the divinities Mitra, Varuna, Indra, and Nasatya (an alternative appellation of the Ashvins, the celestial twins) in the Sanskrit language of the Aryans of India.[7]

How can this curious epigraphic fact be explained? Scholars have generally assumed that the Mitanni ruling elite was made up of Vedic Aryans. However, another explanation is that the Mitanni had the same deities as the Vedic Aryans because they came from a common cultural background. The fact that these names sound so close to Vedic Sanskrit also need not mean that the two linguistic groups separated recently. We know that from earliest times there had been a steady commercial traffic between India on the one side and the

Middle East and Anatolia on the other side.

Indo-European names also are found in Egyptian documents of the same period. Moreover, the elite of the Kassites, who ousted the Semitic rulers of Babylon about 1600 B.C., bore Indo-European names as well. Still earlier references to Indo-Europeans are found in the Chagar Bazar tablets of Samsi-Adad in northern Syria, which have been dated to 1800 B.C. This evidence suggests that Indo-Europeans were on the move in those days. But does this necessarily mean that they were newcomers to Asia Minor?

According to Renfrew, the late arrival of the Indo-Europeans in Asia Minor and India is merely one possibility. He refers to it as "Hypothesis B," which envisions the homeland of the Indo-Europeans in the Eurasian steppes. His own preferred explanation, however, is "Hypothesis A," which assumes the presence of Proto-Indo-European dialects in central and eastern Anatolia as long as nine thousand years ago. From there the Proto-Indo-European speakers gradually extended their sphere of linguistic and cultural influence to Iran and northern India, as well as westward into Europe.

Renfrew considers the possibility that actual history may be explainable by a combination of both hypotheses: While Proto-Indo-European speakers may have been a prominent presence in Anatolia, Iran, and northern India prior to the rise of the great civilizations, there also may have been later invasions of the civilized areas by Indo-European nomadic tribes.

At any rate, the same facts that allow us finally to retire the century-old model of the Aryan invasion into India also present us with an exciting new picture of the ancient world, in which the Indic civilization obviously played a crucial role. What is emerging, and not only in regard to India, is a world that was thoroughly imbued with sacred traditions—traditions that have by and large been forgotten and ignored but that contain vitally important insights into the human condition.

Clearly, the Aryan-speaking communities had to be located somewhere on this planet. But on what grounds was their homeland placed in Central Europe, as Gimbutas would have it, or in South Russia (or, alternatively, Scandinavia), as Childe insisted, or in eastern Anatolia, as Renfrew thinks? Why not, as one Indian savant seriously suggested, at the North Pole? The reasons given are primarily linguistic and cultural rather than archaeological. By comparing phonetic and grammatical changes in diverse Indo-European languages, scholars have invented a series of hypothetical steps, suggesting a certain sequence among the languages involved. Moreover, reconstructing the lost Proto-Indo-European mother language, they also hoped to learn something from the reconstructed vocabulary. What kind of social, cultural, and natural environment did it suggest?

The problem with such linguistic reconstructions is that they are purely hypothetical. The meaning of reconstructed words in Proto-Indo-European is completely unprovable. For instance, the Proto-Indo-European word **reg* (the convention of using an asterisk denotes that the word is purely hypothetical) is thought to mean "ruler" or "king." It was artificially constructed by comparing such words as Sanskrit *rąja*, Latin *rex*, Old Irish *ri*, and Thracian *rhesos*. Yet, some scholars have rightly objected that the Proto-Indo-Europeans may not have had kings but tribal protectors with special charisma or spiritual power. The reconstructed Proto-Indo-European vocabulary is similarly controversial when it comes to descriptions of the natural environment, such as plants and animals. J. P. Mallory critically surveyed the evidence and concluded the following:

> *If we try to draw the environmental evidence together . . . we arrive at a landscape which included some trees and certainly enough to provide forest environments for a number of wild mammals. A river-bank or lake-side orientation is discerned from some of the animals and birds, although in terms of prehistoric settlement this is hardly surprising. That a number of the trees such as birch and willow are so closely linked with temperate climates does suggest a region of at least seasonally cold temperatures. Beyond this we cannot fairly go other than to conclude that to set the Proto-Indo-Europeans exclusively in the open steppe (and not forest steppe or river valleys), or in a desert region, would seem to be incongruous with the Proto-Indo-European vocabulary.*[8]

This is not really very much to go by, especially when we consider that local ecosystems and climates are subject to variation over the long time span in question. The British archaeologist Stuart Piggott summarized the vagaries of linguistic comparisons very poignantly thus:

> *The method has its dangers—the great Sanskrit scholar A. B. Keith once remarked that by taking the linguistic evidence too literally one could conclude that the original Indo-European speakers knew butter, but not milk; snow and feet, but not rain and hands!*[9]

As we have shown, the era postulated for the original Indo-Europeans prior to the divergence into different languages has been steadily pushed back. At first it was maintained that the split occurred about 1500 B.C. Now a more realistic date several thousand years earlier is widely accepted.

Mallory, for instance, places the people who spoke Proto-Indo-European in the era from 4500 B.C. to 2500 B.C. Thereafter their language became fragmented into dialects (known as the various Indo-European languages). The cause of this linguistic divergence is said to have been the exodus of the Proto-Indo-Europeans from their original homeland over many centuries. The Aryans who allegedly moved into India in the second millennium B.C. belonged to a late wave of Indo-European migrants.

Other scholars have suggested that the Indo-European language dates back to the Stone Age![10] Renfrew's much-debated argument is that the original Indo-European speakers lived in Anatolia and from there introduced agriculture to the rest of Europe around 6000 B.C. or somewhat earlier. According to him, immigrant farmers brought the new art. By perhaps as early as 3000 B.C., Indo-European was spoken throughout Europe, with pockets of non-Indo-European speakers (including languages like Basque, Etruscan, and Iberian).

Archaeological evidence does not seem to support completely Renfrew's immigrant agriculturalist model, but at least it seems a step in the right direction. At any rate, it is quite likely that Europe adopted agriculture far more slowly than Renfrew assumed, possibly stretching over several millennia.[11]

Aryan Patriarchal Culture and the Matriarchal Cultures of "Old Europe"

Renfrew's ideas run counter to Gimbutas's model, which has had a certain popular appeal among contemporary paganists and Goddess worshipers. In Gimbutas's reconstruction of history, "Old Europe" prior to 4500 B.C. was exclusively inhabited by people who spoke non-Indo-European languages and had a culture that was "matrifocal and probably matrilinear, agricultural and sedentary, egalitarian and peaceful."[12] The worship of the Mother Creatrix in her various forms was at the center of the worldview of those pre-Indo-Europeans.

After that golden era, Indo-European invaders from the steppes of Russia invaded Europe in three major waves between 4500 and 2500 B.C. Gimbutas characterized the intruding culture as "patriarchal, stratified, pastoral, mobile, and war-oriented."[13] She called these invaders Kurgans—from *kurgan* meaning "barrow" in Russian—because they buried their dead in round barrows.

Gimbutas believes that when the Indo-European invaders largely replaced the Goddesses of Old Europe with male divinities, they effectively interrupted a continuous cultural tradition that had its roots in the Upper Paleolithic twenty thousand years earlier. As a result of these violent Indo-European invasions, the traditions of Old Europe and the Indo-Europeans became inextricably mingled, with the latter dominating the former. As Gimbutas observed:

> *We are still living under the sway of that aggressive male invasion and only beginning to discover our long alienation from our authentic European Heritage—gylanic, nonviolent, earth-centered culture and its symbolic language, whose vestiges remain enmeshed in our own system of symbols.*[14]

Gimbutas's model has not remained unopposed. Invasions are difficult to prove on the basis of archaeological artifacts alone. It is quite possible that Proto-Indo-Europeans entered Europe long before the first Kurgan wave of invaders. Renfrew argued that "a change in iconography does not necessarily betoken a profound change in the underlying belief system" and also that "a change in belief system in no way need correlate with a change in language."[15] He cited the example of the Myceneans who have at times been regarded by Gimbutas as descendants of the gylanic belief system of Old Europe but who spoke an Indo-European language. In other words, while Gimbutas's Kurgans may well have been Indo-Europeans, this does not mean that the societies of Old Europe were inevitably non-Indo-European.

It is perfectly feasible that Old Europe, as Gimbutas uses the term, was a mixture of languages and cultures before the arrival of the Kurgans. That is to say, to contrast a matrifocal, egalitarian, and peace-loving Old European culture with a patriarchal, stratified, and war-mongering Indo-European culture may be too much of a stereotype.

In looking back into the remote past we have to be prepared to live with a certain degree of uncertainty. Many things will never be known for sure. Others will be misinterpreted and perhaps corrected later on. In a way, all historical reconstruction is simplification, and all we can do is be on our guard against gross oversimplification.

Following this excursion into the dimly lit world of the Indo-Europeans and Proto-Indo-Europeans, we next turn to one of the most exciting archaeological discoveries of this century. It brought to light an astonishing civilization—the so-called Indus civilization—that at least for a while seemed to neatly confirm the Aryan invasion theory. But only for a while . . .

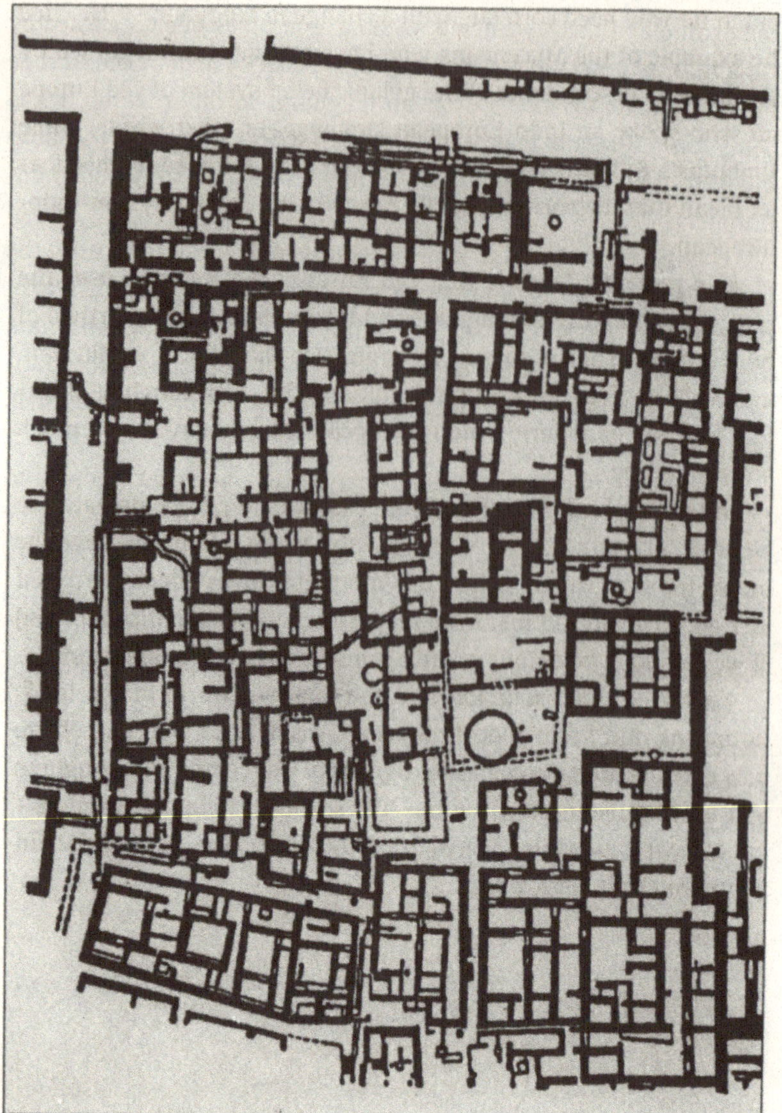

FIG. 7. *A street block in Mohenjo-Daro showing a mazework of houses, with major roads to the top and the left.*

CHAPTER 4

An Archaeological Surprise: The Cities of the Indus Valley

How the Indus Cities Were Discovered

THE LARGE MOUNDS OF HARAPPA IN WHAT IS NOW Pakistan had long been known as concealing the ruins of an old town. What was not understood was that these hidden ruins represented one of the most advanced and important cities of antiquity. As early as 1826, Charles Masson reported on this site, which is located at the river Ravi, a tributary of the Indus in the north of Pakistan. However, its true importance was not appreciated until, in 1921, the Indian archaeologist Daya Ram Sahni conjectured it might belong to the pre-Mauryan era. The Maurya empire was established at the time of Alexander the Great's invasion of India. Candragupta, the first Maurya emperor, usurped the throne of Magadha in 320 B.C. As archaeologists were to discover, Harappa was far older than anyone might have guessed, preceding Candragupta by two-and-a-half millennia.

A year after Daya Ram Sahni's conjecture, R. D. Banerji opened a trench in Mohenjo-Daro four hundred miles to the south, and what he saw compelled him to suggest that these ruins were related to the Harappa site. Experts working on Mesopotamian antiquities pointed out connections with finds from that area which went back to the third or fourth millennium B.C. Mohenjo-Daro is located on the right bank of the Indus River nearly two hundred miles north-east of Karachi, which is at the Arabian Sea. Excavations at Mohenjo-Daro, which perhaps means "hill of the dead," started in 1922 under Sir John Marshall and continued until 1931. After the partition of India and Pakistan in 1947, further archaeological work was conducted by Sir Mortimer Wheeler.

The Harappa site was in a poor state when archaeologists finally began to excavate it seriously. When the Lahore-Multan railway line was built, engineers had mined the ancient bricks to lay the one-hundred-mile-long roadbed. What invaluable evidence was destroyed in that plundering for progress will never be known.

Since the archaeological discovery of Harappa and Mohenjo-Daro, hundreds of other sites have been discovered. These include major sites at Ganweriwala, Rakhigarhi, Dholavira, Kalibangan, and Lothal, the first three comparable in size to Mohenjo-Daro. The Harappan world appears to have covered an area of around 300,000 square miles, stretching from the Himalayas in the north to the Godavari River in modern Karnataka in the south, and from the Indus River valleys in the west to the plains of the Ganges and Yamuna Rivers in the east. Additional sites have been found in Afghanistan to the Amu Darya River, thus bringing part of the Iranian world into the Harappan cultural field. A recent count has identified over 2,500 settlements belonging to various periods. Most of the sites are situated on the eastern side of the greater Indus plain. This plain, which is now mostly desert, was formerly watered by several rivers, including a river that was larger than the Indus—a fact that, as we will show, has crucial bearing for our understanding of ancient India.

The Harappan culture area—some scholars even speak of an empire—by far exceeds in size the combined area occupied by the Sumerian and Egyptian civilizations. It also is more than twice the size of the already huge area claimed for the Maya civilization in the early post-Christian Era. The enormous size of the early Indic civilization was not merely because of northwestern India's fertile soil around the rivers but also because of the age of that civilization and its correspondingly large population. As we will show, it can be traced much farther back than the two great cities of Harappa and Mohenjo-

Daro. Rather, these thriving urban centers seem to be the final flowering of a civilization with a protracted history that began, as far as we know, with the town of Mehrgarh. We say more about this early Neolithic settlement in Chapter 8 and show the lines of development from there to the world of Harappa and Mohenjo-Daro.

The Golden Age of Harappa

The ancient Indic civilization, commonly though misleadingly referred to as the Indus civilization, is now widely thought to have reached maturity during the period from 2700 B.C. to 1900 B.C., generally called the Harappan Age. In 1931, Sir John Marshall had proposed the period from 3100 B.C. to 2750 B.C. as the golden age of Harappa. Thirty years later this date was modified by Sir Mortimer Wheeler to 2500 B.C. to 1500 B.C. Other scholars have fixed the beginnings to 2800 B.C. and the terminal date to 1800 B.C. More and more the consensus moves toward 1900 B.C. as the date for the conclusion of the flowering of the great cities. However, their beginnings are still shrouded in darkness.

In any case, during the span of nearly one millennium, the landscape of northwestern India was dotted with numerous villages and towns, as well as several large urban centers. Archaeologists have furnished various counts for these settlements. In 1968, only around one hundred sites were known. Today some counts go as high as 2,500, and the number is likely to increase further, perhaps dramatically. Of course, these did not all exist at the same time, though many will undoubtedly have coexisted for many generations.

The settlements of the far-flung early Indic civilization, like most ancient civilizations, all lay at or near rivers. The two best-excavated towns to date are Harappa and Mohenjo-Daro. Both show a striking similarity of design. Both sites, which are roughly three miles in diameter, were geometrically arranged into a grid pattern. In both towns, to the west lies a "citadel," some 400 by 200 yards in extent and erected on a high platform constructed of mud and brick and defended by crenelated walls. One of the most remarkable structures of the citadel at Mohenjo-Daro is the Great Bath, which is thirty-nine

FIG. 8. *Mohenjo-Daro's citadel, with living quarters in the foreground.*

feet long, twenty-three feet wide, and eight feet deep. It is sunk into the paving of a courtyard and water-proofed with bitumen; it is approachable from the north and the south by brick steps with possible wooden stair treads. The floor of the bath slopes to an outlet that leads in turn to an arched drain deep enough for an adult to stand upright.

Just north of the pool, archaeologists discovered eight small bathrooms drained by small outlets in the floor. Each bathroom has its own staircase leading to the second story. If the whole complex served a purpose similar to the tanks of the later Hindu temples, we may assume that the second story had cells for the priests and that the baths were designed for their daily ritual ablutions.

To the east of this settlement area lies the lower city with straight unpaved streets, some of them thirty feet wide. The streets have brick-lined sewers fitted with manholes for easy access. Only the Romans, more than two thousand years later, had a comparable drainage system. The streets divide the city into large blocks, and the blocks in turn are served by narrow curving lanes. The lower city appears to have been the residence of the common people—merchants, artisans, and laborers.

The houses, which are often two or more stories high, are built of standardized baked bricks. Each house has several rooms, arranged around a square courtyard. Brick staircases lead to upper floors or flat rooftops. Better appointed houses have bathrooms, which are connected by drains to the sewers under the main streets. The design of the bathrooms suggests that the early Indians cleaned themselves

FIGS. 9-11 *(from top). The Great Bath in Mohenjo-Daro, probably serving as a public forum for the kind of ritual ablutions that devout Hindus still perform every day; view of a typical street in Mohenjo-Daro, carefully constructed with sewers; a close-up view of the brickwork characteristic of many buildings in Mohenjo-Daro and other towns.*

by pouring water over their heads from pitchers—as do their descendants in modern India. The narrow windows, which are placed high on the buildings, are screened with grilles of terra-cotta or alabaster. In many cases, the doors open onto side lanes. This architecture is reminiscent of a traditional Punjabi town in contemporary Pakistan and India.

The largest building uncovered at Mohenjo-Daro, which is 230 feet long and 78 feet wide and includes the Great Bath, has been identified as a palace, governmental administrative center, or a priestly college. Perhaps it served all these functions, as appears to have been the case of the great architectural complexes of Minoan Crete. As Nanno Marinatos argued convincingly in her important monograph *Minoan Religion*, the monumental buildings of Crete at Knossos, Phaistos, Malia, and Zakros were in all probability not, as widely assumed, royal palaces but ritual centers. She writes:

> *The quality of the art and architecture of Minoan Crete shows that it was a major and sophisticated civilization like Egypt and the Near East. Yet the "high cultures" of the Orient possessed one feature which is absent from Minoan Crete: temples. . . . And yet, evidence of religious activity abounds in Crete. . . . This seeming paradox has led one scholar to suggest that urban shrines were not important in Minoan Crete, and that religious activity was, for the most part, confined to "house cults." Thus, a strange picture emerges. On the one hand, there exist monumental palaces and mansions; on the other, modest, if not outright poorly constructed, town shrines. But how to fit the ostentatious cult paraphernalia (obviously manufactured for a social elite) into this model. And could a highly urbanized culture have dispensed with monumental sacred architecture?*[1]

Marinatos continues:

> *The answer to the riddle may, in fact, be very simple. We may have missed Minoan temples, or functionally equivalent structures, because of conceptual biases. It may be that what*

have been termed "palaces" are, in reality, the monumental sacred buildings that we are looking for.[2]

Marinatos's remarks apply with surprising poignancy also to the Indian situation. Although the Minoan temples were all constructed in the period from 1900 B.C. to 1450 B.C., her elegant solution to the Minoan riddle may well provide an answer to the question of the nature and purpose of the much older architectural complexes of Mohenjo-Daro, Harappa, and other towns.

At the Harappa site a building twice the size of the sacred complex at Mohenjo-Daro was found, and archaeologists have identified it as a granary. Granaries and storage areas also have been found at the so-called palaces of Minoan Crete and have been taken to indicate the control of food surplus by the priestly elite. As Marinatos suggested, this surplus could have been used for feasting, as a relief during famine, or in payment of labor rendered to the temple complex.

The site of Dholavira, where excavations have begun recently, has yielded a town plan that is somewhat different from other major sites. An interesting architectural feature here is the use of polished stone pillars. New inscriptions also have been discovered, which include a large wooden board inscribed with Indus signs.[3] The large towns of Rakhigarhi and Ganweriwala are still unexcavated and may well contain further intriguing artifacts.

FIG. 12. ***Ten still undeciphered glyphs found on a wooden signboard in the town of Dholavira.***

The excavations so far have not brought to light any monumental art in the manner of pharaonic Egypt. Also, few smaller objects of artistic merit comparable to the art of Sumer, Egypt, or Akkad have been dug up. Most of the finds are roughly modeled terra-cotta figurines, primarily cattle (though, for unknown reasons, never cows). The abundance of artistic artifacts in the case of Egypt has no parallel anywhere in the ancient world. No tombs filled with splendid treasures like the burial chamber of Tutankhamen have been found in India. Nor have Harappa, Mohenjo-Daro, or any of the other sites surprised archaeologists with colorful murals, inscribed steles, or richly decked coffins. The tropical Indian climate has not been kind to whatever objects the early settlers might have left behind in their houses, public buildings, or graves. However, we must consider that archaeologists

FIG. 13 *(above). The excavations in the Indus Valley have yielded many roughly fashioned clay figurines such as this one.*

FIG. 14 *(right). This soapstone image of a bearded man, who was probably a chief priest, is one of the most remarkable artifacts found in Mohenjo-Daro.*

have excavated only a fraction of the known sites, which may yet yield invaluable treasures from the past.

So far the digs in India have produced at least three striking pieces of art, which demonstrate the tremendous sophistication in sculpting attained at that early time. The first artifact, made out of soapstone (steatite), is a sculpture of a man who is some kind of official—perhaps a priest or overseer. He is bearded, with eyes half-closed, looking rather stern or meditatively withdrawn. He has a headband and a similarly styled ornament on his upper left arm. The garment draped over his left shoulder is decorated with a large trefoil pattern.

FIG. 15. ***This male torso shows the sculptor's superb artistic skill and gives the modern viewer a sense of the inestimable artistic treasures that have been lost.***

The second remarkable object is a male torso, fashioned out of red sandstone, that in its balanced lines compares with the beautiful art of Gandhara two thousand years later.

The third artifact is a small copper figurine that scholars have labeled the "Dancing Girl." The figure depicts a young nude female, standing with a slight arching of the hips. She is probably a prostitute, either of the worldly or the sacred variety. Prostitutes, who offered their services at the temples or in the streets, were a regular feature of social life in Mesopotamia. Temple dancers were, at certain times, also a part of later Indic (Hindu) society. The girls were dedicated at a young age to serve the Gods through their art, and were known as *devadasis*, or "servants of God." It is not known whether this sacred institution actually existed in Harappa and other early Indic towns. However, temple prostitution was widespread in other early civilizations, and we can reasonably expect its presence also in the early Indic civilization. What is certain, though, is that dancing and music were an integral part of the urban life in ancient India. In any event, the dancer's pose prefigures later Indic representations of females.

The excavations also yielded a number of naturalistic miniature sculptures of monkeys, squirrels, and other animals that were used as pinheads or beads. In addition, the artifacts include a number of terra-cotta objects that were clearly toys, such as carts, bird-shaped whistles, and monkeys that could slide down a string.

FIG. 16. *Dubbed the "Dancing Girl," this figurine bears witness to the remarkable continuity of style between the Indus-Sarasvati civilization and later Hinduism.*

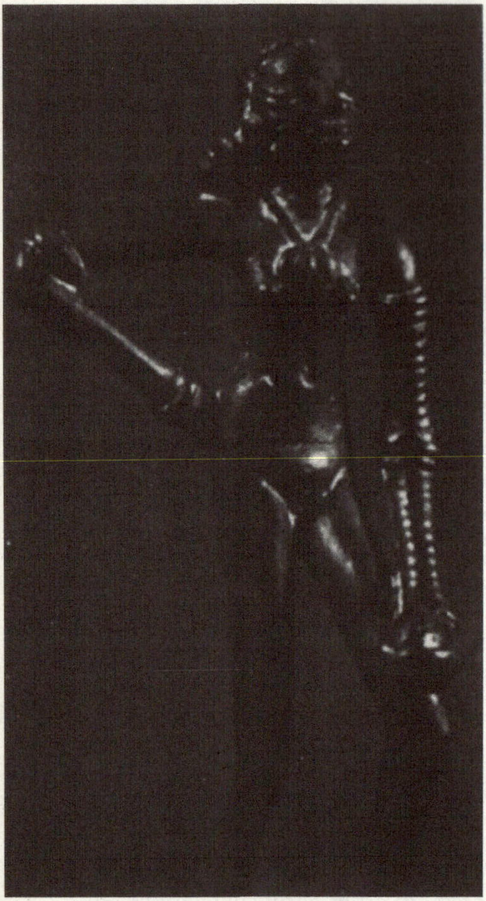

The copper and bronze implements lag behind their Sumerian counterparts in craftsmanship. Perhaps further finds will correct this impression, as certainly the Harappans were skilled metal workers. They even invented the first carpenter's saw with undulating teeth, which allowed an easier cut, since the sawdust could escape more freely.

We must mention here a controversial artifact that has been carbon-dated to the fourth millennium B.C. This is a life-sized bronze head, which has been imaginatively identified as a representation of the sage Vasishtha, who figures prominently in the *Vedas*.[4] The identification was based on the hairstyle of the statue, which the

the *Vedas* describe as having been unique to the family of Vasishtha. The hair is oiled and coiled with a tuft on the right. Vasishtha was chief priest of King Sudas, who defeated a coalition of ten kings in battles on the banks of the Parushni (modern Ravi) and Yamuna Rivers, which mark the region of the Sarasvati River between them.

FIG. 17. ***Known as the "Vasishtha Head," this highly controversial bronze artifact may be the creation of an artisan who lived in the Middle Ages.***

Unfortunately, the Hicks Foundation for Cultural Preservation in San Francisco, the present owners, acquired the head from a dealer in India and so nothing is known about its archaeological context. The carbon-14 tests were performed on the deposits from inside the hollow head, and thus there can be no absolute certainty about the metal casting itself. Metallurgical tests apparently indicate a similar age. The carbon date given was 3700 B.C., with an error of up to eight hundred years in either direction. However, a strikingly similar head from Maharashtra, housed in the Heras Institute in Bombay, seems to belong to a relatively recent time, perhaps 1200 A.D. to 1400 A.D.

The excavations in India have been particularly rewarding in the number of recovered stamp seals. Thousands of them have been found, and they are mostly of square or rectangular shape in contrast to the round seals at the much older town of Mehrgarh, which we will introduce shortly. Many have animal motifs, though some depict humans. Not a few carry glyphs of the neatly designed Indus script. The animals realistically depicted on the seals include the humped bull, water buffalo, goat, tiger, rhinoceros, and elephant.

One seal in particular has stirred the imagination of scholars. It has been dubbed the *pashupati seal*, after the Hindu God Shiva, who is characterized as the "Lord of the Beasts," *pashu* meaning "beast" and *pati* meaning "lord." This seal shows a seated figure with horned headgear, surrounded by an elephant (facing the opposite direction from the other animals), a rhinoceros, a buffalo, and a tiger. Beneath his thronelike seat are a pair of antelopes. The figure's face is masklike and could be that of a buffalo. What has often been interpreted as an erect phallus could be part of the belt. On the chest are either ornaments or, more likely, painted marks reminiscent of the kind of sectarian signs displayed on the foreheads and chests of holy men, or sadhus, in later Hinduism.

FIG. 18. ***Most experts agree that the figure on this soapstone seal is very likely an early representation of God Shiva as Lord of Beasts (Pashupati).***

There is a fascinating side to these seals, which sheds light on the historical significance of the early Indic civilization. For, typical Harappan seals have been found far afield in Oman, Mesopotamia, and the Maldives. These finds bear witness to the enthusiastic initiative of the early Indic peoples as seafaring merchants. More will be said about this in Chapter 6 in connection with our discussion of the picture as it emerges from a careful reading of what Gorden Childe called the "priceless document" of the *Rig-Veda*.[5]

Inland, the Harappans (as the early Indic people have been called collectively) moved their goods using wheeled carts, camels, and river boats. Their products would have included fine pottery wares, jewelry (especially beads fashioned from a variety of materials), copper and bronze vessels, and not least woven cotton goods. The variety and extent of their trade suggests that credit-keeping and calculations were very important to the Harappans.

Weights found at Mohenjo-Daro, Harappa, and other sites have revealed a remarkable accuracy. The weights, which are uninscribed, follow a binary-decimal system: 1, 2, 4, 8, 16, 32, up to 12,800 units, one unit weighing approximately 0.85 grams. Thus some of the weights are so tiny that they could have been used by jewelers to measure gold; others are so enormous that they must have been hoisted by ropes.

FIG. 19. ***The finely tooled scale and the range of the displayed weights show that the merchants of Mohenjo-Daro took their business very seriously.***

Measurements were principally based on a decimal system, reminding one of the fact that the decimal numerals we use today came from India. In Mohenjo-Daro a scale was found that is divided into precise units of 0.264 inches. The "foot" measured 13.2 inches (equalling 50 x 0.264). From Harappa a measuring rod is known that shows units of 0.367 inches, which suggests that the early Indic peoples knew more than one system of measurement. The second system was apparently that of the "cubit" (of 20.7 inches) found also in Egypt, Babylonia, and elsewhere. The buildings of Harappa and Mohenjo-Daro were all laid out in cubits.

All this suggests that the Indic peoples were skilled in arithmetic and presumably also geometry. The scientific knowledge of Neolithic humanity has been systematically underrated by scholars, who simply failed to see that the ancients used arithmetic and astronomy in a ritual context and that ritualism and scientific knowledge are not inherently opposed to each other. Very probably, science started out as the special domain of knowledge of the priestly elite, which, in order to ensure the preservation of the moral order, had to be able to read the language of the divinities inscribed in the regularities of the starry firmament.

Largely based on the meticulous geometric layout of the towns and the carefully maintained weights and measures over a large area, many scholars have expressed the view that the so-called Indus civilization was rigidly governed by a sacerdotal elite. Certainly the overall impression one gets is one of conservatism, which prompted the British scholar Stuart Piggott to pass this harsh judgment:

> *The dead hand of conservatism in design, rather than in technique, lies heavily on all the Harappa products. Complex technical processes were known, but the output suffered from standardization and an almost puritanical utilitarianism.*[6]

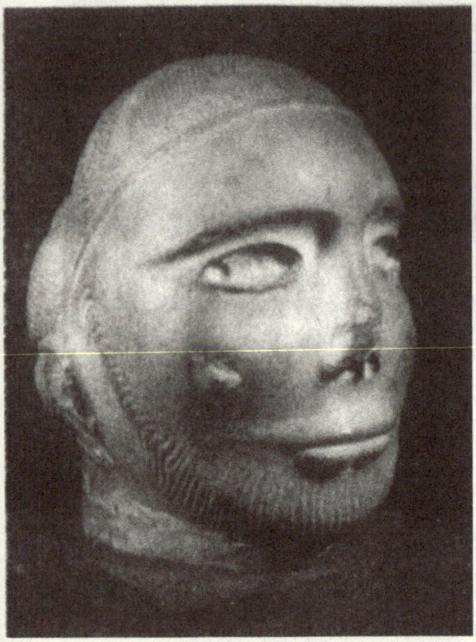

FIG. 20. *This head, found in Kalibangan, is highly stylized, yet preserves the individual expression of the model who was probably a religious official.*

From our point of view, the uniformity pointed out by Piggott, which recent finds show was not as complete as he had thought, is striking rather than "repellent," as he put it. It indeed suggests central organization and traditionalism. It could even be that the very traditionalism of this civilization prevented the preservation of many artifacts, since the Harappans, like the modern Hindus, probably passed on their sacred objects rather than leave them in graves. In that case they might have disposed of them only after they were broken and no longer useable. It is also interesting to note that the Harappans practiced cremation, as do the later Hindus as a general rule.

Archaeologists and historians have proffered all kinds of speculations about the social, economic, and political structure of the so-called Indus civilization. Most of their ideas have so far remained pure speculation and for the most part are not based on the new evidence presented in this book. In light of the remarkable continuity between the so-called Indus civilization and later Hindu civilization, we may reasonably assume that the people of the early Indic civilization were guided by a priestly elite, as happened elsewhere in the ancient world. It is likely that there were leaders among the priests who enjoyed greater charismatic power than others but that on the whole the control by the priestly estate was neither total nor rigid.

We also do not have to assume the existence of a caste system, which appears to have been the product of a much later age. We may, however, reasonably postulate a social stratification into a priestly elite, warrior estate, and general populace—in keeping with what we know from other early civilizations and corresponding to the Vedic division into brahmins, kshatriyas, and vaishyas. In addition, the early Indic society might well have included a servile estate, corresponding to the Vedic shudra class.

Remarkably, war technology is not well represented in the archaeological artifacts, and there is no evidence of any extensive military conflict, which is also true of Sumer for the period prior to around 2000 B.C. The early Indic civilization appears to have been largely peace-loving. As Jonathan Mark Kenoyer, a professor of anthropology at the University of Wisconsin, observed:

> *Episodes of aggression and conflict probably occurred, but armed conflict was not a major activity, nor does the integration of the Indus Valley seem to have been achieved through military coercion.*[7]

If not the might of the sword, what held this expansive urban civilization together? We would probably be not far off the truth to assume that cohesiveness was achieved by a shared religious worldview according to which everything had its proper place and station in life. Rebellion and revolution were not a part of traditional societies, as they seem to be of our own modern societies. Unless the ruling elite squashed the people by prolonged unreasonable demands, everyone bore the burdens of life in silence. The pronounced tendency of accepting the established order was tied in with the reigning cosmology according to which the social order was divinely appointed or a mirror image of the heavenly harmony.

What has seldom been properly appreciated is the strong possibility that the early Indic society, like the Hindu culture to which it has given rise, was complex and diversified, allowing for regional variations.[8] After all, this pioneering civilization extended over an area that, as noted above, has been estimated at around 300,000 square miles. This is an area bigger than the size of the state of Texas or the African Republic of Zambia. By comparison, early pharaonic Egypt, despite its length of 570 miles, is estimated at having comprised an area of under 13,000 square miles. Even when the 1000 miles between the first cataract of the Nile and Khartoum are included, the area would still be under 15,000 square miles because the desert formed an absolute boundary. Sumer, which the schoolbooks continue to hail as the cradle of civilization, was even smaller.

Thus, in the early Indic civilization we are confronting the most populous and geographically expansive culture of the third millennium B.C.—a formidable generator of ideas and skills. In subsequent chapters we will reveal just how unique were the knowledge and achievements of that early civilization. But first we will investigate the terrible fate that seems to have stricken cities like Mohenjo-Daro and Harappa.

CHAPTER 5

The Great Catastrophe and the Reconstruction of the Early Indic Civilization

The Aryan Invaders and the Big Cities of the Indus

UPON THE DISCOVERY OF THE INDUS CITIES, ARYAN INvasion theorists promptly scouted around for signs of battles between the invading Aryans and the settlers of the Indus River. In a late layer at Mohenjo-Daro, archaeologists discovered the skeletal remains of thirty-eight individuals in contexts suggesting violence. Four individuals were found in a room containing a well. Two of them were apparently trying to climb the stairs to the street when they were killed.

In another house, thirteen adults and a single child were found. One of the skulls bore a long cut that could have been made by a sword. Another skull showed similar marks of violence. Five more skeletons—three men, two women, and a child—were found sprawling amidst the bricks of a collapsed wall, ash, and broken pottery. In a lane, six more skeletons—including that of a child—were found, but archaeologists have yet to provide a description. The same is true of a single skeleton dug up in another street.

A group of nine skeletal remains—including those of five children—was found under a mound of debris. Archaeologists have suggested that they were hastily buried. They also speculated that this group could have been a family of ivory workers, since two elephant tusks were found with them.

Hypnotized by the Aryan invasion theory, archaeologists summarily attributed the death of these urbanites to a "final massacre" at the hands of marauding bands of Aryan nomads. In the words of Sir Mortimer Wheeler:

> *The general inference from the thirty-eight derelict corpses at Mohenjo-daro is that from the moment of death the place was uninhabited. The absence of skeletons (so far) from the citadel may imply that the raiders, whoever they were, occupied and cleared this commanding position for their own momentary use. For the rest, it may be suspected that sporadic fires in the sacked city kept predatory animals at bay.*
>
> *Looking back on the macabre scene we may perhaps conclude that, since seventeen of these skeletons seem definitely to belong to the latest occupation and the remainder present the same aspect and have not been found in inconsistent circumstance, we have here in fact the vestiges of a final massacre, after which Mohenjo-daro ceased to exist. Who were the destroyers? We shall not know. It may be that some hill-tribe fell upon the enfeebled city and put it to the sword.*[1]

In his earlier publications, Sir Mortimer Wheeler had pointed the finger not vaguely at "some hill-tribe" but decisively at the Aryan-speaking invaders. While taking note of his peers' massive criticism launched at this interpretation in the intervening years, he made it clear in a passing comment that he continued to favor his original hypothesis. However, the circumstances in which the Mohenjo-Daro dwellers died are by no means certain, and the poorly recorded excavations leave the date of the various groups of skeletal remains in doubt. Specifically, the correct archaeological layers to which they belong are not known, which makes nonsense of the massacre theory.

However, anxious to vindicate their invasion theory, scholars like Wheeler referred to hymns from the *Rig-Veda* that speak of the destruction of fortresses or strongholds (*pura*) and the Aryans' hatred toward the Dasus or Dasyus, whom scholars identified with the Harappans. They completely ignored, however, contradictory references to the Vedic people as *builders* of cities, as agriculturalists, and as fighting *intertribal* battles rather than wars against indigenous non-Indo-European peoples. They also overlooked the fact that the epithet "conqueror of cities" is widely applied to overlords of fully sedentary communities in other parts of the ancient world. We must not limit it to nomadic rulers.

Most importantly, those subscribing to the Aryan invasion theory were hard-pressed to match the dating for the invasion (1500 B.C. to 1200 B.C.) with the archaeologically established chronology of the cities. Harappa and Mohenjo-Daro had been in decline or were abandoned many centuries prior to the alleged intrusion of nomadic Aryans. Reluctant to discard their pet theory, scholars now pushed the time for the invasion back to coincide with the destruction of the cities.

Clearly, something happened to bring this great civilization to its knees, but it was not any brutal invasion by nomads from the northwest. The catastrophe that befell the people of the Indus cities was of an entirely different order and far more devastating than any pillaging tribes could ever be. As we will show, the cities and their inhabitants succumbed to unpredictable Nature herself in a catastrophe of gargantuan proportions.

The Lesson of Catastrophes

In our own era, Nature has bared its bloody tooth on more than one occasion. However, mythmaking in the grand, archetypal style of our ancestors is no longer an art form with us. Otherwise, some more recent natural disasters might have been fixed in the collective memory by the creation of vivid, full-blooded myths. It would seem that our mythologizing propensities do not serve the purpose of making the sacred more visible but that of concealing truth and gaining power or advantage over others, as is overwhelmingly demonstrated in contemporary politics and corporate business. Besides, we tend to forget Nature's escapades very quickly, unless we ourselves were among the victims or suffered loss from them. Our protected urban lifestyle has thoroughly alienated us from Nature, and we know nothing of its rhythms and raw energy. When Nature intrudes into our lives, we tend to react by denial, which is most apparent in the way we deal with death.

Even though natural catastrophes have in modern times been far less severe in magnitude than the cataclysms that spasmed the Earth and terrorized humankind in prehistory, they can still have a planetwide effect, altering climate and vegetation. Modern Western society has so far managed to absorb these upheavals without too much trouble. Government agencies and insurance companies take care of immediate needs, collapsed houses are rebuilt within a year or so, and soon life and business continue as usual.

Thus few of us remember the eruption of the volcano on the Indonesian island of Krakatau in 1883, which caused a tsunami that traveled as far as England. We certainly tell our children no stories about it. It happened to "someone else." An even more powerful eruption occurred sixty-eight years earlier on the Indonesian island of Sumbawa when the Tambora volcano exploded. No universal legends are woven around that event either.

Yet these disasters contain an important lesson for all of us. The Earth is a living, breathing organism, and the thin skin of land that protects us from its hot interior is rather flexible and porous. There are constant seaquakes and earthquakes around the world, which cause tidal waves and floods. Numerous volcanoes above ground and in the depths of the world's oceans erupt periodically. The continents are floating on giant plates around the globe, and where these plates rub against each other, much activity—as yet barely understood—constantly endangers human civilization. Moreover, the gaseous mantle that keeps our lungs filled with air is prone to tornadoes, hurricanes, and blizzards, which can cause considerable destruction.

Nevertheless, according to orthodox scientific opinion, the progress of human civilization has been ensured by a relatively stable environment: All the great geological upheavals belong to the time of pre-sapiens history. Since the ice sheet receded from Eurasia and North America eleven thousand or so years ago, Nature has shown humankind a rather benign face. The story goes that, apart from occasional hiccups in the form of rather localized earthquakes and volcanic eruptions, Nature has thrown no big tantrums in civilized history. This scientific assumption is just that—an assumption, a belief that is not borne out by the facts.

In pointing out this flimsy scientific credo, we must remember that, before anything else, scientists are human beings and therefore they are liable to making the same errors and entertaining the same prejudices as any other human beings. This comes as a surprise only to those who think that the scientific ideal of objectivity is a reality rather than an ideal to be aspired to by scientists. In practice, scientific research frequently falls far short of the demanding standards of objectivity. Indeed, philosophers of science have raised serious questions about whether perfect objectivity is possible in principle. Bertrand Russell, one of the great philosophers and mathematicians of our time, noted:

> *Human beings cannot, of course, wholly transcend human nature; something subjective, if only the interest that determines the direction of our attention, must remain in all our thought.*[2]

No doubt with an eye on his own discipline, the renowned British historian Arnold Toynbee said much the same when he observed, "There are many angles of vision from which human minds peer at the universe."[3] Thus when we look into the past we always look at it through the lens of the present, inevitably distorting what we see. As we become more aware of the distorting properties of our particular lens, we can begin to retract some of our projections and misconceptions about the past.

According to a minority opinion, human civilization has not been spared large-scale natural catastrophes. On the contrary, this small dissenting voice asserts, Nature's cataclysmic changes have shaped much of early culture and thought—leading to the creation of astronomical/astrological and calendrical/divinatory sciences at an early phase in the history of civilization. Our Neolithic (and possibly late Paleolithic) ancestors were anxious to predict the volatile behavior of our planet. They kept careful and remarkably accurate records of the motion of the luminaries in the sky, because they felt that there is a connection between the events in the celestial vault and the events on Earth. As the esoteric maxim ascribed to Hermes Trismegistus states: As above, so below.

Besides, now and again—far more frequently than scholars like to admit—travellers from the heavens streaked across the sky and slammed into the body of our planet as if it were made of gelatin. The shock waves always devastated large areas and certainly did not bypass populated cities. Perhaps this is why, around the time of Jesus' birth, the astronomers/astrologers watched the sky with apprehension. For we now know that they were witnesses to a rare supernova. Our own sky watchers caused moderate excitement in the news media when they reported the close passage of the minor planet Hermes in 1937 (half a mile in diameter) and of a large asteroid labeled 1989FC fifty-two years later—both passing at a distance of little more than twice the distance to the Moon.

We know that climatic spikes occurred at around 8000 B.C., 6000 B.C., 3100 B.C., and 1100 B.C. Temperatures also were unusually low during the "Little Ice Age" period from 1200 A.D. to 1800 A.D. Tree-ring analysis revealed that 536 B.C. started a fifteen-year decline in tree growth, which has been associated with a meteorite impact. According to the statistical analysis of British astronomers Victor Clube and Bill Napier, during the past five thousand years there were several dozen collisions with meteorites weighing tens of thousands of tons and several collisions in the 100- to 1,000-megaton range.[4] Especially the large meteorites would have interrupted civilized life for a period of time. If we have no written records of these traumatic events, it is largely because our knowledge of the past is tantalizingly fragmentary. We do, however, have scribal testimony of other natural disasters of gargantuan proportions, as we will explain shortly.

The Flood and Other Remembered Catastrophes

Apparently all the sacred literatures of the world remember a catastrophe—the Great Flood—that, long ago, wiped out most of civilized humanity. It is conceivable, though not very likely, that the story of the deluge originally recorded a relatively local disaster which then was disseminated from culture to culture through the flourishing oceanic interconnections that existed at a very early date. It is also conceivable that memories of several or many large local disasters contributed to the universal flood legend. Let us also take into account the fact that even a comparatively minor disaster claiming human lives looks like a major catastrophe to those involved and is likely to be remembered as such for a long time, especially in cultures relying primarily on the oral transmission of knowledge.

All this is not to say that the story of the Great Flood may not refer to an actual dramatic superevent in remembered history. There have been large-scale catastrophes in historical times that changed the destiny of whole cultures, which demonstrate that our planet is far less stable than many geologists would have us believe.

For instance, about 1250 B.C. extensive flooding seems to have occurred in Anatolia (modern Turkey), burying the Bronze Age city of Tiryns. About the same time an earthquake destroyed the rich merchant city of Troy (archaeological level VI). It is quite likely that the two events were connected.

Three hundred and seventy-eight years earlier (according to tree-ring analysis validated by radiocarbon dating), the volcano on the small Greek island of Santorini (Thera) blew up and triggered earthquakes and a tsunami that devastated large areas of land not only on mainland Greece but across the Mediterranean in Egypt and Palestine. This catastrophe brought down the fine Minoan civilization, centering on the large island of Crete. Dwellings, temples, and "palaces" were destroyed by fire, ash, or flooding. The resulting social, economic, and political chaos appears to have been exploited by ruthless kings from mainland Greece, who seized the opportunity to deal the deathblow to the Minoan civilization. Although the death was slow, it was certain, and by 1200 B.C. this great civilization, which had emerged around 3000 B.C., was no more.

This particular natural disaster might even offer an explanation for an important event in the remembered history of the Hebrews: Moses parting the waters of the Sea of Reeds (often erroneously translated as the Red Sea). Could it be that the earthquakes associated with the eruption of Thera temporarily drained the Sea of Reeds and that this catastrophe became merged with the Exodus story? In light of the other phenomena described in the Hebrew literature as part of this catastrophe—from fiery ash raining down to thunderous noise and enveloping darkness—there is a high probability that this explanation is correct. This is corroborated by the well-known Ipuwer Papyrus, which contains a haunting account paralleling the Hebrew texts. The fairly precise date now available for the final explosion of Thera—1628 B.C.—obliges Egyptologists to recalibrate their dynastic chronology, which has long been recognized as rather shaky. "When Thera exploded," wrote Charles Pellegrino, who summarized the available evidence, "it changed the history of the world."[5]

Volcanic eruptions followed by radical climatic changes, leading to a three-hundred-year-long drought, are now thought to also have been the cause of the collapse of the Mesopotamian empire of Akkad. The country reached its golden age under Sargon (2371-2316 B.C.), who ruled for fifty-seven years, and continued to flourish under his son Rimush and his grandson Manishtusu (2307-2292 B.C.). Then suddenly, after a century of supremacy, the empire mysteriously collapsed. Towns were abandoned when a failing agriculture could no longer sustain them.

Judging from their legends, the Mesopotamian people blamed the haughty Manishtusu for the empire's demise. Modern geologists, on the basis of microscopic analysis of soil samples, believe that the real culprit was volcanic activity, possibly in nearby Turkey, which covered the region in ash. They do not even consider the ancient theory that a "good" king staves off such disasters by his very goodness. There is no place in geology for any thought that connects natural events with human consciousness. Some avant-garde quantum physicists are not so sure. In any case, after a hiatus of three centuries, both the rains and the people returned to the middle region of the Tigris and Euphrates, creating the Babylonian Empire.

An earlier catastrophe occurred before 3000 B.C. in the heartland of what was then Sumer and what is now the coastal area of Iraq. Digging at Ur in the late 1920s, Sir Leonard Woolley sunk a shaft down to a level corresponding to roughly 3000 B.C. Thereafter, to his utmost surprise, he encountered twelve feet of mud before finding further strata of artifacts. He calculated that the mud was deposited by a flood no less than twenty-five feet deep, perhaps reflecting the fifteen cubits mentioned in Genesis.

It is difficult to know the exact extent of this natural disaster. It undoubtedly affected the Sumerians and possibly some of their neighbors in a profound way. Sir Leonard concluded that he had discovered archaeological evidence for the Great Flood mentioned in the Gilgamesh epic, which apparently served as the model for the biblical account of the deluge. The Sumerian equivalent of Noah is Uta-Napishtim who was instructed by God Enki to build an ark and save himself and his loved ones.

It was after the flood that, according to the Sumerian sources, kingship was sent down from on high. The first dynasty of the ancient city of Ur is thought to have been established around 3100 B.C., but a slightly later date is equally possible. The first ruler was Mesannipadda, who reigned for eighty years.

In Sir Leonard's assessment, the level of artistic accomplishment was higher around 3500 B.C. than in dynastic times—that is, there was a decline that may have been caused by economic and other setbacks resulting from the flood.[6] A similar cultural decline has been noticed also for pharaonic Egypt, suggesting a progressive drying up of this country's original inspirational forces, which were no doubt anchored in its spiritual heritage.

There is a fascinating parallel between the emergence of the dynastic houses of Sumer and the beginning of the pharaonic dynasties. The first dynasty of Egypt has widely been fixed around 3180 B.C. Yet, there is no unanimity among scholars, and some Egyptologists place it two or three centuries later. In India, the beginning of our present world age—the *kali-yuga*—is traditionally assigned to 3102 B.C. This date may coincide with the advent of the reign of Manu Vaivasvata, as fixed by some scholars. The flood, according to ancient Indian sources, occurred shortly before Manu's rulership.

A third and final parallel, which can hardly be coincidental, comes from a civilization on the other side of our planet—the Maya of

Mesoamerica. The Maya named the date 13.0.0.0.0 4 Ahau 8 Cumku as the beginning of the present world cycle. According to the Goodman-Martinez-Thompson correlation, this date corresponds to August 12, 3113 B.C.[7]

Most interestingly, Mayan cosmology knows of five world cycles. The first world was destroyed by the earth element, the second by the air element, the third by fire, and the fourth by water (the Great Flood). We are now in the fifth world cycle, which is destined to be destroyed by earthquakes on December 24, 2011 A.D.

Whatever we make of these curious chronological agreements, what is certain is that the world's mythologies and literatures remember geological changes, often sudden in nature, that traumatized, paralyzed, or destroyed their cultures. Such events were undoubtedly formative experiences, shaping both the consciousness and culture of early civilized humanity. Some observers of human nature have suggested that the dysfunctional character of all civilizations—manifesting in aggression, wars, and ecological destructiveness—goes back to an original trauma: an unknown catastrophe of massive proportions.[8]

History as Myth, Myth as History

Our picture of the ancient world tends to be somewhat monochrome, filled with a succession of raids, conquests, and wars; power-hungry emperors and corrupt nobility; oppressed and manipulated masses; starvation and pestilence; technological achievements accomplished by the sweat and blood of the many to the glorification of the few.

Our history books say little about the truly great accomplishments of our remote ancestors, notably their high level of morality and spirituality, as well as metaphysical insights and aspirations. These mean little to our consumerist culture. However, if we want to put true color into our picture of the past, we must begin to shed our preconceptions and learn to look at the facts. Our history books know nothing of the primordial tradition of spirituality—the legacy left behind by our remote ancestors through the oral traditions of India,

Sumer, Egypt, and other cultures. That primordial tradition revolved around three things: first, the intercourse between humanity and the divine or higher powers; second, human beings who represent the good and those who are "fallen"; third, cycles of civilization that end in various cataclysms.

For a long time, critical-minded readers of the Bible have looked upon the Israelite's escape across the Sea of Reeds as little more than a pious legend that has no substance in historical reality. Today we stand corrected, thanks to the painstaking efforts of archaeologists, biologists, and geologists. Many other biblical references, previously dismissed as incredible or imaginative, have meantime been substantiated. Evidently, we must assume a more respectful attitude toward the writings of the ancients. "What if," asks William Irwin Thompson in his eminently readable book *At the Edge of History*, "the history of the world is 'a myth,' but myth is the remains of the real history of earth?"[9] Then again, we must not take the mythical recollections of humanity too literally either but allow for both poetic license and vested interest.[10]

The purpose of the preceding consideration of cataclysms in historic times was to set the stage for our discussion of the ancient Indic civilization in the next section. Sometimes Earth's catastrophes are truly gargantuan, lifting or dropping large areas of land and shifting forever the course of rivers with disastrous consequences for entire cultures. This appears to be what happened in ancient India nearly four thousand years ago. The Indian subcontinent experienced a traumatic alteration that had a deep and lasting impact on human civilization in that part of the world. The geological changes caused a major upheaval in the existing culture, leading to the collapse and/or abandonment of numerous cities and villages in the region.

The Great Catastrophe: When Rivers Vanish

The Indus River meanders from the Himalayas to the Arabian Sea—a stretch of 1,800 miles. Most of the land to the immediate east of the Indus is barren land. Extending over roughly 100,000 square miles, the Thar Desert, which is comparable in size to the Syrian

Desert, forms a natural divide between the Indus and the Gangetic valleys. It also is the untouched grave of a large part of the early Indic civilization, which collapsed after around 1900 B.C.

The discovery of Mohenjo-Daro on the west bank of the Indus River some 200 miles from the shores of the Arabian Sea and of Harappa about 350 miles further north encouraged archaeologists to look for other sites along the fertile banks of the Indus. Their search was rewarded with such sites as Chanhu Daro, Amri, and Kot Diji. Hastily, they named these sites collectively "Indus civilization."

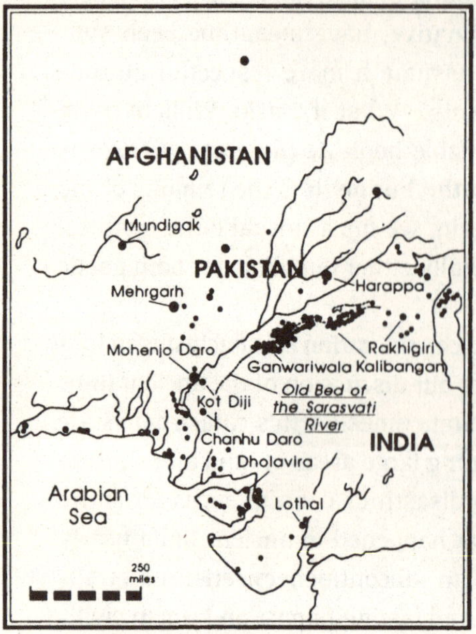

MAP 3. *Select settlements of the Indus and Sarasvati Rivers, showing a larger number of towns and villages along the Sarasvati.*

What they did not know then, but which is well-established fact today, many more sites of that civilization are located not along the Indus but in the middle of the desert, buried under mountains of sand.[11] Obviously, when these vanished towns were still going concerns they could not possibly have thrived in a desert environment. Indeed, as satellite photographs have revealed, what is now the Thar Desert, also known as the Great Indian Desert, was once traversed by a great river with its own fertile banks. Geologists have identified this moribund river, an extension of the present-day Ghaggar, as the Sarasvati mentioned in the Vedic scriptures. This great river flowed from the Tibetan Himalayas into the Arabian Sea, covering a distance similar to the Indus.

Clearly, the Sarasvati and its many tributaries, which also show up on satellite photographs, formed an immense system that supplied a large area with ample water and fertile soil. More than that, the photographs revealed artificial canals carrying water to more remote locations for the cultivation of crops.[12] Scientists are as yet undecided whether the canals were filled only during the monsoon months or throughout the year.

If archaeologists had looked beyond the ruins and artifacts they were able to recover from the soil around the Indus River, and had taken note of the most ancient and sacred Hindu scripture—the *Rig-Veda*—they would not have been surprised by the treasures hidden beneath the sands of the sprawling Thar Desert. The *Rig-Veda* unquestionably speaks of a mighty river—the Sarasvati ("She who flows")—that should not be identified with the Indus but the Ghaggar (or Hakra, as another portion of it is known in Pakistan). For the composers of the *Rig-Veda*, the Sarasvati was the largest of seven rivers forming the life support of the Vedic civilization.

The area of northwestern India, which was the heartland of the early Indic civilization, is today known as the Punjab. The Sanskrit equivalent is *panca-ap*, meaning "five waters," referring to the Jhelum, Chenab, Ravi, Beas, and Sutlej, which flow into the Indus. In ancient times we find no reference to a five-river region. But the texts speak of a seven-river region, which was called *sapta-saindhava* or "land belonging to the seven rivers," of which the largest and most central was the Sarasvati.

The name *sapta-saindhava* is derived from the Sanskrit *sapta* ("seven") and *sindhu* ("stream"), the latter giving rise to the modern words *Indus* and *Sindh*. This expression suggests that in Vedic times the Punjab as we know it today did not exist and that the center of the seven-river region was further east on the Sarasvati. Often mentioned in the early Sanskrit scriptures are the Indus itself, the Sarasvati, the Parushni (modern Ravi), and the Yamuna (Jumna). The Drishadvati, which has been identified with the now small rivers Chautang and Naiwala, has but a single reference in the *Vedas*. According to the *Manu-Samhita* (II.17-18), the "land of the brahmins" once lay between the Sarasvati and the Drishadvati.

The mightiest of all the rivers of northern India was the Sarasvati, which the Vedic seer-bards praised in the following words:

O best mother, O best river, O best Goddess Sarasvati. . .
(*Rig-Veda* II.41.16)

And:

She, Sarasvati, flows with a nourishing stream, Sarasvati, for our support, like a copper fort. In her greatness the river drives away, like a charioteer, all other [rivers].

Unique among rivers, Sarasvati flows pure from the mountains to the ocean. Revealing wealth and the world's abundance, she has yielded milk and ghee for [King] Nahusha [and his descendants].
(*Rig-Veda* VII.95.1-2)

FIG. 21. *In later Hinduism, Goddess Sarasvati is worshiped as the deity of learning and the arts.*

The phrase "yielded milk and ghee" in the above Rig-Vedic verse reminds one of the biblical expression, "the land where milk and honey flow." It was applied to the fertile region in which the Hebrew tribes finally settled after their forty years of wandering in the sun-baked desert. Both expressions suggest plenitude, because of the presence of precious water that renders the soil fertile for livestock and gardens. Like Ganga in later Hindu mythology, Sarasvati was personified as a Goddess and was said to have descended from heaven. That is to say, she brought divine sustenance—what the Hebrews called *manna* (probably from *man*, "gift")—for the Vedic peoples.

Originally, the Sarasvati flowed through Rajasthan and poured itself into the Gulf of Kutch near the Kathiawar peninsula. Kutch itself was once an island at the mouth of the Sarasvati. It did not cease to be an island until about two thousand years ago, as the ancient

Greeks recorded it as such. One of the Sarasvati's main tributaries was the Yamuna River, which now flows into the Ganges (Ganga). The further back in time we go, judging from the ancient Vedic scriptures, the more magnificent a river the Sarasvati appears to have been. Geologists are beginning to confirm the scriptural evidence.

What, then, caused the disastrous drying out of the Sarasvati/Ghaggar/Hakra River, its tributaries, and the countless artificial canals? What happened to stop the flow of life in the numerous towns once fed and interconnected by this large riverine system? How was all the fertile soil that once framed the river replaced by sand? What changed dramatically the life of one of the earliest flourishing civilizations, whose central domain stretched all the way from the Yamuna River in the east to the foothills of Afghanistan to the west, and from the Arabian Sea in the south to Kashmir in the extreme north?

A growing number of geologists converge on the following explanation: Around 1900 B.C., over a comparatively short period of time, major tectonic shifts occurred possibly accompanied by volcanic eruptions, which drastically altered the flow of rivers. Prior to its final demise, the Sarasvati River had shifted course at least four times, gradually turning the region around it into inhospitable desert. Such geological changes are endemic to northern India and result from the pressure of the Indian plate pushing into Asia and raising the Himalayas, which is occurring at this very moment. Various speculative scenarios are possible for the extinction of this mighty river. Here is our own reconstruction of that catastrophic event:

Around four thousand years ago, the earth buckled under a large area of northwestern India, as it is still prone to do today. But at that time, the buckling was sufficiently pronounced to have far-reaching consequences. Perhaps the ground under the cities, towns, and villages of the early Indic civilization rose imperceptibly, and the devastating effects became apparent only over a number of years. Perhaps the buckling announced itself locally in a series of devastating earthquakes, followed by long-term geographic and climatic changes.

We favor the second explanation, because northwestern India is known to be prone to earthquakes. While we have as yet no clear-cut evidence of Harappan sites having been destroyed by earthquakes, a number of sites were destroyed or damaged by floods, and many others were abandoned because of changing river courses. The event would have had to take place rather quickly to allow for sites to be abandoned altogether, particularly those on the Indus where water continued to be available. At any rate, the geological alteration caused the drying-up of the Sarasvati River and most of its tributaries.

Picturing the Past: A Possible Scenario

If the change was indeed relatively sudden, we can propose the following scenario: We can envision tidal waves randomly flooding large areas, and broken dams and walls of water bearing down on unsuspecting townsfolk and villagers, sweeping them miles away from their homes, together with panicky livestock, uprooted trees, boats torn loose from their anchor points, and the debris of houses. We also can imagine the water from the Himalayas seeking new pathways, causing a similar devastation in other areas. The Indian scholar Ram Nath Kak has suggested that, as part of this cataclysm, the natural dam holding the waters in the Kashmir Valley, which was originally a giant lake, broke;[13] this made the valley habitable, but the immense volume of water coming down the Indus River flooded riverine cities such as Mohenjo-Daro, hastening their demise. Floods were also caused by the Sutlej, which shifted its course from the Sarasvati to the Indus.

The cataclysm left behind desiccated river beds, empty canals, parched soil and, finally, abandoned towns and villages. Gradually, as trees and crops died for lack of water, wind-blown sand filled the gaping river beds, crumbling canals, and vacant towns and villages.

Drying rivers became stagnant pools of undrinkable water, too shallow to navigate with trade vessels and soon bereft of fish for food. Once arable soil became baked and sterile under the hot Indian sun, yielding no more sustenance for either the peasant families or the urbanites. With the disappearance of the once lush vegetation, the climate changed as well, yielding fewer and inadequate rains that never allowed the soil to recover.

Family after family was forced to relocate. We can imagine that many people succumbed to illness as a result of malnutrition or from exhaustion or misfortune during their exodus from the cities and villages. Some families must have headed north toward the Himalayas. Others may well have braved the trek westward across an increasingly deserted landscape, until they reached relatives or friends in the settlements of the Indus. Yet others must have migrated south in the hope of land and livelihood nearer the ocean.

Those heading westward will have found that the region of the Indus River had suffered great adversity as well. We can imagine dams breaking under the stress from the tectonic uplift and flooding the towns and smaller settlements along its banks. In fact, the earth has continued to shift under the Indus settlements. The three lowest levels of occupation at Mohenjo-Daro are under water, preventing archaeologists from recovering the telltale signs of their history.

Most people appear to have migrated not toward the Indus but eastward into the fertile valley of the Ganges and its tributaries.[14] The Gangetic valley had been inhabited at least since 5000 B.C. It is possible that some of the families might have had relatives in that part of India. At any rate, the emigrés encountered new difficulties and dangers there. For the thickly forested and swampy area, with heavy monsoon rains, was teaming with wild beasts. The refugees from the calamitous Indus-Sarasvati region had to clear the forests in order to build new settlements, plant gardens, plow fields, and create grazing land for their livestock.

But as the pioneering spirit surfaced in them, they found the strength to rebuild their civilization—unlike the people left behind along the Indus River who, after the collapse of the larger civilization, never succeeded in reconstructing a comparable urban civilization. The point of gravity of the early Indic civilization shifted from west to east, from the Sarasvati to the Ganges.

In the *Shatapatha* ("Hundred Paths")-*Brahmana*, we encounter a vivid description of the conquest of the swampy area east of the Ganges, either after the collapse of the Sarasvati towns or somewhat before.[15] Since this scripture speaks of the events as happening at the time of its composition, we can date this particular passage of the *Shatapatha-Brahmana* to around 1900 B.C. or earlier:

> *Mathava, [king of] Videgha, was at that time on the Sarasvati. He [God Agni] thence went burning along this Earth [eastward] and Videgha Mathava and [his chief priest] Gotama Rahugana followed him from the west as he was burning along. He burned out all these rivers. Now the [river] that is called Sadanira flows from the northern mountains [i.e., the Himalayas] he did not burn over. That one the brahmins did not cross in former times because it had not been burnt out by Agni Vaishvanara.*
>
> *Nowadays (*etarhi*), however, there are many brahmins to the east of it. At that time it [i.e., the land] was most uncultivated. . . .*
>
> *Mathava Videgha then said [to God Agni], "Where am I to live?" He said to him: "To the east of this [river] be your abode!" Even now this [river] forms the boundary of the Kosalas and the Videhas.*

The phrase "burned out" (*atidadaha*) by God Agni does not refer to any artificial conflagration created by the brahmins. It is probably a metaphoric statement about the rivers drying out through the agency of Agni in the form of the scorching sun, of which this deity is a manifestation. Alternatively, it could be a reference to the ritual purification of the rivers and their surrounding land by means of proper sacrifices in which God Agni played a leading role. In the opening hymn of the *Rig-Veda*, Agni is called God of the sacrifice.

In an earlier verse of the above passage from the *Shatapatha-Brahmana*, King Mathava is said to have carried Agni in his mouth and therefore did not speak when spoken to by his chief priest. However, when the sagely Gotama Rahugana, his chief priest, forecefully invoked God Agni, the deity leaped forth from the king's mouth. This is supposed to have occurred when Mathava was still at the Sarasvati River. From there Agni is said to have moved eastward. Possibly this legend was meant to account for the desiccation of entire rivers at that time. Only Agni was thought capable of the terrifying power of evaporating, "burning out," their massive waters. The *Rig-Veda* portrays him not only as a manifestation of the sun but also an offspring of the waters, meaning the oceans (which is where the sun is "born" in the east).

Because the *Shatapatha-Brahmana* does not mention the drying up of the Sarasvati itself as the reason for the eastward migration of the brahmins and their people, we may assume that this migration likely took place prior to 1900 B.C. Perhaps it occurred several hundred years earlier when the signs of spreading environmental disaster were becoming obvious to the inhabitants of northwestern India. It is curious that the passage does not remember the migrations as a tragic necessity but more as an opportunity to cultivate the land to the east of the Sarasvati.

After the worst of the great catastrophe had happened, wherever people may have gone in search of a better fortune, the society and civilization they once knew was no longer. Beyond question, the dispersal left people traumatized—a trauma that was surely passed on for several generations, until a family or clan had established itself firmly in the new country. We can only guess at the response of the governing elite, which saw its power base undermined with the devastation of the land and the emigration of the work force. Northern India's humanity entered a period of relative dormancy, marked by the struggle for survival and psychic recovery.

The Indian peninsula is still shifting and tilting. Earlier this century, the Bolan River in eastern Baluchistan shifted course westward. This time the disaster was fairly local, but, to the chagrin of archaeologists, it led to the flooding of the oldest part of the Mehrgarh site, which will be introduced in Chapter 8. On the other hand, the shift of the Bolan River exposed hitherto buried Neolithic settlement structures. Similarly, it seems likely that the buckling that caused the death of the Sarasvati River system also caused more positive geological changes elsewhere, such as new rivers or better flows in existing rivers. No doubt, in the coming years geologists will invest all the necessary ingenuity in exploring such questions.

Life after the Catastrophe

The massive hydrological changes and their climatic consequences in the Land of the Seven Rivers had far-reaching sociocultural repercussions. The early Indic civilization was laid to sleep in northwestern India. The cities and towns along the Indus River ceased to flourish and were finally abandoned as well. With the death of the heartland in the Sarasvati River system, the western region lost a vital stimulus, which spelled its own decline over a period of a hundred years or so.

But life is incredibly resilient, and, given the slightest opportunity, will recover even from a great trauma. We can see this, for instance, in the case of the collapse of the classical Maya civilization around 900 A.D. The collapse did not spell complete and utter destruction, even though numerous cities were abandoned and left in ruins. Rather, the Maya civilization continued to thrive in a transformed manner until the infelicitous Spanish conquest. In fact, it continues to exist in rural Mexico and is even tentatively undergoing a spiritual renewal.

Similarly, the ancient Indic civilization did not become extinct but simply shifted its center of vitality eastward toward the Ganges. It took, however, thirty or more generations before what has been called a "second urbanization" in the Ganges and Yamuna Valleys took place, starting around 1000 B.C. or perhaps a century later, though the Dwaraka site of 1500 B.C. suggests at least a smaller intermediate period of urbanization as well. Remembrance of the period of forest living in the Gangetic region before this second urbanization may be contained in the sacred books appropriately called *Aranyakas*, or "forest books." The *Aranyakas* and the *Upanishads*, by this reckoning, should belong to the second millennium B.C.

This apparently was also the time of the further development of the doctrines about reincarnation, karma, and spiritual liberation. Scholars have often presented these teachings as complete novelties. However, a closer study of the earlier sacred literature, as embodied in the four Vedic hymnodies, shows that the *Upanishads* by and large merely disclose and, to a degree, elaborate secret teachings that

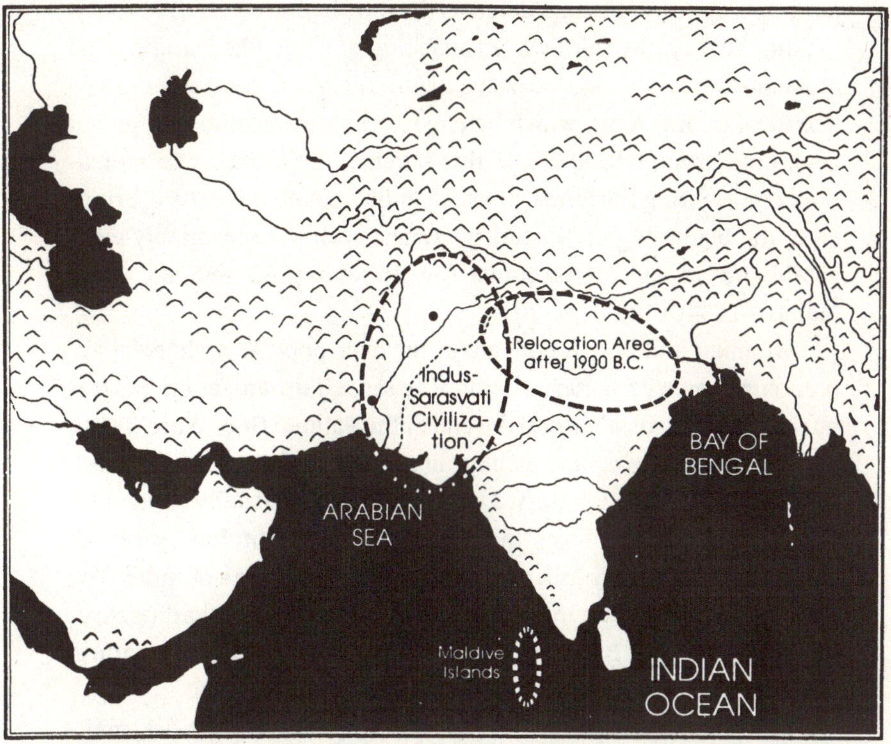

MAP 4. ***After the great catastrophe of circa 1900 B.C., the center of the early Indic civilization shifted from the Indus and Sarasvati rivers to the Ganges.***

had a long preceding history. But we can expect that the social and political restructuring after the catastrophe had some unquantifiable impact on the introspection in the forest hermits and their explanations of age-old teachings.

It is important to understand, however, that the reconstruction was a natural evolution from the earlier world. There was a continuing celebration of the glory days of the third millennium B.C. Even now the Vedic ritual requires the use of copper implements and barley that had been used before the catastrophe. Later art shows no break with the Indus-Sarasvati art.

If we consider the evidence of the Neolithic town of Mehrgarh, which will be discussed in Chapter 8, the second urbanization should more appropriately be considered as the fourth phase in India's town-making history, the third wave consisting of cities like Harappa and Mohenjo-Daro. The second wave of urbanization comprises towns like Balakot and Amri, which belong to a two-thousand-year period beginning around 4000 B.C. In this schema, the Gangetic urbanization, representing the fourth phase in India's urban adventure, brings us to the beginning of "historical" times, with the reasonably well-established dates for Gautama the Buddha (563-483 B.C.) and Mahavira (540-468 B.C.).

We must add here a note about the ever-popular archaeological preoccupation with pottery shards. The second urbanization has frequently been associated with the end of the Painted Gray Ware (PGW) phase (1200-800 B.C.) and with the introduction of the Northern Black Polished Ware (NBP) pottery. Late Harappa was partially contemporary with the PGW phase. In other words, a continuous series of cultural developments link the two early urbanizations of India. The PGW pottery has been interpreted as the property of invading Aryans from the west. But more recent scholarship views it as a natural development in craftsmanship from earlier pottery styles.

In a similar vein, there is a distinct difference in the brick-making of the two urbanizations. Yet, the difference cannot be explained by the intrusion of extraneous cultural elements. The Harappans are known to have used several brick sizes: 30 x 15 x 7.5 centimeters and 40 x 20 x 10 centimeters being the most common, where in these cases and others, the length, breadth, thickness ratio is about 4:2:1. The bricks used during the second urbanization of the Gangetic valley are not according to this ratio. One type encountered there has the ratio 7:4:1. But this departure is most likely a result of the popularization of one of the existing styles in a multiethnic and multicultural society. Again we do not observe a complete break with the earlier tradition but only reorganization and readjustment. Perhaps scholars are beginning to appreciate that past civilizations have had their own changes in fashion, which need not necessarily have been triggered by outside influences.

All the evidence points to a striking continuity between the early urban culture of Mehrgarh and the second urbanization witnessed in the fertile valley of the Ganges, which gave rise to the modern Hindu civilization. India's humanity has undergone many trials and tribulations. More than anything else, the repeated cataclysmic alterations in the course of the rivers of northern India have both tested and strengthened the resilience and creativity of the Indic people. The modern Indian nation can look back upon the longest continuous cultural history in the world—a fact that should inspire confidence in its people in dealing with the massive problems and challenges of today.

Chapter 6

The Vedic Peoples in the Land of the Seven Rivers: The Literary Perspective

Overview

WE HAVE LOOKED AT THE ARCHAEOLOGICAL EVIDENCE, which revealed to us a unique civilization that, before its time of tribulation around 1900 B.C., had risen to a high level of urbanization in such cities as Mohenjo-Daro, Harappa, Ganweriwala, Rakhigarhi, Kalibangan, Dholavira, and the harbor town of Lothal at the Arabian Sea.

We also have shown that the popular model of invading, Sanskrit-speaking Aryan nomads who broke the back of the early Indic civilization by demolishing these splendid cities is nothing more than scholarly fiction. The skeletons found in the streets of Mohenjo-Daro were at first taken to be a sure sign of the violence done to the urbanites at the hand of the Aryan invaders in the final days of that big city. More recently, archaeologists have dropped this interpretation of a massacre, since it received no support from other evidence found in Mohenjo-Daro and other sites. They also recognized that the skeletons belonged to different levels of occupation, which were not adequately distinguished by the pioneering excavators.

When we combine this with the fact that Indo-European speakers are now thought to have been present in Anatolia at the beginning of the Neolithic age, we arrive at an astonishing conclusion.

Modern researchers who have looked at all the evidence dispassionately now believe that the Vedic Aryans—a branch of the Indo-European-speaking world—in all probability lived in India long before they are supposed to have arrived there. *This completely turns topsy-turvy our view of ancient India and ancient history in general!* Small migrations of Indo-European-speaking groups as well as other peoples may well have occurred in Harappan times, as they have throughout India's history, but when they arrived in India they encountered a society that had a prominent, if not dominant, Indo-European contingent—the Sanskrit-speaking Vedic peoples.

Thus the key question now is: What was the relationship between the Vedic peoples and the civilization reflected in the great cities of the Indus and Sarasvati Rivers and their tributaries?

The early Indic civilization, as we know it from towns like Mohenjo-Daro and Harappa, but even from the much earlier settlement of Mehrgarh, was multiracial and multiethnic, similar in composition to the groups living in India today. Skeletons found at those sites have been identified as belonging to the Proto-Australoid, Mediterranean, Alpine, and Mongoloid races. We cannot rule out intermarriage between these races and ethnic groups in an intense urban environment. The Mediterranean race, such as most of the people in India today belong to, including the so-called Aryans and Dravidians, appears to have been the majority group.

We also must not pin particular languages to any of these racial groups. Thus the idea that the Indo-European-speaking Aryans were of the Nordic type is inherently misleading, since in simplistic fashion it equates language with race. The people of Harappa, Mohenjo-Daro, or Lothal may well have spoken various languages, and may have had a lingua franca intelligible to all ethnic groups. However, as we explain in the next chapter, statistical analysis of the Harappan script strongly suggests that the language imprinted on the numerous soapstone seals was Indo-European rather than Dravidian. But this does not rule out the presence of other languages in those cities, or even on some of the seals.

As stated above, the scholarly notion that the Vedic Aryans entered the Harappan world as intruders from beyond the mountain ranges of Afghanistan is no longer tenable. All the evidence points to their original home in India itself. Today we must consider the Vedic peoples as an integral part of the early Indic civilization. They walked the streets of Mohenjo-Daro and Harappa, if not old Mehrgarh, and had their businesses there and in other towns and villages along the Sarasvati and Indus Rivers and their many tributaries. It is even quite likely that they were the principal creators and sustainers of the Indus-Sarasvati civilization.

If this picture is essentially correct, we have in the *Vedas*, the sacred scriptures of the Vedic Aryans and later Hindus, a most impressive body of documents about the life and culture of a representative segment of the early Indic civilization. In other words, we no longer need to feel regret that our only source of information about the Indus-Sarasvati civilization is a script that defies decipherment and archaeological artifacts that raise many more questions than they have answered so far.

The *Vedas* are a remarkably faithful record of many of the beliefs and practices of that civilization. More than that, as we will explain, the *Rig-Veda* is the oldest surviving body of work of *any* civilization. It fills the gap between the early culture of the Neolithic town of Mehrgarh and the subsequent civilization of the Indus and Sarasvati Rivers. Clearly, it deserves our full attention and unprejudiced study.

The *Rig-Veda*: Hymns of Praise, Hymns of History

The British Vedicist Jeanine Miller has called the *Rig-Veda* "not only a highly important religious and literary document" but "also a work of art and a source of inspiration and edification."[1] It certainly is one of the most astounding relics of ancient humanity, for it discloses to us a cultural universe and a deep spirituality at a time for which oral or written documents are unavailable in all other known civilizations of the world.[2] The great Sanskrit scholar Max Müller, who translated the *Rig-Veda* in its entirety, said of the Vedic hymns that "they are to us unique and priceless guides in opening before our eyes tombs of thought richer in relics than the royal tombs of

Egypt" and that "they have their own unique place and stand by themselves in the literature of the world."[3]

While Müller rightly considered the Vedic hymns more ancient than the oldest Babylonian and Akkadian hymns, he wrongly judged them as being more primitive. He felt that "there are thoughts in those ancient Mesopotamian hymns which would have staggered the poets of the Veda."[4] Yet, the passages he quoted from the Mesopotamian literature fail to support his appraisal, despite their monotheistic flavor for which they had undoubtedly been selected by him.

अग्निमीळे पुरोहितं यज्ञस्य देवमृत्विजम् । होतारं रत्नधातमम् ॥१॥
अग्निः पूर्वेभिर्ऋषिभिरीड्यो नूतनैरुत । स देवाँ एह वक्षति ॥२॥
अग्निना रयिमश्नवत्पोषमेव दिवेदिवे । यशसं वीरवत्तमम् ॥३॥
अग्ने यं यज्ञमध्वरं विश्वतः परिभूरसि । स इद्देवेषु गच्छति ॥४॥
अग्निर्होता कविक्रतुः सत्यश्चित्रश्रवस्तमः । देवो देवेभिरा गमत् ॥५॥

FIG. 22. *Sanskrit text of the opening hymn of the* Rig-Veda, *dedicated to Agni, the God of Fire.*

Müller remained by and large unaware of the deeper spiritual significance of many Vedic hymns, preferring like most academic Vedicists a literal interpretation over a deeper metaphoric reading. He also failed to appreciate the historical clues in the *Rig-Veda*, which would have shown him that his dating for this hymnody was off the mark by at least a whole millennium.

Consisting of 1,028 hymns, the *Rig-Veda* is history in poetic form. Many of its skillfully composed hymns are replete with statements that have great relevance for the careful student of early Indic history. The most significant conclusion drawn from the geological references contained in this archaic hymnody is that the sagely composers of the *Rig-Veda* must have lived prior to the great cataclysm around 1900 B.C., for they still knew of the "seven rivers," notably the Sarasvati.

Thus we may take 2000 B.C. to be the lower limit for the composition of the *Rig-Veda*. Very probably it is considerably older. The subsequent Vedic literature—particularly the *Brahmanas* and *Aranyakas*—reflect a geography that is different from the one depicted in the *Rig-Veda*. Although some *Brahmanas* mention the Sarasvati River as an important place of habitation, these later works show signs of an eastward migration of the Vedic peoples. As the later Vedic literature unfolds, the Sarasvati recedes more and more into the background and the Ganges gradually comes to the fore. The *Puranas*, composed in post-Vedic times, have almost totally forgotten about the Sarasvati and give all praise to the Ganges River. Unfortunately, we no longer have the original *Purana*, which is mentioned in the early Vedic literature. We could expect its geographical information to confirm that of the *Rig-Veda* and other early Sanskrit works.

Be that as it may, from internal references in the Vedic literature we can now state with some certainty that the *Rig-Veda* was not composed, as maintained by many scholars under the spell of the Aryan invasion model, around 1200 B.C., but *at least* more than eight centuries earlier. The hymn composers knew of an environment that simply ceased to exist around 1900 B.C. What more concrete evidence could anyone wish for?

Similarly, the *Brahmanas* and *Aranyakas*, which are sacred scriptures based on the *Rig-Veda*, did not originate around 1000 B.C. to 800 B.C. but around 2000 B.C. to 1500 B.C. This makes them contemporaneous with the thirteenth to seventeenth dynasties of the "middle kingdom" in Egypt, which saw the disintegration of the unified state and the alien rule by the Asiatic Hyksos. However, the earliest *Brahmanas* and, perhaps the original *Purana* (the source of all the other *Puranas* of later times), appear to antedate the final systematization of the *Rig-Veda*. If that is the case, then a considerable part of this literature also must belong to the third millennium B.C.

Significantly, certain hymns in the *Rig-Veda* suggest a much earlier date than 2000 B.C. Thus statements in the *Vedas* refer to astronomical configurations that could only have occurred in the period from 2000 B.C. to 6000 B.C.[5] As we explain in a later chapter, the Vedic peoples were well versed in astronomy. Therefore, their statements should be given appropriate weight.

Due to the precession of the equinoxes, the pole star is not always the same. Around 3000 B.C. it was Alpha Draconis rather than Alpha Polaris, our current pole star. Alpha Draconis, also known as Thuban, is a medium-bright star in the tail of the constellation Draco, the Dragon, which winds halfway round the celestial pole. At that time, the seven main stars of the Big Dipper also were close to the polar axis, which may explain the prominence of the "seven seers" (*sapta-rishi*) associated with that constellation. Alpha Draconis was considered to be the eighth seer, who, according to the *Taittiriya-Aranyaka* (I.7.20), does not depart from Meru, the cosmic mountain, corresponding to the celestial pole. We will say more about the Indic peoples' knowledge of astronomy and especially the precessional phenomenon in Chapter 12.

References to the rising constellation at the time of solstice also allow us to assign certain dates. Already Hermann Jacobi, a renowned German scholar of the Vedic literature, noted that one of the hymns of the *Rig-Veda* (V.18-19) suggests a stellar pattern that could only have occurred in the period from 4500 B.C. to 2500 B.C., indicating a time in which the winter solstice occurred with the full moon in the Phalguni constellation, marking the later portion of the sign Leo and the early portion of the sign Virgo.[6] It is clear from this hymn that its author was not referring to some distant past but to his own time. This reading is confirmed by passages from later *Brahmana* works. Jacobi, in contradiction to most other scholars of his day, correctly placed most of the Vedic hymns in that early period.

Unfortunately, Jacobi's more famous compatriot and fellow Vedic researcher Max Müller ignored astronomical and calendrical allusions in the *Rig-Veda*. Instead he favored, quite arbitrarily, the date of 1500 B.C. to 1200 B.C., based primarily on Indo-European documents from the Middle East and the erroneous Aryan invasion model. Müller's view, though vehemently criticized by several eminent scholars of his day, won not only because of his overwhelming authority in the field of Indic studies, but because of the prevailing Eurocentric climate of opinion that did not want to see India as central to world civilization.

Surprisingly enough, many contemporary books on the history of India still echo this outdated view. For instance, the authors of a recent work on the history of India still claim that the dates furnished by Müller "tally very well with modern archaeological research showing at least half a millennium between the decline of the Indus civilisation and the immigration of a new nomadic population which might be identified with the Vedic Indo-Aryans."[7] Nothing could be more misleading than this statement, which simply perpetuates a nineteenth-century scholarly bias. There is no archaeological evidence for any significant migrations into India during the Post-Harappan era. It is also curious to note that in this revised version of the Aryan invasion theory, the Aryans are no longer accused of despoiling the Indus cities, which had perished prior to the demarcation date of 1500 B.C. They have suddenly become peaceful invaders!

The astronomical references in the *Rig-Veda* were first taken seriously by Bal Gangadhar Tilak, a celebrated late nineteenth-century scholar and politician of India. However, his views have been summarily dismissed by most other researchers. The fact that the *Rig-Veda* mentions a stellar configuration that corresponds to a date from 6000 B.C. to 7000 B.C.—the astronomical Ashvini era—must not be merely denied but properly explained.[8]

From what we now know about the dispersal of the Indo-European peoples at the beginning of the Neolithic age, we have every reason to assume that they were at least present in Mehrgarh, if not, what seems more likely, its creators. In its oldest portions, the *Rig-Veda* thus allows us a glimpse of the culture at the very beginnings of the Indic civilization. We are of course not able to identify all the most ancient hymns, though as a body the hymns of the *Rig-Veda* precede the abandonment of the Indus and Sarasvati towns and villages. Many of the hymns may well go back to the fourth millennium B.C.

Scholars have identified the second and seventh book of the ten books or *mandalas* (lit. "circles") of the *Rig-Veda* as containing the oldest Vedic hymns. Other books, such as the first and the tenth book, have been judged more recent. However, this chronology is questionable. When we examine the Vedic index, including the list of the seers who composed the hymns, many of the oldest seers are found in the first book and sometimes the tenth. For example, Gotama, who is the father of Vamadeva (the main seer-sage of the fourth book), contributed hymns to the first book. Other reputedly ancient seers, such as Hiranyastupa, Kanva, Kutsa, Kakshivat, Dirghatamas, and Agastya, also have their hymns in the first book. The attempt by previous scholars to read a progression of thought into the *Vedas* often overlooked the most basic facts of the Vedic lineages, which do not reflect this idea at all.

Whatever the truth may be, the Vedic hymns all attained a sacred status long ago and for millennia have been reverently looked upon as revelation. Fortunately, this reverential attitude obliged generations of the priestly families of India to memorize the sacred hymns with the utmost fidelity. Children were trained early on by their fathers in the art of memorization. Some were expected to learn all the hymns of the *Rig-Veda*. Especially gifted individuals managed to learn not only the *Rig-Veda* but also the other three Vedic hymnodies. The Vedic hymns were not only used during rituals but also were studied in themselves as treasured sources of spiritual knowledge and moral guidance.

Given the astonishingly faithful transmission of the lore embodied in the *Rig-Veda*, we must consider it as a primary source of knowledge for the early Indic civilization, which is even more important than the archaeological remains. For the artifacts dug up by archaeologists more often than not leave us guessing about their true meaning and place within the larger social and cultural context of the era to which they belong. By contrast, words—recorded with such fidelity as those of the *Rig-Veda*—provide many more clues than any artifacts ever could.

The Indus-Sarasvati artifacts and the testimony of the *Rig-Veda* and the other Vedic collections can illuminate each other, and, taken together, they represent a formidable body of evidence for an era in which we encounter only pervasive silence in the rest of the world.

The Vedic Peoples as City Builders and Seafaring Merchants

What picture emerges from a careful reading of the *Rig-Veda*? Who were the Vedic peoples? What was their environment like? How do they relate to the big excavated cities?

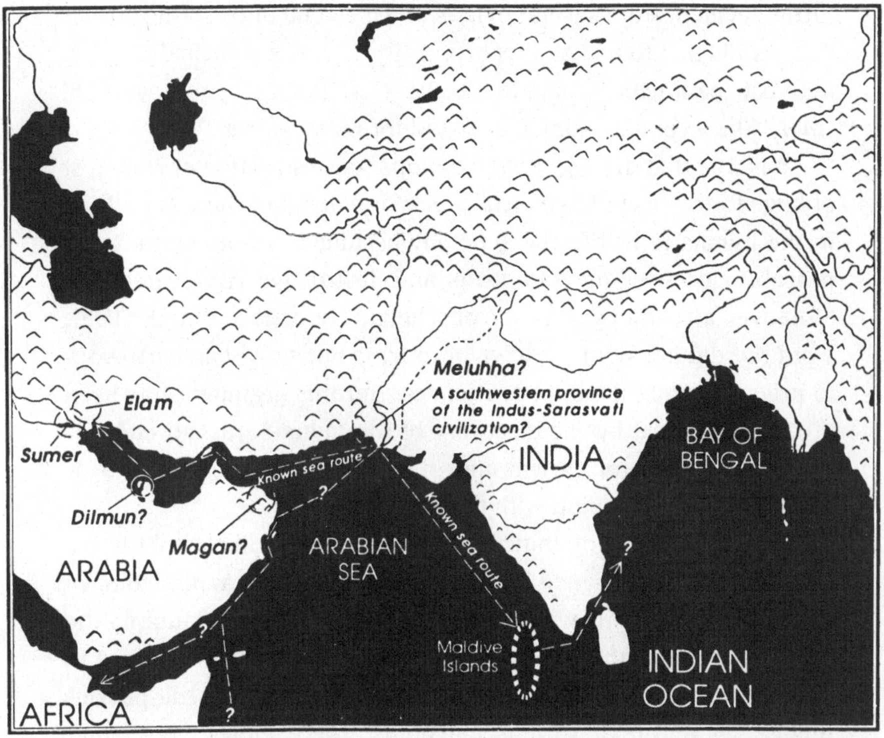

MAP 5. *The merchants of the Indus-Sarasvati civilization early on extended their trade by sea to other countries.*

According to a popular scholarly stereotype, the Vedic Aryans were cattle- and sheep-breeding seminomadic pastoralists. This may well be an accurate portrayal of a certain section of the Vedic society. However, the Vedic Aryans were more than wandering herders. They also were city dwellers and enthusiastic seafarers and merchants whose business took them the whole length of the great Sarasvati and Indus Rivers, as well as out into the oceans.[9]

As we have repeatedly emphasized, the Vedic peoples did not come as conquerors and destroyers from outside India, but lived in and even built the cities in the Land of the Seven Rivers. In several Rig-Vedic hymns, God Agni (associated with fire) is invoked to protect the Aryans with a hundred cities.[10] If they had no cities, the prayer would be nonsensical. The positive attitude toward cities is further evident from several hymns in which one or the other Aryan deity is likened to a vast supporting city. Indra, a principal deity of the Vedic pantheon, is said in the *Rig-Veda* (VII.26.3) to govern all cities "like a common single husband for many wives."[11]

It is true that the *Rig-Veda* mentions the destruction or conquest of large fortresses or towns (called *pur* or *pura*), but there is nothing in the hymns to justify the generally assumed dichotomy between peaceful city-dwelling Harappans and destructive Aryan nomads. Moreover, an earlier generation of scholars has argued that the Vedic word *pur* did not signify a town or fortress but simply an earthwork to protect against flooding or enemies. But this argument has been greatly weakened by the discovery of the Indus-Sarasvati civilization with its numerous towns and, of course, by our present identification of that civilization with the Vedic peoples.

Politically, the early Indic civilization was very likely split into a number of tribally aligned kingdoms, some of which appear to have been quite large. This was still the case at the time of Gautama the Buddha in the sixth century B.C. Evidently, the wars mentioned in the *Rig-Veda* were chiefly intertribal conflicts among the Vedic peoples themselves and their various kingdoms. The enemies were either fallen Aryans (groups deviating, perhaps only temporarily, from Vedic values) or non-Aryans (tribes perhaps not speaking an Indo-European language or sharing the moral values of the Vedic peoples). But we have no way of determining whether the antagonists belonged to the first or second group, as they are nowhere differentiated in the *Vedas* in those terms. From the Vedic point of view, all human beings are descendants of Manu who, like the biblical Adam, is considered to be the common ancestor of all human beings.

Thus the enemies of the celebrated Vedic King Sudas are described in the *Rig-Veda* as being both Aryans and Dasas or Dasyus. Both groups are traced to the same Vedic ancestors and their tribes.[12] In classical Sanskrit, the word *dasa* means "servant" or "slave," but in those early times it must have stood for the exact opposite of the word *arya* ("noble"). In other words, the Dasyus were ignoble folk, people lacking the spiritual vision of the Vedic Aryans. The Iranians provide further illumination here. For *daha*, the Iranian equivalent of *dasa*, represents the common Aryan people. It is for this reason that scholars have suggested that the Aryan-Dasa conflict might just represent a struggle between the Indic and the Iranian Aryans. In most instances, however, the conflict appears to be entirely mythological.

Thus in several hymns, the Dasyus are described as dark-skinned, and this has often been taken as a telltale sign that they were a Dravidian-speaking race. However, such references are not so much racial descriptions as metaphors, referring to the symbolic battle between light and darkness, as it is described in most ancient mythologies. For instance, the battle between light and darkness is mirrored in the struggle between the Egyptian solar deity Ra and the demons of darkness, in the war between the deities of the Greek pantheon and the Titans, and in the biblical battle between God and Satan. This mythological motif is most evident in the Zoroastrian (ancient Persian) conflict between Ahura Mazda and Ahriman. In many of these myths the enemy can be equated with the principle of evil, the dark forces of existence. It seems strange that, in the case of India, scholars should have turned this cosmological-theological myth into a racial war.

In one instance, the hymn composers call the Dasyus "noseless" (*anasa*), which some modern interpreters of the *Rig-Veda* have understood in deprecating racial terms as "flat-nosed," taking this to be a reference to the Dravidians of South India. But it is not the Dravidians who are racially low-nosed but the aborigines of India. At any rate, the term *anasa* does not mean "flat-nosed" but "without nose" or "noseless." This descriptive adjective applies not to any human group but to the serpent race of Vedic mythology, as further designations of the Dasyus as "handless" and "footless" indicate.[13] The Dasyus are usually a group of serpentlike demons, and only occasionally is this epithet used as a metaphor for evil people.

It is also curious that this designation, whose meaning is actually in dispute and which occurs but a single time in the entire Vedic literature, should have become one of the cornerstones of the Aryan invasion theory. If the same strategy were used in regard to other rare and disputed terms in the *Vedas*, we could create any number of bizarre theories. In any case, the identification of the Dasyus with the Dravidians or some other non-Aryan group is disproved by the fact that, in some contexts, the name Dasyu is applied to fallen Aryans, who could often be reinstated as Aryans once they purified themselves.

It is clear from the Vedic hymns that the tribes conquered by King Sudas had the same culture but were deemed renegades, who followed different priests, perhaps challenging the ruling orthodoxy and, above all, who were led by kings considered to be unrighteous. The Dasyus are usually described as fallen *kshatriyas*, or members of the warrior class, who have become unspiritual, flouting the proper rituals. In hymn VII.7 of the *Rig-Veda*, the Dasyus are identified with the Panis, the well-to-do merchants who are said to be harmful in their speech and without faith. Perhaps, from the point of view of the Vedic orthodoxy, they were what we would now call materialists. They may have been blinded by the allurements of the cities and were possibly a little jaded from their travels in foreign lands, where they encountered other customs and beliefs. The Panis's greed knew no bounds, for elsewhere in the *Rig-Veda*, they are denounced as cattle thieves.

Some researchers, including one of the present authors (David Frawley), have speculatively associated or equated the Vedic Panis with the Phoenicians. It appears that both were enterprising merchants. The Phoenicians called themselves Canaanites and spoke a Semitic tongue closely related to Hebrew. Racially, they were also close to the Hebrew-speaking tribes. The Greeks called them Phoenike and the Romans spoke of them as the Poeni. Their Greek name, first used by the bard Homer, is the familiar *phoenix* in the singular, which originally referred to a dark red or purple color. Perhaps it was applied to the Canaanites because of their brownish skin color.

The Phoenicians were a great maritime nation and were famed for their nautical skills. They had succeeded in circumnavigating Africa and there is some evidence that they might even have sailed (or drifted) across the Atlantic to the New World. It is feasible that they also reached India at an early age, though this is pure speculation. Although the origins of these industrious people are a mystery, they were busy pursuing international commerce already before 3000 B.C. When, around 2200 B.C., their seafaring power was temporarily interrupted by military attacks upon their coastal cities, the Egyptians complained about the lack of cedar wood for their sarcophagi. The connections between the civilizations of antiquity are only poorly understood, but we know that they existed and possibly were far more intensive than we can gauge from the scant evidence available. Judging from the Vedic literature, the Panis seemed strongly motivated by profit, and perhaps a hunger for adventure, and in their maritime trade had carved out a lucrative niche for themselves for literally thousands of years.

At the same time, we cannot ignore the fact that the early Vedic references to the Panis are heavily mythologized, and it is difficult, if not impossible, to reach any definite picture of them as actual people.

King Sudas's war against the ten kings, mentioned above, was a defensive battle against hostile forces that had formed an overpowering coalition, which was seeking to strangulate Sudas's righteous kingdom at the Sarasvati River. As the Vedic hymns relate, Sudas miraculously triumphed over his enemies—not least thanks to the prayers of the chief priest Vasishtha, if we can believe his own testimony, as given in the *Rig-Veda* (VII.33.3). Vasishtha and his fellow priests apparently enabled Sudas's army to cross the river during a flood, while the priesthood of the hostile alliance failed to do the same, thus causing the drowning of even the swiftest warriors. Much later, Moses is credited with working a similar miracle for the Hebrews, who safely crossed the Sea of Reeds, whereas the pursuing Egyptian force was annihilated by the waves. As noted earlier, there may be a naturalistic interpretation for this miracle, which in itself need not discredit the biblical view of this extraordinary event. After all, if miracles are not wonderful coincidences, what are they?

Sudas, head of the Tritsus, is also said to have destroyed or conquered seven towns, which appear to have been cities of his adversarial kinsmen.[14] The civil war fought by Sudas supposedly claimed the lives of 66,660 enemies, reminding one of other Vedic battles that speak of 60,000 or 100,000 among the conquered. With ten hostile kingdoms involved, this figure is not impossible, though it is more likely that such numbers encode certain characteristics and are not to be taken literally.

In later Vedic literature we learn that the sons of Sudas themselves fell from the Aryan way of life and consequently were called *rakshasas*, or "demons." They are accused of killing the hundred sons of the great seer Vasishtha, who guided Sudas. We also learn that the Kavashas, who had been among those defeated by Sudas, were reinstated and became the chief priests (*purohita*) of the Kuru dynasty, the most celebrated of the royal dynasties of ancient India. One of the Kavashas, Tura Kavasheya, even heads an important list of Upanishadic sages! Clearly, *arya* and *dasyu* are terms describing not race but behavior. As the behavior of a group or individual changed, so did the label.

Another, earlier king by the name of Divodasa is mentioned in the eighth book of the *Rig-Veda* as the destroyer of the hundred towns of Shambara. Aided by God Indra, Divodasa also "caused the seven rivers to flow to the sea." Some interpreters have taken this to mean that he demolished the artificial dams regulating the flow of the rivers in northern India, with the result that the land below the dams was devastated by flooding. However, the release of the seven rivers appears to have primarily a spiritual significance. It is possible, though, that in addition to its symbolic message the myth remembers a huge flood. Be that as it may, we have no firm historical information about either Divodasa or the conquered King Shambara, but both lived before Sudas.[15]

In another Rig-Vedic hymn (IV.61.2), Divodasa is described as defeating the Turvashas and the Yadus, two of the five main Vedic tribes, suggesting that Shambara was of the same group. This idea is confirmed in various *Puranas*, where Divodasa, king of Kashi (Varanasi or Benares), is reported as having defeated the Yadus. As a matter of fact, most of the battles mentioned in the *Purana* literature are against the Yadus, who are the branch of the Vedic people most frequently called Dasyus or given other similar derogatory names. The sixth incarnation (*avatara*) of God Vishnu, who bears the name Parashu Rama ("Rama with the Axe"), is specifically said to have come into being in order to defeat the Yadus. The great king Sagara of Ayodhya is also said to have defeated them after they had overrun all of northern India.

Even demon-ruler Ravana, who was defeated by King Rama, is related in the *Ramayana* epic to the demon Lavana, who ruled Mathura, one of the main cities of the Yadus. Furthermore, the first people from northern India to come to Sri Lanka (formerly Ceylon), where Ravana ruled, are said to have hailed from Gujarat, a land of the Yadus. Significantly, the *Ramayana* speaks of Ravana as a brahmin and a chanter of the *Sama-Veda*. Incidentally, even Vritra, the Vedic archdemon who is killed by Indra, is thought to have been a brahmin. It is also important to note that the eighth incarnation of Vishnu, Lord Krishna, took birth among these same Yadus, who also produced a number of pious kings and sages. In light of this evidence, it is safe to assume that the Vedic and Puranic battles—when they are not purely allegorical—are among peoples of the same culture but of different spiritual status as a result of their behavior.

We also want to emphasize that mere pastoralists, as the Aryans have always been described, do not build towns or ships, establish kingdoms, or maintain organized armies. They certainly do not venture out into the ocean in pursuit of commerce with other nations. But this is exactly what we know about the Vedic people from the hymns of the *Rig-Veda*, which mention the two oceans to the east and the west (probably the Bay of Bengal and the Arabian Sea), just as they mention ships and maritime trade.

FIG. 23. *Soapstone seal, clearly showing the kind of ship in which the merchants of Mohenjo-Daro and the other towns carried their precious cargo, not only inside the borders of their extensive civilization but also across the ocean to the Middle East and other areas.*

Bhujyu, who is one of the main ancestral figures of the Vedic people, is said in the *Rig-Veda* (I.116.5) to have been brought home safely in a ship with a hundred oars.

Although Bhujyu is one of the many names of the sun, the mention of a ship with a hundred oars may not be mere fantasy. The idea of a houseboat is implied in several hymns, and so is ocean travel over a period of many days. The Vedic people were well aware that the Indus and the Sarasvati poured their water into the ocean, that the ocean roars, is ever in motion through its waves, and encircles the land masses.

The picture of the Vedic people as seafaring merchants meshes perfectly with the archaeological evidence of the Indus-Sarasvati civilization. Apart from foreign artifacts in the Indus cities and Indus artifacts overseas, there are also steatite seals depicting seaworthy vessels. The Aryan invasion model, which is predicated on the notion that the Vedic Aryans were seminomadic cattle breeders, can offer no valid explanation for the numerous references to maritime interest in the *Vedas*. However, when we realize that the Vedic people and the Harappans represent one and the same culture, we can perfectly understand the extraordinary parallels between archaeological artifacts and literary evidence.

The seafaring nature of the Hindus is well known from later sources. King Hiram of Tyre (Phoenicia) in 975 B.C. traded with India through the port of Ophir (Supara) near modern Bombay. What most historians have failed to notice in this is that Supara is a Sanskrit name, thus placing the Vedic people on the coast of south central India before 1000 B.C. We also know that Aryans from northern India began migrating to Sri Lanka before the time of the Buddha (563 B.C.). Additionally, inscriptions in the Brahmi alphabet have been found in Indonesia from the third century B.C.[16] These accomplishments would be highly improbable if the Aryans had been land-based nomads, who conquered India gradually after 1500 B.C.

In Chapter 7, we will speak of the archaeological discovery of stamp seals from the early Indic civilization in the Middle East and elsewhere. A script resembling that of the Indic civilization has been found on the remote Easter Island. Although the origin of the Easter Island glyphs remains an enigma, as does the origin of the islanders themselves, most scholars have a priori excluded the possibility of maritime travel in the ancient world. Yet, the Polynesians, who are racially mixed (including a strong European strand), long ago crossed the oceans in seemingly precarious boats to populate the islands in the middle of the Pacific.

The truth is that the capacity for sea travel among ancient peoples has been systematically underestimated. There is mounting evidence that they were in fact well accomplished in maritime navigation, crossing thousands of miles of open ocean, guided by the stars and handed-down navigational charts.[17]

Harappan seals discovered at several Mesopotamian sites have been dated to about 2400 B.C. Judging from the available evidence, the flow of goods seems to have gone primarily from India westward to Mesopotamia, rather than from Mesopotamia to India. Early Indic merchants very probably made their home in the towns of the Middle East, acting as importers of goods from India. Unlike India, Mesopotamia is not rich in natural resources. Although the Sumerians knew how to drain the marshes and irrigate the land, they and their Akkadian descendants heavily depended on imports. Sumer's soil was so arid that it did not even produce trees, and was almost without stone. The timber for houses, ships, and temples had to be laboriously transported from far away, which bespeaks of the Sumerians' industriousness, creativity, and resolution. They have occasionally been portrayed as a somewhat unreligious people, but the central position of the temple in each Sumerian city hardly bears out this judgment. However, their religiosity may not have been the deep, spontaneous spirituality of the Vedic people, as we can glean it from the *Rig-Veda* and other sacred scriptures. Rather the Sumerians, who called themselves "black-heads" (*sang-ngiga*), appear more restrained, formal, and perhaps even prosaic in their orientation to religious matters. If this impression is correct, they anticipated the attitude of the Romans by three thousand years.

The Mysterious Lands of Meluhha, Magan, and Dilmun

The Mesopotamians knew of the great countries of Meluhha, Magan, and Dilmun. The identity of Dilmun is still a mystery. However, most scholars today tentatively identify it as the island of Bahrain in the Arabian/Persian Gulf, and perhaps the nearby coastal land on the Arabian peninsula. By the middle of the third century, Bahrain was densely populated, serving as a stopover for seafaring merchants, especially of Indic origin. The renowned British archaeologist Geoffrey Bibby, who directed the early excavations in Bahrain, made the following significant statement in his book *Looking for Dilmun*:

> *A puzzle remained. Why had Dilmun used the standard weights of the Indus Valley? The Babylonians and Sumerians used a completely different system . . . Either the first commercial impulses to have reached Dilmun must have come not from Mesopotamia but from India, or else India was a far more important commercial connection with Dilmun than was Mesopotamia.*[18]

It is probable that Dilmun was either a colony of the Indus-Sarasvati civilization or a vitally important outpost for its merchants. The first mention of Dilmun is in a cuneiform text from Ur-nanshe, king of Lagash, in South Babylonia. The king, who lived about 2520 B.C., notes in his inscription on the tablet that "the ships from Dilmun, from the foreign lands, brought me wood as a tribute." It is likely that the source of the timber gifted to the ruler of Lagash was in fact India, which had immense forests.

The significance of the island of Bahrain, which is smaller than New York City, can be seen in the fact that it has more than 100,000 burial mounds (*tumuli*)—from thirteen to sixty-six feet in diameter—each covering a stone-built burial chamber containing only a single body, together with funerary offerings. Dilmun, or Bahrain, was regarded as a sacred land by the ancients, and many undertook the long pilgrimage from Mesopotamia and Arabia to be buried there. Sadly, over the centuries, grave robbers emptied the chambers, so that they yield few finds. Fortunately, however, only a handful of the mounds have been excavated, so that there may still be wonderful surprises in store for archaeologists.

The great Sumerologist Samuel Noah Kramer remained skeptical about the placement of Dilmun in Bahrain. He favored a different location, stating that "there is even some possibility that Dilmun may turn out to include the region in Pakistan and India where a remarkable urban, literate culture flourished toward the end of the third millennium B.C., the so-called Harappan, or Indus Valley, culture."[19] His main argument is that the Sumerian texts generally refer to the blessed land of Dilmun as "the place where the sun rises," which does not fit the island of Bahrain, located to the south of Sumer.

Kramer equated Dilmun with what the Sumerian scriptures call "The Cedar Land," arguing that it lay east of the kingdom of Elam. The solar deity Utu is said to rise there. Curiously, in Sanskrit, the word *udu* means "star," with *udu-pati* designating the moon. The Vedic solar deity is Surya, who is understandably described in rather similar terms to Utu. In particular, both deities seem to be associated with a predatory bird. On one Sumerian cylinder seal, Utu is shown rising between two mountains, with flames emerging behind him. On his right a winged being (identified as the Goddess Inanna/Ishtar) can be seen hovering in the sky. To his left is a hawklike or eaglelike creature. In the *Rig-Veda*, significantly, Surya is often symbolized as a bird and is called "fine-winged" (*su-parna*). He too is associated with the primal mountain (or mountains).

Wherever Dilmun's location may turn out to be, as Kramer stressed, it "is not just a literary fiction, a never-never land created by the fertile imagination of the Sumerian bards and poets."[20] The country's name appears too frequently in the Sumerian and Akkadian tablets, recording incoming shipments of timber, gold, copper, lapis lazuli, ivory, and other valuable commodities.

Equally historical are Meluhha and Magan (or Makan) mentioned in the cuneiform texts, though their identity is even less certain than that of Dilmun.[21] Some authorities have located Magan as far south as the Sudan or Ethiopia. The consensus of scholarly opinion identifies this country, which was the source of much of Mesopotamia's copper, as Oman at the bottom of the Arabian peninsula. There copper mines were worked as early as the fifth millennium B.C. Recently, an inscription in the Harappan script has been found at Ras al-Junayz on the Omani coast. Because of the intensive copper export, the members of the Omani elite were incredibly wealthy, which may have attracted the attention of the maritime merchants from the Indus and Sarasvati Rivers.

Meluhha (or Melukhkha) has been identified with eastern Iran and western Afghanistan or, what is more likely, with the Harappan civilization or its southernmost province bordering on the Arabian Sea. The Mesopotamian texts specify Meluhha as the source of its imported carnelian, which is a beautiful mineral of translucent red color. This helpful hint narrows down the choice to what is today Rajputana, which is exactly the area of the former Sarasvati River and the present-day Thar Desert.

The cuneiform texts also mention the import of tables and multi-colored ivory birds from Meluhha, and the materials from which these exports were fashioned was available in ample quantities in the Indus-Sarasvati civilization.

The emerging scenario is of the early Indic peoples as skilled seafarers and enterprising merchants. Maritime trade seems to have been one of the foundations of their economy. The Mesopotamian records speak of ships from Meluhha bringing wealth to the people of the Tigris and Euphrates, never of their own ships heading eastward. It appears that the early Indic civilization in the third and early second millennia played a role similar to the Phoenicians in the first millennium B.C. It will be remembered that the Phoenicians were not only skillful merchants, whose ships sailed the world's oceans, but also the inventors of the alphabetic script of twenty-two letters. The merchants of the Harappan civilization probably exported the same goods that the earlier merchants of Mehrgarh traded overland with countries to the west. The main export article to Mesopotamia was probably cotton which was cultivated in India already in the seventh millennium B.C.

The Religious World of the Vedic Harappans

If the Vedic peoples and the Indus-Sarasvati civilization were entirely different cultures, we would expect to find few, if any, parallels between their religious worlds, as they can be reconstructed from the archaeological and textual evidence. But this is not at all the case. On the contrary, when we look closely enough, we find an abundance of significant overlap. Even those researchers who dismiss the notion that the Vedic people may have lived peaceably with their Harappan neighbors or, as we and several other scholars claim, were in fact one and the same people, have often remarked on the astonishing parallels between Indus artifacts and Vedic scriptural testimony.

What do we know about the Indus religion? The honest answer must be not very much, and what we know is largely inferred from the artifacts. Most researchers are agreed that, in the words of the British archaeologist Stuart Piggott, there is "more than a hint that the priesthood of some religion played a very important part in the regulation of Harappa economy from within the walls of the citadels of the two capital cities."[22] A similar emphasis on the priesthood is also found in the Vedic literature and is central to Hinduism.

The numerous clay figurines of mostly nude women suggest to most scholars the presence of a Mother Goddess cult, which would have played a part in household shrines rather than public temples. A representation of a female from whose womb a plant issues strengthens this idea of a Goddess responsible for fecundity. Such Goddesses are common in rural Hinduism even today. Goddesses are even mentioned in many hymns of the *Rig-Veda*, thus clearly contradicting popular scholarly opinion, which characterizes the Vedic religion as male oriented. Much of this view came from a lack of understanding of Vedic Sanskrit in which words with feminine case endings, which are nearly as numerous as masculine words, often refer to Goddesses.

There are several steatite representations of a horned male deity, seated in a yogilike position on a podium and surrounded by wild beasts. Art historian Stella Kramrisch made the following observation about this seal:

> *Although the enthroned figure with its large head and sex organ defies identification, it is like the other unidentified figures shown in a yoga posture. On either side of the enthroned yogi and above his arms, a tiger and an elephant*

are on his right, a rhinoceros and buffalo on his left, and two antelopes are below, that is, in front of his throne. The composition of this steatite relief is hieratic. The horn-crowned and enthroned yogi figure forms an isosceles triangle whose axis connects the middle of the bifurcating horns, the long nose, and the erect phallus of the deity.[23]

Kramrisch particularly emphasizes the figure's bovine facial features reminiscent of a mask. Almost all researchers see in this figure a prototype of the great Hindu deity Shiva Pashupati, who is Lord of the Beasts and archetypal yogi. Rudra/Shiva is the most prominent deity of the *Yajur-Veda*, perhaps linking the Harappan religion with this later Vedic text. However, other Vedic deities, like Indra, Agni, and Soma, also are sometimes called Lord of the Beasts and many are given the epithet "bull" (*vrisha*).

Polished stones of up to two feet long and pierced stones have been taken to represent male and female generative organs respectively—*linga* and *yoni*. And this affords another remarkable continuity in religious imagery and presumably ritual, notably in the tradition of Tantrism. Worship by means of standing stones and pillars is a common feature of Vedic religion and the religions of many other ancient civilizations. Some scholars see in the mortar and pestlelike *soma* stones of Vedic times the basis for the *linga-yoni* stones of Hinduism.

FIG. 24. ***This seal combines two favorite motifs—tree and unicorn.***

There also is evidence of the practice of what has been mislabelled "tree worship" in Harappan times, for one of the seals shows a deity standing in the branches of the sacred fig tree, which is still regarded as a sacred tree and is mentioned as such in the *Rig-Veda* (I.24; I.164) and also in the *Atharva-Veda* (IV.37; V.5; XIX.31). The ritual worship, of course, relates not to the tree but to the spirit or deity associated with the tree. We will say more about this particular seal in the next chapter.

Numerous seals depict a variety of animals, which may have held a sacred significance for the Harappans. Piggott singled out the humped or Brahma bull (*Bos indicus*), a species that is allowed to roam freely and unmolested in India's villages and towns even today. He also mentions animals standing in front of "mangers." The Indic scholar I. Mahadevan has furnished an ingenious interpretation for those images.[24] He believes that the mangers were sacred devices for filtering the Vedic ambrosia (*soma*), which played a crucial role in the ancient Vedic rituals. The animal in front of the filter is usually a humpless bull (possibly a descendant of *Bos primigenius*) portrayed with a single horn, which has often been called a unicorn. The large forward-pointing horn is very probably the result of the bull's portrayal in profile, which conceals the second horn. The bull symbolizes the Vedic ambrosial draught, which in the *Rig-Veda* is frequently compared to a bull.

FIG. 25. *With the help of the symbolism of the* Vedas, *the enigmatic bull-unicorn on this seal can be interpreted convincingly.*

Some scholars think that none of the archaeological buildings can positively be identified as temples. But recently two archaeologists have plausibly argued that one of the larger buildings at Mohenjo-Daro, with a central courtyard and symmetrically arranged rooms, was used as a fire temple.[25]

In his book *Prehistoric India*, Piggott expressed the consensus of scholarly opinion at the time when he noted that possibly Hindu society owed more to Harappa than to the Sanskrit-speaking invaders. Yet he, and others, conveniently overlooked the fact that there is nothing in the above catalogue of religious elements that would irrefutably demonstrate that the Harappans and the Vedic Aryans were entirely different cultures.

On the other hand, when we drop the Aryan invasion model, we find that there is in fact good reason to assume the identity of the

Indus-Sarasvati civilization with the Vedic culture. In that case, the alleged survivals in Hinduism of symbolic elements and ritual practices from the "pre-Aryan Harappans" turn out to be simple continuities within the same civilization. In other words, Harappan tree worship or the Mother Goddess cult did not surreptitiously sneak into Hinduism but have been an integral part of the Hindu religion since ancient times. We also want to emphasize that the *Vedas* preserve the priestly religion of the times. One would expect that the common people may have entertained slightly divergent beliefs and practices, as they do in rural India today.

There is strong supportive evidence for the Vedic nature of the Indus-Sarasvati civilization. This concerns the fire altars found at several Indus sites. It must be appreciated that at the core of the Vedic religion is sacrifice. It was thought to duplicate the cosmic process itself, since all things of the world are sacrificed in the fire of time. Sacrifice, however, involves ritual and, for the Vedic priests, ritual meant the construction of altars out of bricks. Sun-dried or burnt bricks were common in the Indus-Sarasvati towns.

The Vedic altar was regarded as a miniature representation of the cosmos and was assembled piece by piece. The single most important sacrificial ritual in Vedic times and later was the fire ritual (*agni-shtoma* or *agni-hotra*). The Vedic literature is pervaded by a rich mythological symbolism revolving around the central notion of the sacrificial fire, which was understood to be a representation of the sun and, by further extension, of the blinding radiance of the transcendental reality.

Sacrificial altars have been excavated in Indus towns over a large area, from Baluchistan in the west to Uttar Pradesh in the east and Gujarat in the south. In the citadel at the site of Kalibangan, which lies at the confluence of the famous Sarasvati and Drishadvati Rivers of Vedic lore, seven rectangular fire altars were found. They stood in a row, aligned north-south, beside a well. This parallels the six Vedic *dhishnya* hearths that are lined up in the same way; the seventh hearth could be one of the additional hearths used for cleaning the ritual implements. Circular and ovoid altars also have been discovered. Some of them contained the ashes of charcoal and offerings of beads and gold. One altar has five layers, just as a Vedic fire altar would.

When we assemble all the available pieces of the puzzle, we obtain a discernable pattern—not yet complete but certainly adequate enough to demand a new way of looking at India's ancient history. When we look with open eyes and an open mind at the puzzle, as it slowly but surely is emerging from piecemeal archaeological reconstruction, we find increasing certainty that the Indus-Sarasvati civilization was not pre-Aryan but essentially Vedic.

There is nothing in the *Rig-Veda* that starkly contradicts what we know about ancient India from the archaeological excavations. On the contrary, there are many parallels in geography, culture, and chronology between the Vedic society, as mirrored in the hymns, and the Indus-Sarasvati civilization, as reflected in the archaeological artifacts. These two bodies of evidence strongly suggest the conclusion that the two civilizations were one and the same. In other words, we may with reasonable certainty assume that the Indus-Sarasvati civilization was thoroughly Vedic or, conversely, that the *Rig-Veda* and the other related sacred hymns, were the product of the religious genius of the people who created the urban civilization of the Land of the Seven Rivers.

CHAPTER 7

Deciphering the Indus-Sarasvati Script

Beyond Oral Transmission

THE *RIG-VEDA* AND THE THREE OTHER ANCIENT VEDIC hymnodies are traditionally regarded as "superhuman" knowledge, revealed by seer-sages (*rishi*) in a heightened state of awareness. The four sacred Vedic collections were from the beginning orally transmitted within priestly families. Some brahmins were able to memorize the thousands of verses of only one Vedic hymnody; others, two, three, or all four—a truly astounding feat.

Because of this emphasis on oral transmission and the absence of ancient written records, some scholars have assumed that the Vedic peoples were illiterate. In the preceding chapters, we have shown that we are no longer justified in differentiating the Vedic Aryans from the creators of the Indus-Sarasvati civilization. They were one and the same people. Of course, not everyone lived in the towns along the Indus and Sarasvati Rivers and their many tributaries. On the contrary, as in modern India, the majority of the Vedic population probably lived in small villages scattered throughout the countryside wherever there was soil fertile enough to grow barley and other crops and to pasture cattle. These villagers, then as now, very likely could neither read nor write.

But the Vedic city dwellers were probably a literate or at least semi-literate folk. To be sure, the presence of a strong oral tradition does not preclude literacy. On the contrary, it may show a concern with

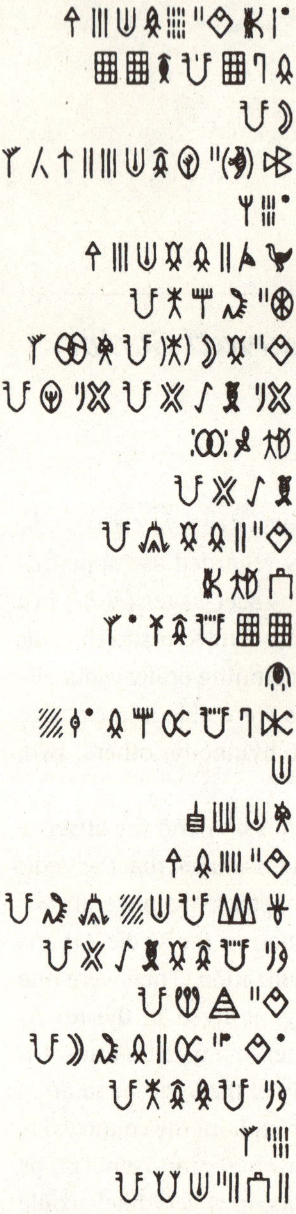

FIG. 26. *A sampling of words or phrases found on Harappan seals in the still undeciphered script.*

faithfulness in the transmission of knowledge, which requires something more, not less, than the written word. Evidence for writing in Vedic times is found in an overlooked reference in the *Rig-Veda* (X.62. 7) itself. Here the strange compound *ashta-karṇyah*, or "eight-eared," is applied to cattle. This phrase has generally been understood in the sense of "broad-eared" or "fully grown." However, more likely it refers to cattle that had their ears branded or marked with the numeral eight. The symbolic significance of eight is not clear, though the numeral is rarely mentioned in the *Rig-Veda.*

There also is a fascinating statement in the *Atharva-Veda* (XIX.72.1) that the Veda is to be replaced in the chest (*kosha*) from which it was taken. Admittedly, this particular Vedic hymnody is somewhat younger than the *Rig-Veda*, but it still belongs to the era coinciding with the last phase of the Indus cities.

Although the memory of the ancients appears to have been phenomenal, it is nonetheless difficult to believe that the massive corpus of Vedic literature was transmitted by oral tradition alone, without the help of written documents. In this regard we must note that the *Vedas* commonly speak of the "word" that is seen as well as heard, as for instance in the *Rig-Veda* (X.71.4). While this has been taken to imply intellectual seeing (or understanding), we cannot rule out the possibility of the written word.

Thus the Vedic poet-seers are often said to fashion or carve their hymns like a craftsman does a chariot.[1] This fashioning or carving—the verbal root *taksh* is used—need not be a poetic metaphor only but could refer to actual writing. It seems that without a script, the Vedic poets would have found it exceedingly difficult to meet the rigorous standards of Sanskrit metric composition.

तत् सवितुर् वरेण्यं
भर्गो देवस्य धीमहि
धियो यो नः प्रचोदयात् ॥

FIG. 27. *Sanskrit text of the famous* gayatri-mantra.

The bards knew no fewer than fifteen distinct meters, though employed only seven of these frequently. Approximately one quarter of the total number of verses in the *Rig-Veda* are composed in the *gayatri* meter, which has three sections of eight syllables each, the first four syllables of which are free while the last four have a prescribed cadence. This meter derives its name from the most famous Vedic mantra, which reads *tat savitur varenyam, bhargo devasya dhimahi, dhiyo yo nah pracodayat*. In English translation, this sacred utterance means, "Let us contemplate the beautiful splendor of God Savitri, that he may inspire our visions." To this day, pious Hindus recite this mantra at dawn and at dusk to receive the blessings of the divine Light manifesting in the luminous orb of the sun.

The *Taittiriya-Samhita* (V.2.8) of the *Yajur-Veda* speaks of the "divine sign" (*deva-lakshman*) that is written threefold (*try-alikhita*), which could well be a reference to the sacred sign *om*, which has three constituent parts. In some old rites, the syllable *om* has to be written out on the ground or traced in water—a tradition that may have had its origin in Vedic times.

The *Shukla-Yajur-Veda* (XVII.2) mentions the names for numbers from 10 to 1,000,000,000,000. Mathematics involving such large numbers is impossible without some form of written annotation. Incidentally, as C. W. Ceram pointed out long ago in his famous book *Gods, Graves and Scholars*, the concept of one million did not become common in the West until the nineteenth century.[2] The Christian Middle Ages were notoriously averse to long strings of numerals and would have been horrified at the familiarity with which the Indic peoples and the Mesopotamians, as well as the Maya, handled large numbers.

Furthermore, the geometric design of the Vedic fire altar involved mathematical calculations that could not possibly be done in the head, unless we assume the priests were *idiot savants* in the field of arithmetic. The Vedic astrologers, too, had to resort to writing in order to cast their horoscopes. If we grant the Vedic peoples the ability to write numerals, we should also entertain the possibility that they—or an elite group—were literate.

In any case, writing in Sanskrit is not the late invention it has always been considered to be. The *Aitareya-Aranyaka* (V.3.3), which is more than three thousand years old, clearly refers to writing. Several *Upanishads* describe various aspects of the alphabet. What is more, ancient India produced the most extensive grammatical science the world has known until twentieth-century linguistics. Although the genius grammarian Panini is thought to have lived around 500 B.C., it is unlikely that such a sophisticated tradition could have arisen in the absence of writing, or by a culture that was only newly literate (as the Aryan invasion theory requires).

As in later times, writing was probably executed on highly perishable material, such as palm leaves or wood (birch bark). Given the remoteness of the Vedic age and India's climate, it should not come as a surprise that no books from that early period have survived. The same holds true of other ancient civilizations, apart from texts etched in stone. What is truly curious is that while scholars have tended to give credence to traditions about lost texts from ancient Greece and Rome, they have generally dismissed similar traditions among the Hindus. For example, the great grammarian Panini himself mentions a number of grammatical works prior to his date, showing that he came at the end of a long line of development rather than the beginning. Yet some scholars have refused to take Panini seriously on this. Also, the *Mahabharata* epic speaks of lost *Vedas* apart from the four hymnodies that have survived the vicissitudes of time.

The Language of the Seals

Turning to the archaeological evidence from Mohenjo-Daro, Harappa, and other sites, there are around 4,200 inscribed objects, many of which are duplicates. These are mainly carvings on seals, small pieces of soft stone, and a few copper tablets. They reveal a surprisingly mature system of writing, quite distinct from the scripts of Sumer and pharaonic Egypt.

There are close to four hundred different signs, including numerals as well as conjuncts of more basic signs. Most texts are very brief, the average length being five signs. The longest text, on a three-sided amulet, is only twenty-six signs long. The longest inscription on a single side is seventeen signs, extending over three lines on a seal. This severe brevity of the available texts has greatly hampered the efforts at decipherment.

While the inscribed copper tablets may have been worn as amulets, the steatite seals appear to have served primarily as marks of ownership. A large number of seal impressions on clay also have survived. These are likely to have served as tags that were attached to bales of goods, for the reverse sides often show traces of packing materials.

Thus, as in other civilizations of that formative period, writing appears to have been principally connected with commercial life. However, the absence of written documents of a religious nature does not necessarily mean that writing was deemed unfit as a medium for the communication of deeper knowledge. It is generally believed that the sacred lore was not put down in writing until post-Vedic times. The spiritual knowledge was then, as it is today, communicated by word of mouth. Millennium after millennium, the sacred tradition was faithfully handed down from teacher to disciple by oral transmission. Even today, with the Vedic texts readily available in critical editions, this time-honored custom is followed in parts of India. Yet, as we have noted, the sacred knowledge was very probably not exclusively entrusted to human memory, however prodigious, but we no longer have actual written texts from that early period. Nevertheless, the proven fidelity of the orally transmitted *Vedas* allows us to look upon them as artifacts equal, for instance, to the Pyramid Texts of ancient Egypt or the Sumerian king lists inscribed on clay tablets.

The pictorial motifs that accompany the writing on the seals include the humped bull, humpless bull, water buffalo, elephant, tiger, rhinoceros, crocodile, antelope, fish, and tortoise. Geometric designs include the *svastika* (a solar symbol), spoked wheel, and a circle with a dot. These pictures are similar to the ones that show up on seals two thousand years later.

Indian scholars like Fateh Singh have pointed out many striking parallels between the Indus-Sarasvati pictures and Vedic images.[3] We already mentioned the much-debated Pashupati seal that expresses many attributes of Shiva. Another well-known seal shows two birds looking up from opposite sides of the branches of an *ashvattha* (sacred fig) tree. In a riddle-filled hymn of the *Rig-Veda* (I.164.20), the seer-bard speaks of two birds, "friends joined together," who are perched on a tree. One bird is tasting the tree's sweet fruit, while the other simply looks on. This striking image has elicited many different interpretations from scholars. According to some researchers, it expresses a key Vedic idea: that the individual spirit and the universal spirit both are of the same essence.

FIG. 28. *The bull-unicorn is a frequent motif found on Harappan seals.*

The most common Indus-Sarasvati seal image is that of a single-horned animal, which some have identified as a humpless bull. However, this identification is far from certain. The creature is drawn in such a way that we must assume either that the craftsmanship is inferior to the realistic depictions on the other seals or that the figure is a composite creature of mythology. The latter interpretation is preferable, because if the creature does indeed represent a unicorn, we have a direct link to the Vedic heritage. First of all, the notion of the animal with the single horn—the *eka-shringa*—occurs relatively often in the later Hindu literature.[4] The strange-looking elongated body of the creature could conceivably be a composite of bull and horse, in which case we can see in it a representation of God Indra as Vrishashvapati. The name means literally "Lord (*pati*) of the bull-horse." In Vedic mythology, Vrishashva (bull-horse) —from *vrisha* ("bull") and *ashva* ("horse")— is Indra's mount.

FIG. 29. ***The bull was a favorite artistic motif for the sculptors and other artisans of the Indus-Sarasvati civilization.***

Bull and horse are symbols of fertility—both on the material plane and the psychic or spiritual level. More particularly, the bull is a symbol of the sacred *soma* draught, which is the gateway to the luminous world of the deities and the Divine itself. In one hymn of the *Rig-Veda* (IX.3.3), the sacred soma is said to be adorned by the priestly chants as a horse for battle. In another hymn of the *Rig-Veda* (IX.13.6), the soma juices flowing through the filter into the receptacle are likened to horses urged to battle. One hymn (I.164.35) speaks of the soma as the semen of the stallion. Elsewhere in the *Rig-Veda* (IX.21.4), the dripping soma juices are compared to horses harnessed to a cart, since they bring all kinds of desired blessings. Thus we have a direct connection between the bull as a light-bringer and the horse as a swift carrier of good fortune.

Both bull and horse, moreover, are associated with the sun, as is the soma juice, or heavenly ambrosia. The sun itself is a visible symbol for the Light beyond. Thus we have a whole cycle of symbolic associations. Bereft of the wisdom of the ancients, we can barely comprehend the thoughtful connections and magical correlations with which the creators of the Vedic hymnodies were thoroughly familiar.

We can, however, glimpse enough of their worldview to appreciate that the symbolism found on the soapstone seals does not contradict what we encounter in the *Vedas* but, on the contrary, seems to match it well enough.

In another much-discussed seal, we see a horned figure standing amidst a bifurcated tree. To the left is a kneeling figure with arms extended forward in a prayerful or invocatory gesture. Behind it is a creature with curved horns extending sideways, which some scholars have seen as a bull, others as a goat. Below this scene is a row of seven figures standing upright, shown in frontal view. Each figure wears a long tuft of hair draped over the left shoulder and a peculiar headdress. The horned figure standing in the tree is very probably a deity, and the eight other human figures could be the seven sacrificial priests associated with some Vedic rituals (as mentioned in *Rig-Veda* IX.10.7; 15.8), with the eighth figure possibly being the sponsor of the sacrifice or the head priest. In one Rig-Vedic hymn (X.114.9), the composer poses this riddle:

FIG. 30. *Seal depicting a ritualistic or mythological scene.*

> *What sage knows the application (*yoga*) of the meters? Who utters the words appropriate to the functions of the various priests? Whom do they call the eighth priest, the superior (*shura*)? Who has honored Indra's [two] steeds?*

The Indian scholar P. V. Pathak offered a divergent and quite intriguing interpretation for the symbolism of this seal, which demonstrates the tentative nature of all such explanations.[5] He related the seal to a motif found in the *Atharva-Veda* (IV.37). This particular hymn was chanted to drive away malevolent spirits, and the plant called *aja-shringi* ("goat-horned") was somehow used during this incantation ritual. According to Pathak, the kneeling figure is preparing an extract from the aja-shringi plant, which he identified as the foul-smelling species *Onida pinnata*. As he saw it, the smell of the plant and its hornlike leaves provided the ancients with an immediate correlation to the animal kingdom in the form of a goat. He also identified the bifurcated tree as the common pipal tree.

Particularly suggestive are a number of seals depicting a human figure fighting a serpent or dragonlike creature. In a paper read at the World Archaeology Congress convened in New Delhi in 1994, Pathak convincingly argued that these images are depictions of the central myth of the *Vedas*: the slaying of the serpent-dragon (*ahi*), or Vritra, by Indra, the principal deity of the Vedic age. Mesopotamian seals depicting a similar motif have been dated to the ninth century B.C. and are thus much more recent than the Indus-Sarasvati seals.

We must keep an open mind about this and other similar explanations, but they are pointing in the right direction. The pictorial seals clearly contain motifs that held great symbolic or mythological fascination for the Indus-Sarasvati people. When we examine the seals of the post-Vedic period, from the time of Emperor Ashoka onward, we find that they too carry brief inscriptions. In almost all cases the inscriptions end in the genitive case, signifying ownership. The exceptions are where no case ending is used or where the ending is nominative, as in religious formulas. The impressions from these seals, like the earlier seals of the Harappan period, were used to authenticate records, or to serve as signatures.

The question is, what language is encoded in the Indus-Sarasvati script? During the ascendancy of the Aryan invasion model, many scholars favored the arbitrary view that the enigmatic Indus-Sarasvati glyphs were in a non-Indo-European language, such as Dravidian. With the retirement of that model due to the new archaeological evidence and the reinterpretation of the Vedic scriptures, the world of scholarship must now confront the revolutionary fact that the language on the seals and other artifacts is very probably Indo-European after all.

This view is fortified when we consider the evolution of writing in India. Indic scripts have undergone continual change for centuries and by medieval times the earliest scripts had been quite forgotten. One of these scripts, Brahmi, was used by the Buddhist emperor Ashoka in the third century B.C. to inscribe his edicts on stone pillars around the length and breadth of India. Brahmi was deciphered by James Prinsep in 1837, and the language on the edicts turned out to be a Prakrit dialect. Some authorities have suggested a Semitic origin for the Brahmi alphabet, but current evidence clearly shows that it is a descendant of the Indus-Sarasvati script.

In Brahmi, as in later Indic scripts, each letter represents a consonant combined with the vowel *a*. Combinations with other vowels are represented by the use of distinctive marks which modify the basic sign. Two consonants together were expressed by placing the signs for the two one on top of the other. This process of combination yields a total of 330 distinctive Brahmi signs for the 33 consonants alone, without taking into account any consonant conjuncts. In light of the theory put forward in this book, it is not surprising that the Indus-Sarasvati inscriptions should turn out to have a total of about 400 signs. Moreover, many of these signs appear to be modified in exactly the same regular manner as in the much later Brahmi script.

It is logical to assume that a systematically designed script such as Brahmi would represent a simplification of an earlier script. Moreover, with the parallel of ancient Egyptian writing in mind, one may further assume that, in addition to the phonetic signs, the ancestor of Brahmi probably included logograms as well as determinatives. A logogram is a single sign for a word, while determinatives are signs added to the logogram to qualify it in some fashion. In ancient Egyptian, for instance, the determinatives indicate grammatical categories; thus an egg shape following a name indicates a feminine name, and a name in a cartouche represents royalty. Assuming the Indus-Sarasvati script to be the ancestor of Brahmi, one would expect a core syllabary together with many logograms and other signs. The decipherment would best proceed by concentrating on this syllabary first.

We may add that pottery marks in the late second millennium B.C. are strongly reminiscent of the Indus-Sarasvati signs. It is reasonable to assume that this was the period when the logosyllabic Indus-Sarasvati script was being reorganized into an early form of the Brahmi script.

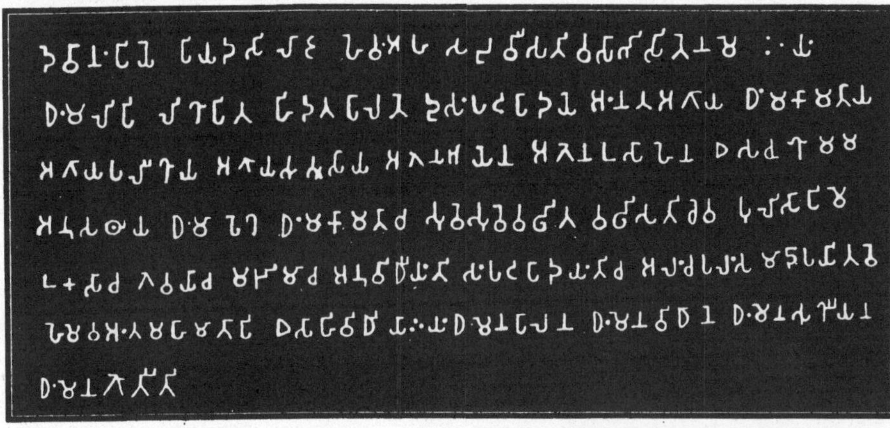

FIG. 31. *An edict of Emperor Ashoka in the Brahmi script.*

The Indus script, like hieroglyphic Egyptian, is generally written from right to left, in a direction opposite to that of Brahmi. On the other hand, there are instances of both scripts being written in *boustrophedon* fashion, reading alternately left to right and right to left in successive lines. The change in the direction of writing does indicate a fundamental shift in orientation. However, it is not clear whether this shift occurred when the Indus-Sarasvati peoples relocated to the Gangetic valley after the urban collapse of 1900 B.C. or during the urbanization that occurred around the time of the Buddha or several centuries earlier.

In 1934, G. R. Hunter published a first study on the relationship between the Indus-Sarasvati glyphs and the Brahmi script.[6] However, this significant research and also the 1978 study by J. E. Mitchiner failed to provide conclusive proof for the existence of that relationship.[7] More recently, one of the present authors (Subhash Kak) renewedly explored this important question from a statistical point of view, using computer-created concordances.[8] This analysis has shown that the most frequent letters of the Indus-Sarasvati and

Brahmi scripts look almost identical and, moreover, share a rather similar frequency of occurrence. The chance that this is a coincidence is so small that one can safely say that Brahmi is derived from Indus-Sarasvati. Furthermore, a structural analysis of the inscriptions indicates that the texts on the steatite seals follow grammatical rules like that of Sanskrit.

Nevertheless, one cannot claim that the script has been deciphered. According to cryptological theory, the texts have to be much longer than those currently available to confirm that a proposed decipherment is the only solution possible. The minimum size of the cipher text necessary to validate a decipherment is called its *unicity distance*. For the Indus-Sarasvati script, the texts will have to be about twenty characters long. It appears, therefore, that a conclusive decipherment will have to await the discovery of longer texts. Given that many known sites are yet to be excavated, one can be quite hopeful that such texts will be found.

Of course, the demonstration that Brahmi is derived from the Indus-Sarasvati script does not, by itself, establish that the urbanites from Mohenjo-Daro and Harappa were Indo-Aryan. Yet, the structural similarities in the Indus-Sarasvati and the Brahmi texts do point to that conclusion. This, in turn, reinforces the other continuities between the Indus-Sarasvati culture and the Vedic peoples that the archaeological discoveries of the past few decades have revealed. Furthermore, such an explanation agrees with the independent proposals by Marija Gimbutas, T. V. Gamkrelidze, V. V. Ivanov, and Colin Renfrew, who posited a dispersal of the Indo-European languages considerably earlier than previously thought.

At the same time, we must not rule out the possibility that some of the Harappan inscriptions may be in a non-Indo-European language, since the population was multiethnic and very probably included speakers of different languages. However, we may reasonably assume that one language served as a lingua franca, especially in the business community.

In any event, the relationship between the Indus-Sarasvati and the Brahmi scripts is one more piece of evidence that interlocks with other similar evidence from archaeology and literature linking the civilizations of the Indus and the Ganges Rivers. It opens up a new direction for a more rewarding study of the Indus-Sarasvati script. New questions on the relationship between the appearance of writing in Mesopotamia and the Indus-Sarasvati world also arise. Archaeology is yet to unearth evidence that will allow us to reconstruct the developmental stages of the Indus-Sarasvati script. Did it evolve from a need for business transactions? Such transactions must have been fundamental to the Vedic world with its extensive maritime and overland trade. If this was the case then one can see the development of the Mesopotamian and the Indus-Sarasvati scripts to have been somewhat related. Another theory is that the symbols represent archetypal patterns and that the development of the Indus-Sarasvati script is to be viewed as a byproduct of spiritual practices rather than mere commercial interactions. Later scriptures from the Indic tradition subscribe to the second view.

It is not surprising that the later Indic tradition represents Sarasvati as the Goddess of learning. This very likely commemorates the development of writing in the Sarasvati region. It also suggests the possibility that the original name of the Indus-Sarasvati writing might have been Sarasvati. The etymology of the term *Brahmi*, applied to the script that has apparently evolved out of the Indus-Sarasvati glyphs, captures its true origin. For, in Hindu theogony, Brahmi is the daughter of God Brahma and Goddess Sarasvati.

The Dravidian Puzzle

One of the main difficulties in interpreting the early history of India concerns the fact that the languages of South India belong to an entirely different linguistic group than those of the North. While Indo-European languages prevail in the northern part of the peninsula, Dravidian languages dominate the southern tip.

This linguistic differentiation has frequently been connected with the ethnographic fact that skin color becomes darker as one proceeds from north to south. The Aryan invasion theory was invented largely to explain these racial and linguistic differences. The invading Aryans were deemed to constitute not only a separate language group but a different race and culture. The light-skinned Aryans allegedly pushed the indigenous dark-skinned Dravidians to the south, creating an Aryan/Dravidian divide. In this model, the Aryans are given the role of barbaric invaders, while the Dravidians represent the indigenous civilized people responsible for the creation of the Harappan cities. Once the Dravidians had been displaced from the north and their cities (notably Harappa and Mohenjo-Daro) had been destroyed—so the theory goes—the seminomadic Aryans took over their fertile land and established their own society, becoming fully sedentary in the process.

The problem with this model, as we have shown, is that it does not fit the known facts. A major displacement of languages hardly occurs without a simultaneous displacement of the speakers of those languages. Yet, we have no archaeological evidence for such a population shift in India, nor for the alleged Aryan invasion. On the other side, if population and culture have remained the same in a given area, which is exactly our argument, more than likely language has remained the same as well.

Furthermore, scientifically speaking, there is no such thing as an Aryan and a Dravidian race. Strictly speaking, the so-called Aryans and the so-called Dravidians are members of the same Mediterranean branch of the Caucasian race. The darker skin color of peoples living nearer to the equator may be no more than an adaptive mechanism in response to the hotter climate.

What is more, it is now known that the various Dravidian languages, which are agglutinative, have much in common with a number of North Asian and European languages, including Finnish, Hungarian, old Bulgarian, Turkish, and perhaps even Japanese, which all belong to the so-called Finno-Ugric and Ural-Altaic branch of languages.[9] Some scholars have proposed that the original language behind Dravidian was spoken in Central Asia. In addition, the ancient city-state of Elam in southwestern Iran, east of Sumer, also has been speculatively related to Dravidian because of its agglutinative syntax.

Thus the same language-based speculations that crystallized into the Aryan invasion theory curiously also led scholars to formulate a

Dravidian invasion theory. According to this theory, the Dravidians—like the Aryans—are invaders who hailed from Central Asia and entered into India through Iran, with one group splitting off to found Elam at the Persian or Arabian Gulf.

As in the case of the Aryans, the Dravidians' own claim to being indigenous to India has been dismissed in favor of doubtful linguistic speculations. At the same time, however, the Dravidian invasion theory brings the Aryans and the Dravidians into contact throughout much of Asia, which makes us wonder whether the two are really different people.

To be sure, the Dravidian invasion theory has as many problems as the Aryan invasion theory relative to the mechanism by which the Aryan and the Dravidian speakers moved from remote Central Asia to South India. Thus, if the Dravidians of India originated in Elam, as a few scholars have maintained, we must ask how a small city-state could move a significant population several thousand miles overland through much treacherous terrain to populate the southern part of the Indian subcontinent? And to do so without leaving any archaeological trace of their exodus. There also is no evidence that the Elamites were a dark-skinned people like the Dravidians. Rather, as the renowned German archaeologist Walther Hinz, who deciphered the Old Elamite linear script, has made clear, the Elamite population was in all probability multiracial.[10] Most probably, it included light-skinned and dark-skinned people, as both are still found in that region in modern times.

FIG. 32. *Manuscripts of the* **Tirukkural**, *a Tamil scripture consisting of short memorable verses for moral edification.*

Moreover, the great linguistic schism between Aryan and Dravidian is breaking down. Today some linguists propose a greater Nostratic family of languages, which includes Indo-European,

Dravidian, and Semitic. The word "Nostratic" was coined by the Danish scholar Holger Pedersen in 1924, from the Latin *nostras* meaning "of our country."

Significantly, when we turn to the Sanskrit and Dravidian sources, we find that Vedic Sanskrit has affinities with Dravidian. While scholars have identified some twenty Dravidian "loan words" in the *Rig-Veda*, the Dravidian languages have "borrowed" at least fifty percent of their vocabulary from (Aryan) Sanskrit. Dravidian history attributes the creation of Tamil, the oldest Dravidian tongue, to Agastya, who figures in the *Rig-Veda* as one of the most prominent sages of his era. The Dravidian kings historically have called themselves Aryans and have traced their descent through Manu, the Hindu counterpart of Noah who repopulated the Earth after the Great Flood. The notion that the same culture—namely the vast and multiethnic Indus-Sarasvati civilization—could not have utilized two distinct language systems appears to us questionable.

Apart from linguistic affinities, northern and southern India share a common culture and religion. There have been attempts to characterize Shaivism (the worship of Shiva) of the South as non-Vedic or non-Aryan. However, God Shiva clearly is synonymous with the Vedic God Rudra, who also shares many features with other Vedic deities, such as Agni, Indra, and Soma. Moreover, God Shiva is a deity most closely associated with the northern river Ganges, which, according to Hindu mythology, cascades down onto his head.

In any case, today the Dravidian invasion theory stands revealed as a mere shadow cast by the Aryan invasion theory, which itself is a distortion of historical actuality. We must jettison both these scholarly models if we want to discover the truth about ancient India.

CHAPTER 8

The Dawn of the Indic Civilization: The Neolithic Town of Mehrgarh

Urban Life and the Neolithic Revolution

IN THIS CHAPTER WE TRAVEL TO A TIME LONG BEFORE the foundation stones of the cities of Mohenjo-Daro and Harappa were laid—back to the dawn of the Indic civilization. Scholars were still debating the implications of the Harappan cities for the Aryan invasion theory when archaeologists made another startling and far-reaching discovery—the town of Mehrgarh in eastern Pakistan (Baluchistan). When fully understood, this discovery will be found to challenge the conventional view of ancient history even more vigorously than the evidence presented in the preceding pages.

The earliest layers of Mohenjo-Daro, which are inaccessible because of groundwater, likely date back to a period before 3000 B.C., coinciding with the earliest beginnings of dynastic Egypt or possibly even with the misty era of the predynastic rulers. Scholars understandably wondered about the origins of the urban civilization reflected in Mohenjo-Daro and the other towns along the Indus River. Who were the people who created these great urban centers? Where did they come from? When did their civilizing efforts begin? The discovery of Mehrgarh furnished them with an immediate answer, but spawned a host of new questions as well.

The excavations at Mehrgarh have yielded the astonishingly early date of around 6500 B.C. This places Mehrgarh in the company of other early settlements like Çatal Hüyük in Anatolia, Jarmo in Mesopotamia, and Jericho in Palestine.

Jericho is a site of many succeeding settlements; as many as twenty-five strata have been identified. The earliest occupation of this oasis has been dated back to around 9200 B.C. when Jericho was little more than a semipermanent camp. It took at least another millennium for Jericho to become a village of little more than ten acres, sheltering a population of around two thousand. Small by our modern reckoning, Jericho was a large settlement for its time. Significantly, it was surrounded by a wall more than twelve feet high, complete with a tower that was over thirty-two feet in diameter and probably stood all of thirty feet tall. The purpose of either wall or tower are not clear. The obvious explanation that they functioned as defensive fortifications shielding the settlement from external attacks by hostile tribes is not necessarily the only or best explanation. The wall, it has been suggested, could also have served to hold back flash floods and encroaching silt and debris from the wadi to the west of the oasis. The tower probably did not serve a defensive function as it is situated inside the wall's perimeter. However, a ritual purpose for its existence is quite possible. At any rate, the original wall was the first of many walls erected throughout Jericho's long existence, including the famous wall mentioned in the Old Testament (Joshua 6:20) that is said to have crumbled at the sound of the Israelites' trumpets.

Jarmo, which originated in the mid-seventh millennium, was a hamlet of no more than thirty houses spread out over four acres. Each house, built of pisé (rammed earth) walls and mud floors, consisted of several small rooms most of which were used for storage. For the first five centuries of its existence, Jarmo shows no trace of pottery making, which is regarded as an important breakthrough in the development of human civilization. Archaeologists distinguish between aceramic (prepottery) and ceramic (pottery) cultures. The word *ceramic* comes from the Greek term *keramos*, referring to potter's clay. This clay is hardened by being baked in the sun or by being fired in a kiln. The inhabitants of early Jarmo used stone vessels and baskets lined with asphalt instead. Later generations knew how to fashion simple clay pottery. Jarmo is considered a typical transitional site between the hunting-and-gathering lifestyle of the Paleolithic (Old Stone Age) and the sedentary lifestyle of the Neolithic (New Stone Age), supported by agriculture and the domestication of livestock.

Of the three contemporaneous settlements mentioned above, only Çatal Hüyük is roughly comparable to the sixth-millennium Mehrgarh in size and significance, and we will address this fascinating cultural parallel shortly. First, however, we need to capture the fact that the date of 6500 B.C. falls into the early Neolithic, which marks the crucial transition from the nomadic or seminomadic life of hunters and gatherers to the sedentary life of agriculturists. The discovery of Mehrgarh considerably broadened our understanding of the Neolithic. An article published in *Scientific American* summarized the new view thus:

> *Already Mehrgarh offers proof of the existence of an early agricultural center close to the Indus valley and strongly supports the hypothesis that the Neolithic revolution was a complex event involving more than simply a single nuclear center in western Asia.*[1]

In other words, the Neolithic revolution was not confined to the Fertile Crescent, the narrow area of the Near East—to settlements like Jericho, Jarmo, and Çatal Hüyük. Nor was Gordon Childe, who coined the concept of a "Neolithic revolution," correct in stating that this was followed by an "urban revolution." For, Mehrgarh is proof that large settlements—which we could call towns—existed already at the opening of the Neolithic age. These served as a prototype for the splendid cities of a later era, such as the large urban environments of Mohenjo-Daro and Harappa. The existence of early settlements like Mehrgarh is yet another indication that we must completely revise our opinion about the level of civilization that existed eight or nine thousand years ago.

Mehrgarh: The Largest Town of Early Antiquity?

The Mehrgarh site is located at the foot of the Bolan Pass in the region of Baluchistan. Estimated to cover an area of over 500 acres,

FIG. 33 *(above and right). These clay figurines from Mehrgarh in all probability served a ritualistic purpose.*

Mehrgarh appears to be an assemblage of villages from different periods. The Mehrgarh of the fifth millennium B.C. covered roughly 168 acres.[2] This is still five times larger than the contemporaneous site of Çatal Hüyük in Anatolia (modern Turkey), which has been called "the largest Neolithic site hitherto known in the Near East."[3] The population of Çatal Hüyük has been estimated at around four thousand individuals. Employing similar standards, early Mehrgarh's population was at least twenty thousand individuals—the size of Tyre, capital of the Phoenician empire, and of the modern university town of Stanford, California. Even if it turns out that at any given time Mehrgarh occupied a somewhat smaller area than the total acreage tentatively mapped by archaeologists, it would still have been a town of considerable size for that period.

By comparison, Egypt's population is estimated as having been somewhere in the vicinity of 30,000 individuals by around 6000 B.C.—just a little more than the population of early Mehrgarh alone! We must remember that this was more than two millennia before the Sumerians settled in the land of the Tigris and Euphrates Rivers and created in a relatively short span of time their astonishing civilization. Prior to their arrival the land had been tilled by the Ubaidians, who lived in numerous small villages along the banks of the two rivers.

At the end of the last Ice Age, around 10,000 B.C., the total world population is estimated as having been around four million. At that time, India is thought to have had a population of only 100,000 individuals. Nor do we have any reason to assume that there was any significant population increase during the interim until the opening of the Neolithic period. By the time Mehrgarh was a thriving town in the sixth millennium B.C., India's population might have numbered around 250,000. Three thousand years later, during the Harappan era, India's population has been calculated at five million. Today it is nearly one billion!

Archaeologists found many burial grounds between the buildings of Mehrgarh and inferred from the number of burials that this town was densely populated. Possibly we can raise the figure to twenty-five thousand individuals. This is not the size of a mere village but that of a town. Depending on our definition, Mehrgarh might even qualify as a city.

To place this finding into proper perspective, one must know that the settlements in the preceding period were seldom larger than six or seven acres. Also, the houses were still round—in imitation of the caves of the Paleolithic—and usually dug out of a hillside and then covered with branches and hides. The oldest known house, at the site of Ein Guev on the river Jordan in what is now Syria, is dated between 14,000 B.C. and 12,000 B.C. This architectural style has been traced down to about 8000 B.C. Thereafter, rectangular construction became the norm in most cultures of the world, suggesting a corresponding radical shift in consciousness.[4]

At the Mehrgarh site, the earliest level of inhabitation is composed of rectangular buildings fashioned from mud bricks—the universal building material in that part of the world—and contains between four and six symmetrical rooms each. As in the earlier roundhouse time, the buildings formed clusters, and each cluster was probably inhabited by members of the same family group.

Over the centuries, life in India—as elsewhere—became increasingly complex. For that early period, this complexification can best be seen in pottery changes. No pottery has been found at the oldest level of occupation at Mehrgarh. When pottery first made its appearance at Mehrgarh, it was rather rough. However, before long it made way for glossy red wares of a finer quality. Then, during the fifth millennium B.C., simple geometric patterns were first applied. By the end of that millennium, pottery showed complex animal decorations and was expertly thrown on the wheel.

The use of the potter's wheel and also of bow drills more than six thousand years ago underscore the impression that Mehrgarh was a center of technological creativity and innovation, as well as a thriving marketplace for imported and exported goods. The town had many buildings with storage rooms and workrooms for artisans like potters, bead makers, basket makers, and stonemasons.

The people of Mehrgarh had domesticated cattle in addition to sheep, goats, and possibly water buffalo. Cattle has always been thought to have been introduced into India by the invading Aryans in the second millennium B.C. The new evidence shows that domestication of cattle occurred in Mehrgarh earlier than other ancient settlements of western Asia. Moreover, there is evidence that cattle were more significant to Mehrgarh's inhabitants than any other large domesticated animals—a cultural trait that has been preserved over thousands of years down to present-day Hinduism.

As the Indian historian Romila Thapar observed, for the Vedic Aryans the cow "was the measure of value and was a very precious commodity."[5] Pertinent as Thapar's remarks are, they are far too abstract to convey to our modern urban intelligence the central importance of cattle in Vedic culture and thought. A few more comments seem therefore in order. The archaic Sanskrit word for both "cow" and "bull" is *go*. The same word when used in the plural can refer to the stars and the solar rays. *Go* also denotes the Earth and, to confuse us moderns even more, human speech, particularly the inspired speech of the Vedic seers.

The phrase *go-kula* ("cow herd" or "cow family") is applied to a temple. *Go-cara* ("cow pasture") can also denote the abstract idea of "range" or "horizon." *Gotra* can stand for "cowshed" as well as "family" or "race." *Go-pati* ("cattle lord") can signify both a bull or the moon. *Go-pala* ("cow protector") can refer to a humble cowherd or a king who rules the Earth (*go*). *Go-bhuj* ("cow enjoyer") likewise stands for "king." *Goshthi*, which is derived from *go-shtha* ("cow-pen"), means "assembly" or "fellowship." And finally, the word *goshpada* ("cow's footprint") can also have the metaphoric meaning of "trifling matter." It is clear from these derivates of the word *go* that cattle were uppermost in the minds of the Vedic Aryans. They prayed and fought for them. But, as is evident from an unbiased reading of the *Rig-Veda*, they used their familiarity with the bovine species also to express the loftiest metaphysical ideas.

FIG. 34. ***To this day, pious Hindus have a reverential attitude toward the cow, which more than any other animal is charged with a deep symbolism for them.***

In this connection, the adjective *gavishti* (from *gavesha* "to look for cows") is important to mention. It means literally "to search for cows," and, as Thapar pointed out, came to mean "to fight."[6] However, *gavishti* also held higher connotations for the Vedic Aryans than cattle raiding. As a noun, *gavishti* stands for "ardor" and "fervor"—the kind of intense passion shown not only in raids and battles but, above all, in spiritual life. For the Vedic seers, *gavishti* meant primarily the ardent quest for visionary experience and elevated insight into the nature of existence.

Given the dominant role that cattle played in the daily life of the people of Mehrgarh, we feel justified in speculating that cattle also figured prominently in their symbolism and mythology. In that event, we may trace a direct line of development from Mehrgarh to Mohenjo-Daro and the *Rig-Veda*.

Mehrgarh's craftsmen mass-produced pottery in the early fourth millennium and at least by the early third millennium exported their ware to eastern Iran. There was extensive trading in the fourth millennium and possibly earlier. In the past, scholars typically underestimated the communication between settlements and between cultures. All the recent evidence from around the world, however, obliges us to think of our Neolithic ancestors as having been rather communicative and mobile. Trading was as essential to them as it is to us moderns, and business seems to have been the catalyst for a number of important cultural innovations, not the least of which was writing. The people of Mehrgarh imported jade and turquoise from Central Asia, lapis lazuli from northern Afghanistan, fuchsite (a jadelike material) from the south of India, shells from the coast of the Arabian Sea, and no doubt a good many other products from elsewhere.

The trade routes were unquestionably also the routes along which ideas flowed from one culture to another. The populations of many of the early Neolithic sites, such as Mehrgarh or Çatal Hüyük in Anatolia, were surprisingly multiracial—again showing that distance was not the obstacle that scholars have been prone to assume. Large villages and towns were attracting a variety of people, just as today's sprawling urban environments are exerting a strong pull on those seeking work or diversion.

Remarkably, cotton was cultivated by the Mehrgarh farmers as early as the fifth millennium B.C., either for its oil content or its fiber. Although no weaving utensils have been found so far, this does not exclude the possibility that cotton was used to make clothes. Some scholars think that India was very likely the birthplace of the fine art of weaving. The oldest textile fragments belong to the Harappan period, but the art of weaving could have been invented well before then.

In what scholars label "period VII" at Mehrgarh, corresponding to 2600 B.C., the excavations indicate the large-scale production of pots. From that period also, larger numbers of human figurines have survived. Most of them are female statuettes, some wearing elaborate hairdos. The male figurines typically sport a turban, which provides an incredible continuity with the customary modern headgear in that region.

Three primitively fashioned human figurines, made out of unfired clay, were found already at the oldest level at Mehrgarh. We must assume that they were not the only ones crafted, either at that time or in the immediately succeeding centuries. But human representation was probably rare until later. At any rate, the three artifacts "are the earliest figurines yet discovered in southern Asia."[7] Another first for Mehrgarh.

Most of the later stylized female figurines, made out of terracotta, are in a seated position. From about 3000 B.C. on, the female figurines underwent a stylistic change. Now the legs were encircled by a coil, the faces became goggle-eyed and bordered by coils resembling elaborate hair dresses, and the breasts became pendulous. A few hundred years later, the standing position became more frequent, and male figurines appear in larger numbers. There is an ongoing debate about whether such figurines were toys or cult objects, not only at Mehrgarh but in other cultures as well. The latter explanation seems more plausible, as children's toys were probably improvised from bits of wood and other readily available material.

Terra-cotta is a brownish-red mixture of clay and sand, which is hardened by fire. It was also used, in addition to bone, to make the first stamp seals in that area. The later seals in the urban centers were fashioned from soapstone (steatite). The small round seals were pressed into soft sealing material to mark someone's property. These stamp seals appear to be an original invention of India. However, the Sumerians may claim the innovation of the cylinder seal, which was rolled over the sealing material to produce a long rectangular impression.

After 4000 B.C., many more towns and villages sprang up in northwestern India, clustering on the rich alluvial soil around the rivers. Agriculture boomed and prepared the ground for the great and populous cities of the third millennium B.C., such as Mohenjo-Daro and Harappa.

According to the American anthropologist James G. Shaffer, the early Indic civilization evolved in four distinguishable phases. The first phase is the *early food-producing era* (6500-5000 B.C.), which is characterized by an absence of pottery. The second phase is the *regionalization era* (5000-2600 B.C.), which is marked by distinct regional styles in pottery and other artifacts. The third phase is the *integration era* (2600-1900 B.C.), which shows a pronounced cultural homogeneity and the emergence of urban centers like Mohenjo-Daro and Harappa.

The fourth phase is the *localization era* (1900-1300 B.C.), which is characterized by a blending of the patterns from the integration era with regional ceramic styles. This era is one of decentralization and restructuring, in which the same traditions continued in modified form (but not the dark age that Aryan invasion proponents have projected).

Another classification system, invented by the Indian archaeologist S. P. Gupta,[8] recognizes the following series of phases: the *pre-ceramic Neolithic* (8000-6000 B.C.), *ceramic Neolithic* (6000-5000 B.C.), *chalcolithic* (5000-3000 B.C.), *early bronze age* (3000-1900 B.C.), *late bronze age* (1900-1200 B.C.), *early iron age* (1200-800 B.C.), followed by the *late iron age cultures*.

The most extraordinary finding of Indian archaeology is that there is no noticeable break in the series of cultural developments from Mehrgarh to Harappa to modern India. The full implications of this fact still need to be grasped. When they are finally understood, we will very likely look at ancient history and the evolution of human civilization with new eyes.

CHAPTER 9

Why the Aryan Invasion Never Happened: Seventeen Arguments

The Facts Speak for Themselves

WE HAVE COVERED ENORMOUS GROUND IN THE PRECEDING chapters—from the rediscovery of the sacred canon of the Hindus to the discrediting of the Aryan invasion theory, to the discovery of the Indus and Sarasvati towns and villages and the likely geological and environmental cause of their demise, and finally to the archaeological surprise of the large Neolithic town of Mehrgarh.

In this chapter we return to the core argument of the first part of this book, which is the dismissal of the long-standing scholarly belief that the Vedic Aryans entered India from outside and demolished the so-called Harappan civilization. As we have shown, far from being the nemesis of the Indus cities, as most scholars have assumed, the Vedic Aryans were in fact their builders and inhabitants. In this connection it is surely not without deeper significance that the macrocosmic archetype of the human being is called *purusha* in the *Rig-Veda* (X.90; X.130) and later literature. For the word *pur* means "town" and *usha* can be derived from the verbal root *vas*, meaning "to dwell" or "to exist."[1] Thus the *purusha*—whether on the macrocosmic or the human level—means "he who dwells in the town." Town-dwelling is thus deemed a primary characteristic of humankind, which supports the evidence for the Aryans' civilized way of life depicted in the *Rig-Veda*.

In order to penetrate archaic symbolism further, we can note that the word *pur* is derived from the verbal root *pri*, meaning "to be full." Thus the Cosmic Man—and, as a reflection, the human being on Earth—is a dweller in fullness. We may interpret this to refer to both the plenitude of the world at large (which is the creation of the Cosmic Man by an act of self-sacrifice) and also the plenty of earthly towns. In the latter instance, plenty can signal both material wealth and multitudinous population, which was probably considered a boon rather than a curse in those days.

Because our reasons for rejecting the Aryan invasion theory are very complex—indeed more complex than can be fully documented in a book intended for a lay readership—we thought it desirable to furnish an overview of our basic arguments to round off this first part of our consideration.

First Argument: The Aryan invasion model is largely based on linguistic conjectures, which, in turn, are founded in archaeological speculations that have been shown to be misguided. As Sri Aurobindo, one of the great spiritual luminaries of modern India, noted in his thoughtful book *On the Veda*:

> *The hypothesis, invented to fill the gap, that these ideas [of the secret teachings of the* Upanishads*] were borrowed by barbarous Aryan invaders from the civilised Dravidians, is a conjecture supported only by other conjectures. It is indeed coming to be doubted whether the whole story of an Aryan invasion through the Punjab is not a myth of the philologists.*[2]

Aurobindo was right, of course, as is clear from the following remarks by the British archaeologist Colin Renfrew:

> *In the Indo-European field, linguists have been willing to follow the archaeological orthodoxy of nearly a century ago, while archaeologists have taken the conclusions of the historical linguists at their face value, failing to realize that*

> *they were themselves based upon archaeological assumptions which had not been questioned, yet which were not in some cases justifiable.*[3]

Recognizing that languages develop far more slowly than previously thought, linguists have pushed the Indo-European family of languages much further back in time. Thus Renfrew made it plausible that Indo-European speakers may have lived in Anatolia as long ago as 7000 B.C., which is at the very dawn of the Neolithic era, or, according to some scholarly reckonings, in the middle of the Mesolithic age, which followed the long Paleolithic age. Even more conservative scholars now assign the earliest Indo-European speakers to at least 4000 B.C. In light of this we need not assume that the Aryans were necessarily foreign to Indian soil until they allegedly invaded it and soaked it in blood around the middle of the second millennium B.C.

The Aryans could just as well have been native to India for several millennia, deriving their Sanskritic language from earlier Indo-European dialects. In fact, this alternative assumption makes better sense of many of the facts known about that time and the early Sanskrit speakers.

Second Argument: It has been widely argued that Indo-Europeans invaded the Middle East in the second millennium B.C. and that these invasions were part of a general migration that also led to the conquest of northern India by the Aryans around 1500 B.C. Especially the famous treaty between a Hittite and a Mitanni ruler, which makes reference to Vedic deities, has frequently been cited as supporting this hypothesis. However, Middle Eastern scholarship now inclines to the view that the Hittites—an Indo-European-speaking people—were in Anatolia by 2200 B.C. Also, the Indo-European Kassites and Mitanni had great kings and dynasties by 1600 B.C., which suggests that the Indo-Europeans had a well-established and ramifying culture in that region, giving rise to the further conclusion that they must have been present in the Middle East for a considerable period of time before then. They certainly were no nomadic barbarians, as popular belief would have it.

Third Argument: The descendants of the Aryans—the Hindus—have no memory whatsoever of having invaded India! There is no record of such an invasion in the ancient scriptures of the Hindus, nor in those of non-Vedic religions like Jainism and Buddhism. The most archaic document in any Indo-European tongue—the *Rig-Veda* composed in an early form of Sanskrit—does not look back on a homeland outside India. The geography, climate, flora, and fauna recorded in the *Rig-Veda* match those of northern India. Nor do we have any record of such an invasion in the collective memory of the Dravidian-speaking peoples who supposedly inhabited India before the Aryans arrived.

Fourth Argument: There is a striking cultural continuity between the archaeological artifacts of the Indus-Sarasvati civilization and subsequent Hindu society and culture. This continuity is evident in the religious ideas, arts, crafts, architecture, writing style, and the system of weights and measures. How can we explain this if the Sanskrit-speaking Aryans were supposedly foreign invaders who leveled the native civilization of the Indus Valley? The suggestion, made by some scholars, that the Aryans adopted lock, stock, and barrel the culture of the Indus people is equally preposterous because in that case the Aryans would presumably have adopted the native language or languages as well. This position is similar to the fanciful creationist belief that when God placed the first human being on Earth, God also simultaneously created the fossil evidence that now misleads evolutionists into believing that humans have descended from animals in a long chain of development.

Fifth Argument: Archaeologists have argued that their digs in the Indus Valley, home of the great civilization that was allegedly destroyed by the invading Aryans, brought no typically Vedic artifacts to light. Many of them have emphasized the marked difference between the nomadic culture they believe to have discovered in the *Rig-Veda* and the urban culture so vividly preserved in the ruins of Mohenjo-Daro, Harappa, and other sites along the mighty Indus River. However, the archaeological site of Mehrgarh, which has been dated to 6500 B.C., brought to light evidence for the use of copper, barley, and cattle at a very early time—all items that resemble the culture of the Vedic people. Additionally, many Harappan sites have yielded fire altars constructed in the same manner as those of the Vedic people, as well as sacrificial implements corresponding to those used in the *soma* sacrifice, central to the Vedic religion. Meanwhile the literary interpretation of the Vedic people as nomadic has also been revealed as an assumption of the invasion theory that is not warranted by a more critical reading of the texts, which show cities as an integral part of the Vedic culture.

Sixth Argument: The Aryan invasion of India was widely thought to have been made possible by the use of horse-drawn chariots, as in the case of the invasions of the Middle East by other Indo-European speakers in the late second millennium B.C. It was also thought that horses were unknown in the Indus civilization. This later assumption has meantime been proved wrong, for there is evidence for the presence of horses in a number of Harappan and pre-Harappan sites. In addition, recently discovered depictions of horses in Paleolithic caves show that the horse was present in India even before the Indus towns were built. Horseback riding has until recently been deemed a relatively late invention. However, evidence from the Ukraine proves that riding was practiced as early as 4300 B.C.[4] Thus, we can dismiss the whole idea that the Aryan invasion, which supposedly depended on the use of horses, could only have occurred about the middle of the second millennium B.C., which is the date of the earliest available depictions of horse-drawn chariots in the Middle East. The whole idea of nomads coming down the passes of Afghanistan in war chariots is anyway fanciful. Chariots are not the vehicles of nomads but of an urban elite, as is clear from their usage in ancient Greece, Rome, and Mesopotamia. They are hardly appropriate for travel through difficult terrain such as mountain passes.

Seventh Argument: In addition to the cultural continuity between ancient and modern India, there is also a striking racial continuity. The excavations at Harappa have brought to light skeletons belonging to members of various racial groups—all of which are still present in India today. It appears that the cities of the Indus Valley were cosmopolitan centers in which different ethnic groups lived together relatively peacefully or came together for commerce. There is no evidence that a new race intruded into north India during Harappan times and that the Dravidian inhabitants of the region were driven to the south. Rather, all the facts point to the continuity of the same people who have generally regarded themselves as Aryan.

Eighth Argument: The *Rig-Veda* of the Aryans describes an environment and particularly river systems that prevailed prior to 1900 B.C. (in the case of the Sarasvati River) and even 2600 B.C. (in the case of the Drishadvati River). The Harappan civilization was therefore located in the same riverine region as the Vedic culture. The Vedic literature, moreover, shows a population shift from the ancient and now dried-up Sarasvati River (extolled in many hymns of the *Rig-Veda*) to the Ganges (as reflected in the subsequent literature of the *Brahmanas* and *Puranas*)—a shift that is faithfully reflected in the archaeological record.

Ninth Argument: Recent research has shown that the sacred *Rig-Veda* is based on an astronomical system and calendar that hark back to the Pleiades-Krittika (Taurean) era of 2500 B.C., or the Harappan era, and still earlier. Vedic astronomy and mathematics were well-developed sciences, which attests to an advanced civilization, not a primitive nomadic culture. This point will be discussed at some length in Chapters 11 and 12.

Tenth Argument: The renowned British archaeologist Sir Mortimer Wheeler suggested that the Harappan cities were destroyed by violence—a speculative comment that was treated as absolute fact by many subsequent scholars. Further excavations have disproved Wheeler's notion. Most archaeologists now believe that the Harappan cities were not destroyed by invading Aryans but were abandoned by their citizens because of major geological and climatic changes. There is no evidence of any Harappan cities having been systematically plundered, destroyed, or burned at any layer. The abandonment of towns along the Indus, as a result of dramatic changes in the flow of the river and related environmental conditions, was not unheard of even in much later times. Thus the Greek geographer Strabo, who died a decade or so before Jesus, reported in his famous *Geography* (XV.1.19) that when Aristobulus was on a mission in India, he saw a country of a thousand towns and villages that had been deserted because the Indus had changed its course to the ocean. The Indian peninsula continues to be a very active tectonic zone.

Eleventh Argument: It has frequently been asserted that the *Rig-Veda* describes battles between the Aryan invaders and the native Indians. However, careful study of the relevant Vedic hymns shows that these battles were largely fought between people of the same culture. Reading an invasion into them is a leap of faith that is quite unsupported by the transmitted Sanskrit text. Such racial wars were part of the milieu of nineteenth-century thinking, which invented the Aryan invasion theory. Modern archaeology considers culture to be a more complex and pluralistic phenomenon that cannot be so easily stereotyped.

Twelfth Argument: Recent excavations at the Dwaraka site, a port city in Gujarat larger in size than the largest Harappan city of Mohenjo-Daro and dated to about 1500 B.C., have revealed architectural structures similar in style to the traditional city of the same name in which the God-man Krishna is said to have lived. The archaeological Dwaraka corresponds to the Dwaraka described in the *Mahabharata* epic as the city of Krishna. The evidence includes the use of iron and the employment of a script that is intermediate between the Harappan glyphs and the Brahmi alphabet of later India. According to the traditional view, Krishna lived at the conclusion of the Vedic period.

Thirteenth Argument: There is a strong morphological link between the Harappan glyphs, as found on numerous seals, and the later Brahmi script, which subsequently gave rise to the *deva-nagari* script in which Sanskrit is mostly written today. This continuity in alphabets reinforces the argument about the cultural continuity between the Harappan civilization and later post-Vedic Hinduism in general.

Fourteenth Argument: The Vedic Aryans have been credited with the use of iron, and it has always been maintained that their use of iron weapons and horse-drawn chariots guaranteed their supremacy over the Indus people. However, the Sanskrit word *ayas*, thought to denote "iron," appears to have stood for "copper" or "bronze." Earliest evidence for iron in India dates back to before 1500 B.C. in association with Kashmir and the newly excavated city of Dwaraka and is considered to be an indigenous development. Vedic *ayas* is associated with a culture of cattle and barley, such as we encounter in pre-Harappan sites.

Fifteenth Argument: Contrary to popular scholarly opinion, the genealogies found in the *Puranas*, which list over a hundred and twenty kings in one Vedic dynasty alone, do fit into the new model of ancient Indian history. The Puranic records are far more trustworthy than has hitherto been assumed. They are the distillate of countless generations of remembered knowledge, especially knowledge concerning the vicissitudes of royal houses. They date back to the third millennium B.C. and earlier. Greek accounts point to the existence of Indian royal lists (perhaps coinciding with those of the *Puranas*) that are reported to go back to the seventh millennium B.C.

Sixteenth Argument: The *Rig-Veda*, the sacred fountainhead of later Hinduism, shows an advanced level of cultural and philosophical sophistication, suggesting a long antecedent development. The Vedic language itself is highly sophisticated, and the Vedic pantheon is as complex as that of later India. In other words, the *Rig-Veda* is by no means the product of a primitive culture but of a people enjoying the fruits of a mature civilization based on age-old traditions—a civilization that could not have been delivered to India on horseback. Whatever the original homeland of the Aryans may have been, they seem to have lived in India long before the alleged invasion occurred, apparently for several millennia.

Seventeenth Argument: The Painted Gray Ware (PGW) culture in the western region of the Ganges has frequently been referred to in support of the Aryan invasion theory. However, carbon-14 tests have yielded dates of little more than 1100 B.C., which is too late for the modified date given for the Aryan invasion, though Max Müller's proposed date of 1200 B.C. would roughly fit if it were not out of sync with the Harappan evidence. At any rate, recent research has revealed connections between the PGW culture, the Northern Black Polished Ware culture, the Black and Red Ware culture, and the Indus-Sarasvati civilization. Moreover, as archaeologist James Shaffer has pointed out, all these labels based on pottery styles are ill-defined and rather confusing and therefore best abandoned.[5]

When we integrate the above arguments and other additional evidence not specifically cited here, we obtain a picture of ancient India that diverges considerably from the inherited Aryan invasion model. It is a picture that is at once more credible and exciting than the infelicitous hypothesis of an Aryan invasion. It removes the heavy, near-impenetrable curtain of ideology that has prevented us from seeing ancient India more clearly and faithfully, and it opens up to our modern vision at least some of the splendor of that early era of human civilization. From this new perspective we are now able to turn our historical imagination upon specific aspects of ancient Indian history and culture.

PART TWO

The Splendor of Ancient India: Its Cultural and Spiritual Legacy

CHAPTER 10

The Spiritual Heritage of Ancient India

Understanding the East

SINCE THE TIME OF CLASSICAL GREECE, IF NOT EARLIER, India has been lauded by outsiders as a land of mystery, mysticism, and metaphysics. Many of the mystical movements that have sprung up in the West during the past two centuries, including Romanticism, Occultism, Thulism, Magic (notably that of Aleister Crowley), Rosicrucianism, Theosophy, and Anthroposophy, have looked to India for much of their secret knowledge, though without always understanding it correctly. Thousands of contemporary Westerners have visited India to savor its mystique or study its spiritual teachings, and many gurus regularly visit the West to teach, or have even taken up permanent residence in Europe and America.

India discovered its missionary spirit in the figure of Swami Vivekananda, who held thousands spellbound with his talks during and after the Parliament of Religions in 1883. It was primarily he who, building on the cultural foundations of Romanticism, introduced the idea of the materialistic West versus the spiritual East—a distinction that may have served a certain purpose at one time but that is breaking down today as part of the growing globalization.

There is as much practical materialism in the non-Western world as there is in Europe and America. However, as an ideology, materialism has been far more influential in the West than it has been in the East. On the other hand, the East did produce spiritual traditions of enormous profundity, diversity, and sophistication, as well as great spiritual teachers. Yet, that Westerners are not inherently materialistic was demonstrated by Vivekananda himself, who attracted and inspired thousands of American men and women.

FIG. 35. *Swami Vivekananda (1863-1902).*

While we do not need to uncritically succumb to India's mystique, as did perhaps the German Romantics, we nevertheless must learn to appreciate that the spiritual geniuses of ancient India have in fact created a pristine wisdom tradition that in its depth and breadth is without parallel in the world. Now as scholars begin to understand the *Vedas* a little better, we cannot fail to recognize the authenticity and power of their spiritual communication. What is more, India continues to gift the world with great teachers, though the finest flowers of its spiritual creativity are not always those who achieve the greatest popularity or notoriety in Western countries.

In reconstructing the history and culture of ancient India, we must not fail to keep the moral and spiritual contribution of the Indic branch of the human family clearly before our eyes. The same Eurocentric bias that led to the formulation of the erroneous Aryan invasion model also is responsible for other distortions, notably the view that we can learn nothing from India or other non-Western countries. Fortunately, this arrogant notion—once widespread throughout the Western hemisphere—is gradually being replaced by a fairer and more sensible attitude. Joseph Needham, the renowned author of a multivolume history of Chinese science and civilization, made the following pertinent comments:

Europe and America must stand ready not only to share with all Asians and Africans those treasures of understanding and use of Nature which modern science and technology have brought forth, but also to learn from them many things concerning individual life and society which they are more than competent to teach. If this is not done, the achievements of Europe (and America) will in any case become the common property of mankind, but our civilization will go down in history as distorted and evil, unwilling to practise what it preached, and worthy of the condemnation of ten thousand generations.[1]

Yoga and the Ideal of Spiritual Liberation

As was the case with pharaonic Egypt and the Mayan civilization, spirituality is all-pervasive in traditional Indic culture. The arts, sciences, and literature of India—from sculpture and dance to astronomy and grammar—have been cast in a spiritual mold and made into spiritual paths. India's traditional social system is imbued with spiritual values, which is not to say that actual behavior necessarily always corresponds to the highest ideals of the cultural heritage. But the highest value is traditionally placed on spirituality. Thus Hindu ethics acknowledges four human goals, which are known as the *purusha-arthas*: material welfare (*artha*), pleasure (*kama*, which includes aesthetic satisfaction as well as sexual fulfillment), morality (*dharma*), and spiritual liberation (*moksha*).

Yoga best epitomizes India's spirituality, and the meditating yogi seated in the beautifully symmetric lotus posture is its most typical expression and symbol. In the Western world, Yoga is generally identified with the various postures (*asana*) of Hatha-Yoga, which is widely misunderstood as a system of health care. All schools and forms of Yoga have the common purpose of facilitating spiritual awakening, whether it be called enlightenment or liberation. This is true even of Hatha-Yoga, which is often reduced in the West to physical fitness training.

The tradition of Yoga, which crystallized at the time of the

Upanishads some three thousand years ago, but which has its roots in the ancient worldview of the *Vedas*, is spectacularly comprehensive.[2] It includes postures and breathing techniques as well as moral disciplines and a wide range of methods of mental concentration and meditation. In their pursuit of enlightenment, the adepts of Yoga have availed themselves of visualization, light, sound, geometric devices (*yantra*), ritual action, and, in its left-hand Tantric variety, even ceremonial sexual intercourse. The yogic scriptures furnish descriptions of—and prescriptions for achieving—higher states of consciousness, including ecstatic merging with the object of contemplation, a practice known as *samadhi*. All these are deemed valuable means to the attainment of transcendental gnosis, or liberation, which is Yoga's ultimate goal and the highest value recognized within the Indic value system. The American philosophy professor Abraham Kaplan wrote about this sublime ideal as follows:

FIG. 36. *A sadhu (virtuous one), who has renounced the world to cultivate inner peace and Self-realization.*

> *The goal of* moksha, *of emancipation, though individual in form (like the Western quest for personal salvation), is thoroughly social in content. In a way, it goes beyond even the prevailing Western conception of moving from egoism to altruism. For the goal is not unselfishness but selflessness, a movement, not from self to other, but from self to Self, in which there is no other.*[3]

Kaplan further commented that the metaphysical truth of the unity of all existence has not remained mere speculation in India. To make his point, he referred to the Ramakrishna Mission, which has a strong social welfare program, and to Mahatma Gandhi's nonviolent politics, as well as Vinoba Bhave's land-reform movement—all springing from a primary spiritual orientation, translated into social action. However, not all spiritual adepts who strive for liberation or have attained it feel the need to express the premier value of moksha by becoming social activists. We must appreciate the fact that there also are those who distinctly prefer a quietistic lifestyle, either passing on teachings to a small circle of disciples or remaining altogether silent. We must not be too hasty in criticizing them for their choice, because their silence may be truly thunderous. If we have learned anything from modern physics, it surely is that much of the universe's most effective action is quite invisible to the human eye. The illumined beings are undoubtedly a force to be reckoned with.

The history of Yoga is filled with examples of great adepts, whether of the activist or quietistic type, whose presence has been a powerful catalyst for the spiritual transformation and moral upliftment of others. But when we examine the typical treatment of world history served to Euro-American school children and college students, we find no mention of India's spiritual heroes and their contribution to the world. Our history books, which are thoroughly secularized, tend to confuse spirituality with religion and are never far from dismissing the earnest spiritual aspirations of cultures other than those of Judeo-Christian descent as being laden with superstitions and unproductive mythology. At best, spirituality is treated as the prerogative pursuit of a gifted elite, which has little relevance to the mainline development of human civilization.

Yet, the deeper we penetrate the ancient world with an unbiased mind, the more we discover at its core a profound spirituality beyond mere religion. Similarly, when we extrapolate from the present moment and look ahead into the future, we find not a resurgence of conventional religion but the timid emergence of a new, globally oriented spirituality that transcends religious dogmatic boundaries. In this book we are trying to make a connection between the spirituality of ancient India and the emerging spirituality that is limited to no particular culture but embraces and enriches all cultures. The emerging global civilization requires the wisdom and knowledge of both hemispheres of the world. As Paramahansa Yogananda wrote in his widely read *Autobiography of a Yogi*:

> *The great masters of India who have shown keen interest in the West have well understood modern conditions. They know that, until there is better assimilation in all nations of the distinctive Eastern and Western virtues, world affairs cannot improve. Each hemisphere needs the best offerings of the other.*[4]

Balance has long been a hallmark of the yogic approach and was emphasized already in the *Bhagavad-Gita*, composed around the middle of the first millennium B.C. By then, Yoga had been an ancient discipline with a long line of teachers extending back into dim antiquity.

The Origins of Yoga

The Hindus have traditionally looked to the archaic *Vedas* as the seedbed of the later Yoga tradition.[5] The Vedic seers are honored as illumined sages who passed down the secrets of meditation and higher consciousness to subsequent generations of spiritual practitioners. Reflecting this idea, the teachers of the school of Classical Yoga, embodied in the *Yoga-Sutra* of Patanjali and his commentators, not only employ Vedic concepts in their teachings but also speak of their tradition as thoroughly Vedic.

The term *yoga* itself first occurs in the *Rig-Veda*, but does not yet have its later technical connotation. In many instances, it simply means "application."[6] The word *yoga* is one of the most flexible terms of the Sanskrit language and therefore has been used in many diverse contexts, in addition to its specific philosophical meaning. In the technical sense of "spiritual discipline," the term *yoga* first made its appearance in the *Taittiriya-Upanishad*, a work belonging possibly to the era around 1000 B.C. or even earlier.

Many of modern India's Yoga adepts believe that the *Vedas* contain the original teachings of Yoga. Thus Sri Aurobindo, arguably the greatest philosopher-sage of twentieth-century India, turned to the ancient *Vedas* for inspiration and guidance. In his important book *On the Veda*, Aurobindo describes how, like most educated Hindus of his day, he used to regard the *Upanishads* rather than the *Vedas* as the fountainhead of India's metaphysics and spirituality. For a long time, he held the view that the *Vedas* were of only small value to the history of thought and to living spiritual practice. All this changed in the course of his own yogic discipline and experience.

> *My first contact with Vedic thought came indirectly while pursuing certain lines of self-development in the way of Indian Yoga, which, without my knowing it, were spontaneously converging towards the ancient and now unfrequented paths followed by our forefathers.*[7]

Aurobindo's study of the *Vedas* in the original archaic Sanskrit gave him insights into his own inner processes, for which later systems of thought and Western psychology simply offered no plausible explanations. He soon realized that the wisdom tradition of the *Vedas* lives on in later traditions, especially Yoga. He wrote:

> *Here we have the ancient psychological science and the art of spiritual living of which the* Upanishads *are the philosophical outcome and modification and Vedanta, Sankhya and [Classical] Yoga the late intellectual result and logical dogma.*[8]

Other renowned Yoga masters, like Paramahansa Yogananda, who felt compelled to share their knowledge and understanding with Westerners, have likewise spoken of the profundity and great antiquity of the Yogic tradition.[9] But few have had either Aurobindo's deep insight into the Vedic heritage or his mastery of the symbolic code of the *Vedas*.

The traditionalist Hindu view about the Vedic origin of Yoga stands in sharp contrast to mainstream Western scholarship, which subscribes to the Aryan invasion theory. In the twilight of this erroneous model, Yoga has been typified either as the product of non-Vedic (non-Aryan) indigenous cultures or as the result of a long osmosis between the cultures of the Aryan invaders and the native non-Aryan population.

Both explanations have been reinforced by the inability of modern scholarship to understand or recognize the spiritual meaning of the Vedic myths and symbols. Even Yoga researchers who are clearly sympathetic to the spiritual traditions of India have generally accepted both the Aryan invasion model and a nonspiritual, mythological interpretation of the *Vedas*, primarily because of the overwhelming influence of the reigning scholarly model.[10] The new evidence, as presented in this book and in academic publications, now obliges everyone to reconsider these issues.

Strictly speaking, the Aryan invasion model implies that the Yoga tradition has a fraudulent history: Yoga was invented by the native cultures and subsequently was borrowed, or taken over, by the Aryan-speaking nomads, who supposedly conquered northern India by force.[11] They then wiped out all traces of this borrowing, as if they themselves had been the true originators of Yoga all along. This notion makes no sense, given what we know about cultural adoptions and adaptations. It makes even less sense in view of the archaeological and literary evidence cited in the present book.

Even non-Vedic traditions such as Jainism and Buddhism have strong Sanskritic and Vedic roots, and have always presented themselves as Aryan. Thus the Buddha, though he certainly did not outwardly follow the *Vedas*, proclaimed his teaching to be the *ariyo atthangiko maggo*, or "noble eightfold path." As in Jainism, the Buddhist scriptures also applied the Pali term *ariyo* (Sanskrit *arya*) to a saintly person or "noble individual," who is receptive to the truth. We have noted earlier that "Aryan" does not connote a racial or linguistic category but a cultural or psychological quality. The Aryans were those who were of noble mind and heart, honoring the timeless sacred tradition of their ancestors. It is surely very significant that this sense of the word should have been retained even in such non-Vedic traditions as Buddhism and Jainism. The significance, in our view, lies in that it belongs to the core of the Vedic culture, which has given rise to the powerful spiritual traditions of

Jainism and Buddhism, just as it has perpetuated itself in the many branches of Hinduism.

The time is ripe for a critical reexamination of the question of the origin of Yoga.[12] In looking for the roots of Yoga in the *Vedas*, we must first of all rid ourselves of the tendency to indulge in what scholars call arguments *ex silentio*; that is, to favor a particular point of view because of the absence of contrary evidence. For instance, we might argue that, because the original Pledge of Allegiance did not contain the phrase "one nation under God," the American people were irreligious prior to 1954 when the Pledge was changed by an Act of Congress. This is clearly absurd, and yet this kind of argument is frequently resorted to by scholars, especially when defending cherished positions.

Thus, if the *Vedas* do not include passages explaining technical Yoga practices in detail, this does not necessarily mean that such practices were unknown at that time. In this connection, we must particularly appreciate the fact that the *Vedas* are not trying to communicate facts but spiritual meanings. They are appropriately composed in a highly evocative symbolic language.[13] The *Vedas* speak of what is secret, hidden, mysterious, and purposely veiled. They emphasize the need for special instruction, initiation, and meditative or ritual practices and disciplines in order to understand their deeper meaning. In other words, the *Vedas* are part of an esoteric tradition that requires special insight and keys, without which we cannot make any real sense of the Vedic revelation.

Many of the standard concepts of Indic spirituality are found already in the archaic *Rig-Veda*, notably the concepts of *eka* (the One), *yajna* (sacrifice), *mantra* (numinous sound), *jnana* (wisdom), *prana* (life energy), *dhyana* (meditation), *karma* (moral action), *tapas* (austerity), *sat/asat* (being/nonbeing), *satya* or *rita* (truth), *vac* (divine speech), *dharma* (moral law), *shraddha* (faith), *brahmacarya* (chastity), *ojas* (spiritual strength), *vrata* (vow), *muni* (sage), *kama* (desire), and *papa* (sin). These provide helpful entry points into the Vedic system of symbolism. Yet, there has been a tendency to underinterpret them in Vedic contexts, on the assumption that they must have evolved over a long span of time. However, this notion was predicated on the incorrect Aryan invasion model and a relatively late date for the *Rig-Veda* (1500 B.C. to 1200 B.C.). We now know that the Rig-Vedic hymns were composed in the third millennium B.C. and earlier. Therefore, there was an adequate length of time for the development of concepts and practices from the Rig-Vedic sacrificial culture to the esotericism of the *Upanishads*. Besides, research has shown that there is a pronounced continuity of ideas between the Vedic era and subsequent periods.

While the Sanskrit vocabulary has obviously changed and grown in the long span of more than four thousand years, many key terms have retained their original core meaning. The failure to realize this is largely due to the bias among Western Vedicists, who see in the *Vedas* primitive poetry or expressions of an unsophisticated naturalist religiosity. The same bias has been responsible for interpreting ancient Egyptian texts as primitive, which bespeaks of an inability to appreciate spiritual and occult symbologies.

For example, a principal Vedic theme is the conflict between light and darkness and the need to cross over the darkness to reach the light—a metaphor for attaining illumination or enlightenment. Under the primitivist bias, not a few Vedic scholars have interpreted this symbolic notion in a naturalistic manner as a primitive fear of darkness, or even in gross political and racial terms as a war between the light-skinned Aryans and the dark-skinned natives. To avoid such distortions, we must endeavor to approach the *Vedas* with the same symbolic sophistication that patently characterizes the Vedic hymns. That is to say, we must look past our modern prejudices and penetrate below the surface, realizing that the Vedic language exceeds everyday language and is profoundly spiritual. As James Newton Powell, representing the new scholarly approach, observed:

> *The* Veda *is a supreme example of a type of poetry in which the life of the symbol corresponds so intimately with the truth it clothes that it is indeed the living form of that truth. There are, residing within the language of the* Veda, *a hierarchy of potencies, indwelling powers of speech which inspire by*

*means of sound and a transcendental logic. These verses were forged by the vibrant poets (*vipras*) who veiled the imperishable in raiment so perfectly fitted and so utterly transparent that the very act of veiling was simultaneously an unveiling. Image, sound and sense were indissolubly united to forge luminous language—symbols capable of conveying the most orient hues of the imperishable. The aim of this language is not to beckon the discursive faculties, but to reveal in swift, strong and sonorous unveiling images the very cognition which gave birth to the initial expression.*[14]

Sri Aurobindo, a renowned sage of modern India who had received a Western education, wrote:

The Veda *is a book of esoteric symbols, almost of spiritual formulae, which masks itself as a collection of ritual poems. The inner sense is psychological, universal, impersonal.*[15]

Yet even Aurobindo, sympathetic as he was to the Vedic revelation, underrated the expressive capacity of the ancient rishis' language. He thought that it lagged behind the language of the subsequent Upanishadic literature. But when we examine the *Upanishads* carefully, we find a language that is perhaps more philosophical though often lacking in immediacy, which is a hallmark of the language of the Vedic poet-sages.

Leitmotifs of Vedic Spirituality

When we reconstruct the Vedic worldview from an empathetic, symbol-sensitive perspective, we find that it agrees in fundamental respects with the core teachings of later Hinduism. The following are ten key cosmological-metaphysical ideas and practices of Hinduism, which are also characteristic of the early Vedic culture:

1. *Self-realization or God-realization*: The goal of human life is enlightenment or liberation, understood as noetic or ontic union with the Divine or the inner Self: The illumined sage *glimpses*, in superlative mystical states, the oneness

of all things, and, beyond elevated cognition, even *realizes* himself or herself to be one and the same as the ultimate Reality.

2. *A universalist approach*: The ultimate Truth lies beyond all possible conceptions of it. For the same reason, the Truth can be approached from many different paths and with the guidance of a variety of teachers and scriptures.

3. *Karma and rebirth*: In maturing and evolving toward Self-realization, the person undergoes many repeated births and deaths. This process is governed by the law of karma, according to which every thought and action has a corresponding reaction, which shapes a person's immediate or future destiny.

4. *Spiritual practice*: In order to attain Selfhood, or to realize the nameless Reality, the person must be aware of the law of karma, producing only such thoughts and actions that are conducive to a spiritually auspicious life. Ultimately, the conditional realms in which the law of karma holds sway must all be transcended. This is possible only by adopting a rigorous spiritual discipline. There are a number of practical paths or approaches to Self-realization, which are widely referred to as Yoga.

5. *Spiritual initiation and guidance*: Spiritual growth is seen as depending on proper spiritual guidance from living teachers rather than on books or figures from the past. Spiritual discipleship commences with a more or less formal initiation in which the teacher makes a deeper connection with the disciple—a connection that involves the direct transmission of psychospiritual energy and consciousness.

6. *Ritual worship*: Rituals are special forms of action that are intended to create higher states of consciousness through

the ceremonial use of images, statues, or other symbolic representations of deities and other elevated spiritual beings, including teachers.

7. *Meditation*: The introversion of the mind is an important aspect of the spiritual path. Meditation helps to focus, clear, and strengthen the mind, so that it becomes more capable of reflecting the ultimate Reality (Self or Divine).

8. *Mantra recitation*: One important way of stabilizing and harmonizing the mind is through the recitation of power-charged sounds called *mantras*, either silently or aloud.

9. *Breath control*: Mind and breathing are intimately connected. Mind control can be directly brought about by means of a variety of breathing techniques.

10. *Posture*: Our inner state is affected by our bodily posture. Hence in order to harmonize the mind, special physical postures are employed as aids to concentration and meditation.

In the next section, we review the spiritual heritage of the *Vedas* in more detail, following the preceding framework of concepts and practices.

The Depth of Vedic Spirituality

1. *Self-realization or God-realization*: The earliest clear articulation of the notion of Self-realization, or the realization of the Absolute (*brahman*), can be found in the oldest *Upanishads*, such as the *Brihadaranyaka*, the *Chandogya*, and the *Taittiriya*. These expound original insights about the identity of the person's essential being (or Self) with the essential nature of the universe at large. They also recommend various moral practices and meditation exercises for realizing that ultimate Essence. In doing so, these *Upanishads* base themselves on the spiritual experiences and revelations of the Vedic

seer-sages (*rishi*). For example, we find the following passage in the three-thousand-year-old *Brihadaranyaka-Upanishad* (I.4.10):

> *In the beginning all this was Brahman. It knew itself only as "I am Brahman." Thus it became everything. He who among the Gods awakened to this likewise became That. Similarly with seers and with [other] human beings. This the [Vedic] seer Vamadeva saw when he stated, "I was Manu and am the Sun."*

In this cryptic passage, the anonymous composer of the *Upanishad* quotes from a chant of the Vedic sage Vamadeva, who is the main seer of the fourth book of the *Rig-Veda*. In the first verse of the twenty-sixth hymn in that book, Vamadeva exclaims in ecstasy his essential identification with everything:

> *I was Manu and now I am the Sun! I am the seer and poet-sage Kakshivat! I am [the sage] Kutsa Arjuneya! I am the poet-sage Ushana! Behold me!*

In the *Vedas*, Manu represents the original Man, the progenitor of the human race in our present world cycle. The Sun, Surya, is not merely the visible luminary but the divine Light, the solar Self—again a potent Vedic notion. Vamadeva ecstatically identifies with various illustrious sages who, before him, had realized the indivisible essential Being, the Brahman, or Absolute. The Upanishadic idea of Self-realization thus has a clear Vedic basis. In the *Aitareya-Upanishad* (IV.5), another early work of this genre, Vamadeva is similarly quoted as an example of Self-realization. His autobiographical statement, which reminds one of certain Egyptian hieroglyphic texts, is as follows:

> *While I was in the womb I searched out and discovered the births of all the Gods. A hundred metal cities oppressed me. Then I flew out with the speed of a hawk.*

The womb of which Vamadeva speaks is Nature herself, cosmic existence, which held him in confinement. Then when he had found the birthplace of the deities—the ultimate Reality as the source of

Gods and humans—he was able to extricate himself from Nature's hold.

A number of seers from the *Rig-Veda* are mentioned in the *Upanishads* as great sages and the originators of various esoteric teachings. These include Manu, Brihaspati, Ayasya, Ghora, Dadhyanc, and Vamadeva. Moreover, a number of Vedic deities also make their appearance in the Upanishadic texts, not for their role in rituals but as symbols of the Self, of prana (the life-force), or other spiritual realities. Among them we find Indra, Agni, Surya, Vayu, and Aditi.

One of the most famous doctrines of the *Brihadaranyaka-Upanishad* (II.5) is the "honey doctrine" (*madhu-vidya*), according to which all aspects of the universe are part of the same ultimate Being—a singular Being that is inherently blissful. The *Brihadaranyaka* explicitly relates this teaching to the honey doctrine of the *Rig-Veda*, as taught by the seer Dadhyanc, son of Atharvan.

2. *Universalist approach*: Self-realization or God-realization presupposes the existence of an ultimate Reality that transcends all finite, temporal forms. This Reality has been given many names. In later Hinduism the various deities like Shiva ("Benign"), Vishnu ("Pervader"), and Devi ("Goddess") are freely identified with each other, and any one of them can represent the ultimate Reality, the Absolute or supreme Self. Chants to one deity may include or change over into chants to other deities. This is because each deity is not a separate divine being but merely a different form or conceptual doorway by which the singular Reality can be approached.

This attitude, which characterizes Hinduism, reflects a sense of universality, which permits the coexistence of multiple expressions for that singular Being beyond all manifest forms. The same attitude is pervasive in the *Rig-Veda*, where the Gods and Goddesses represent different aspects of the supracosmic Intelligence, each of which encompasses all the others as part of an integral reality.

For instance, the *Rig-Veda* explicitly identifies Agni, or the sacred fire, with all the main male and female Vedic deities and with all the powers of nature and aspects of the sacred teaching. But then Agni is praised as the most excellent representation of the ultimate Reality:

> *O Agni, by your vigor you are one with the Gods and, perfectly born, you surpass them.* (*Rig-Veda* II.1.15)

Further hymns identify Indra, Soma, Surya, and several other Vedic divinities with all the other Gods respectively.

> *Poet-sages, great is that beautiful Name by which, O Vishve-Devas, you exist in Indra.* (*Rig-Veda* III.54.17)

The Vishve-Devas ("All-Gods") mentioned in the above hymn strikingly represent the Vedic principle of universality and the perfect interchangeability of the members of the Vedic pantheon. They are combined and integrated in different manners. These Vedic deities include Heaven, Earth, plants, mountains, rivers, oceans, stars, human beings, and animals, as well as different psychological factors, such as intelligence and wisdom.

> *Not one of you, Gods, is like a child or a youth. All of you are truly great.*
>
> *May the All-Gods here, who are Vaishvanara [the universal Fire], grant us and our cows and horses complete rest.* (*Rig-Veda* VIII.30.1 and 4)

In the second quote, the cows and horses are symbolic of the sensory and motor organs, which should be put to rest, or made peaceful, so that higher spiritual vision can blossom. For the Vedic seers all of nature was mirrored within the psyche.

This liberal Vedic orientation, which respects all Gods and Goddesses, must not be confused with polytheism. Rather it is a creative and universalist approach to the Divine that, in contrast to many religious teachings, is free of dogmatic narrowness. Noticing the Vedic custom of identifying the various deities with one another and then singling out one particular deity for praise, Max Müller coined the word "henotheism" to distinguish this theological orientation from both polytheism and monotheism. However, he wrongly believed that henotheism is a historical stage subsequent to polytheistic syncretism, which identifies the various Gods and Goddesses with each other. In other words, he underestimated the Vedic sages' philosophical and theological sophistication. By whatever name they invoked the great Being, they understood its absolute uniqueness.

> *The wise speak of the same One as Indra, Mitra, Varuna, and Agni, and He has beautiful wings and great speed. There is one Truth but the wise call it by different names such as Yama and Matarishvan [and so forth].* (*Rig-Veda* I.164.46)

It is this Vedic idea of the unitary truth, underlying the many paths, that serves as the metaphysical basis for the noted tolerance of later Hinduism. It can also be said to be the glue that holds together the enormous variety of spiritual teachings that compose the tapestry of the Indic civilization. But it must be appreciated that this orientation derives its strength not merely from philosophical insight but actual spiritual experience, or higher wisdom. The Vedic seers spoke with the authority of direct realization, as do the great teachers of modern Hindu spirituality.[16]

3. *Karma and rebirth*: The term *karma* or *karman*, meaning literally "action," is common in Vedic texts and specifically refers to the Vedic sacrificial ritual. The Vedic ritual is a symbolic reenactment of the process of cosmic creation, designed to reconnect the sacrificer with the greater cosmic being. The term *karma* also refers to the process of cause and effect on the moral level. It stands for the influence that our thoughts and actions have on ourselves, propelling us into repeated births and deaths. Karma is the force of destiny, which, in a way, can be viewed as the sacrificial ritual in which the cosmos itself engages, ensuring justice in the complex process of change to which all finite beings and things are subject.

When we study the early *Upanishads*, which first talk about the process of rebirth in a more or less open fashion, we find that the discussion is in terms of the Vedic ritual, which consists of various offerings into the sacred fire. There is even a direct quote from the *Rig-Veda* (X.88.16) in support of the karma doctrine. It is said that there are two life paths or "vehicles" (*yana*)—that of the Gods (*deva-yana*) and that of the fathers or ancestors (*pitri-yana*). The former leads to enlightenment and freedom from rebirth, while the latter leads to rebirth.

Those who are wise enter the flame of the sacred fire and thereby merge into the day, the waxing half of the moon, the bright half of the year, the worlds of the Gods (the powers of the light), the luminous world of the Sun, the worlds of lightning (the realms of direct illumination), and the worlds of Brahman (the dimension of infinite and eternal light).

Those who do good deeds but nevertheless lack true wisdom are reborn. They enter the dark phases of nature—the night, the waning Moon, the dark half of the year, the world of the fathers (or ancestors), and the Moon itself (the Vedic symbol for the mind or principle of thought, which is reflective, as is the Moon's borrowed luminosity). After enjoying their accumulated virtues in subtle realms, they return for rebirth by descending through space, air, water, and earth to reenter a terrestrial womb. As karma and rebirth are explained through the metaphor of the sacred fire, the implication is that the sacred fire ritual reflects the process of rebirth, which is the secret knowledge behind the ritual. The sages voluntarily undergo a spiritual rebirth in order to escape the mechanism of karma and natural rebirth altogether and to attain perfect identification with the transcendental One, or divine Being.

4. *Spiritual Practice*: Self-realization or God-realization depends on a process of inner awakening that is known as spiritual practice. In post-Vedic times, this practice has largely been equated with Yoga. Hinduism distinguishes seven principal yogic paths, which are thought to match the different temperaments of people:

(1) *Jnana-Yoga*—the Yoga of Knowledge, emphasizing spiritual discernment and renunciation of all that has been recognized as being merely finite and temporal.

(2) *Karma-Yoga*—the Yoga of Service, cultivating the person's capacity for selfless dedication to labor for the good of others.

(3) *Bhakti-Yoga*—the Yoga of Devotion, utilizing the person's ability to cultivate love and surrender.

(4) *Raja-Yoga*—the Royal Yoga, focusing on mental control through meditation and ecstatic mergence.

(5) *Laya-Yoga*—the Yoga of Absorption, consisting of techniques, particularly visualization, that impact directly on the psychoenergetic system of the human body-mind, thereby revealing higher truths.

(6) *Hatha-Yoga*—the Forceful Yoga, employing the physical body's potential in order to strengthen and harmonize it, so that it can serve as a fit vehicle for meditation and ecstasy.

(7) *Mantra-Yoga*—the Yoga of Numinous Sounds, consisting of the silent or audible recitation of mantras, or sacred words.

Jnana-Yoga is the fundamental orientation espoused in the *Upanishads*. Karma-Yoga typifies the ideal life of the householder, who, because he or she has a family, is not able to renounce worldly life and pursue meditation in the seclusion of forests or mountains. Bhakti-Yoga is the method recommended above all other approaches in the *Bhagavad-Gita*, which was composed probably in the middle of the first millennium B.C. Bhakti-Yoga always has a theistic flavor, since the Divine is worshipped in a particular form, such as Krishna in the Bhagavata tradition or Devi in the Tantric tradition. Raja-Yoga is a relatively late term, which is particularly applied to the meditation system expounded by Patanjali in his *Yoga-Sutra*, which was compiled between 200 B.C. and 200 A.D. Laya-Yoga is the Yoga most typical of Tantrism, which flourished around 1000 A.D. Hatha-Yoga, which is an offshoot of the body-oriented teachings within Tantrism, is a latecomer in the long history of Yoga. It is concerned with purifying the body in order to spiritualize it. Mantra-Yoga, which is traditionally deemed the easiest path, also acquired prominence through the growing popularity of Tantrism. However, the basic elements of all these yogic approaches, but especially Mantra-Yoga, can be found in varying degrees of elaboration in the *Vedas*.

Thus the four main Vedic deities can be identified with various Yoga paths. Agni, God of the sacred fire, relates to the Yoga of Knowledge. Soma, God of the immortal nectar, relates to the Yoga of Devotion. Indra, who symbolizes prana or the life force, relates to all Yogas directly concerned with utilizing the psychospiritual energy, especially by means of the technique of breath control (*pranayama*). Surya, the solar deity, represents the integral path of Self-realization through enhanced awareness and self-discipline.

Ritual played a significant role in Vedic times. Even though the *Vedas* were used as liturgical texts, they stress the superlative importance of spiritual knowledge or wisdom. This is in fact the very meaning of the word *veda*. A range of other terms for knowledge, understanding, wisdom, and intelligence is present in the Vedic hymns, which points to the gnostic import of the *Vedas*. Tending the sacred fire symbolizes the inner cultivation of the fires of awareness, mindfulness, and wakefulness—the way of meditation. The various Vedic deities are constantly referred to as having special knowledge and as being approachable through knowledge. Knowledge, or wisdom, is the province of the sages, who served the Vedic aspirant as a living example:

> *Being ignorant, I ask the sages who know not as one who knows but [so that I may obtain] knowledge. What is the One who in the form of the Unborn has established the six regions [of the world]?* (*Rig-Veda* I.164.6)

> *I do not know what I truly am. I roam about, mysteriously fettered by my mind.* (I.164.37a)

> *In the supreme space in which all the Gods reside is the [ultimate] syllable (*akshara*) of the chant-of-praise. What can one who does not know this do with the chant-of-praise? Those who know it, they sit together [in harmony] in this [world].* (*Rig-Veda* I.164.39)

The devotional element, or bhakti, also is prominent in the *Vedas*. Most Vedic hymns are devotional chants to the Divine in its various forms. In the *Vedas*, as in the scriptures of later Hinduism, the Divine is worshipped as father, mother, son, daughter, wife, lover, master, and so on. At the same time, the Vedic people worshipped the Divine in animal forms and all the myriad other forms of Nature. God Indra, for example, is related to the bull, Surya to a steed, and Ushas (the Goddess of Dawn) to a mare. The *Vedas* are filled with images of worship involving the mountains, rivers, dawn, wind, earth, and sky. This view is epitomized in the Vedic revelation of Purusha-Narayana, the cosmic Nan or primordial Person, whose body is the entire universe.

FIG. 37. *God Krishna and Goddess Radha, the divine couple, in eternal embrace—a symbol of the path of devotion.*

The principal means of Bhakti-Yoga is surrender, the opening of the heart to the indwelling deity. This process of surrender is ritualized in the practice of *namaskara*, the gesture of placing the flat palms of the hands together in front of the heart. Like the Christian gesture of folding the hands in prayer, namaskara indicates a recognition that the Divine is also present in the person so greeted.

> *Surrender (*namas*) is truly powerful. In surrender I take refuge. Surrender upholds Heaven and Earth. Surrender to the Gods. Surrender is their ruler. By means of surrender, I take refuge from whatever wrong actions [I may have committed].* (*Rig-Veda* VI.51.8)

We say more about this aspect of Vedic spirituality under the heading "Ritual worship" below.

As for Karma-Yoga, the whole Vedic sacrificial spirituality can be viewed as embodying this approach of selfless service. For all the rituals are performed for the larger good. The Gods and Goddesses are worshipped and the ancestors are reverenced in order to maintain the cosmic balance, which ensures everyone's welfare. Even those sacrificial rites that have a more personal objective can be understood to dovetail with and promote this larger purpose, because they depend for their success on the cultivation of universal virtues.

The elements of the other yogic approaches are discussed separately below, under "Meditation," "Mantra recitation," "Breath control," and "Posture."

5. *Spiritual initiation and guidance*: Spiritual life has traditionally been an initiatory path, depending on the transmission of wisdom from teacher to disciple. Hence the teacher who possesses not only scriptural knowledge but living experience is an individual demanding great respect, even reverence.

According to the Vedic tradition, even the Gods had their teacher (*guru*) in the form of Brihaspati, a form of Agni and a master of meditative prayer (*brahman*). The *Maitrayani-Samhita* (I.11.5) calls Brihaspati the chief priest (*purohita*) of the deities. He also is a frequent interceder on behalf of human beings, granting peace of mind to pious sacrificers. In general, the Vedic literature portrays him as a benign, healing influence in the world.

The *Vedas* mention many illustrious sages and seers, the rishis, who gained immortality in the company of the Gods and to whom appropriate reverential offerings are to be made. It is they who, as one Rig-Vedic hymn (X.14.15) puts it, anciently created the spiritual path. Some Vedic sages achieved such fame that they have been remembered ever since, figuring in many later Hindu scriptures. Among these great gurus are Vasishtha, Vishvamitra, Agastya, Bharadvaja, and Vamadeva. Not a few contemporary Hindu teachers trace their lineage or family back to one or the other Vedic sage.

6. *Ritual worship*: The Vedic tradition and subsequent Hinduism are

essentially ritualistic. Rituals are not merely of ceremonial value but are designed to enact various spiritual truths and cosmic processes on the human level. They are understood as effective vehicles of transformation for the participants, putting them in touch with the hidden reality, the realm of the Gods and Goddesses, or the cosmic order. Vedic rituals help purify the psychic environment both individually and collectively and thereby qualitatively change consciousness so as to make it receptive to higher truths. As the Vedic authorities insist, the rituals are not to be done mechanically but with full attention and proper control of body, mind, speech, and breath. In other words, they constitute a form of yogic practice. In later times, the compound *kriya-yoga* (Yoga of ritual action) is applied to this approach.

7. *Meditation*: Various meditation practices are related in the early Vedic texts. The Sanskrit word *dhyana*, the most common term for "meditation" and its numerous cognates are frequently employed in the *Vedas*. *Dhyana* stems from the verbal root *dhi*, meaning "to reflect, conceive, meditate." As a noun, *dhi* denotes "visionary insight," "higher understanding," or "illumined intelligence." As a verb it appears, for instance, in the *gayatri-mantra*, the most famous and most sacred of all Vedic chants, in the *Rig-Veda* (III.62.10) as given on p. 129.

Fig. 38. ***The sacred syllable* om, *the source of all other* mantras.**

Illumination is the crowning achievement of a long process of voluntary self-transformation. This process is often couched in terms of self-purification or catharsis. This idea, which is common to all schools of Hindu metaphysics, is already clearly expressed in the *Vedas*. In one hymn of the *Rig-Veda* (III.26.8), three filters are mentioned by which the mind is purified, so that the hidden treasures of Heaven and Earth can be beheld. The idea of filters stems from the soma ritual in which the sacred soma plant is actually pressed and filtered to produce the ambrosia of immortality. There is thus an exact correspondence between the external ritual and the inner spiritual process.

On the inner level, self-purification is accomplished primarily by means of meditation and mantra recitation. The illumined, tranquil mind is like a highly polished mirror that faithfully reflects the true nature of the universe. Before the sage's inner eye the heavenly domain opens up, yielding its secrets and eternal bliss.

Meditation and recitation were essential to the Vedic sacrificial rituals, as was flawless concentration. Only a perfectly focused mind permitted the extreme punctiliousness with which the sacrifices had to be performed in all their countless details, lest the deities or ancestors should be offended through inadvertent errors of speech or action. We may see in this extraordinary mental focusing the bedrock of the later yogic technique of concentration (*dharana*), which precedes and underlies the meditative state.

As the British Vedicist Jeanine Miller has shown, the Vedic rishis had a sophisticated culture of meditative introspection, which revolved around the practice of what is called *brahman*.[17] Here *brahman* stands for the act and potency of prayerful meditation. As Miller explains:

> *The ancient* brahman *of the* Rigveda *is a drawing forth out of the subconscious layers of the* psyche *of that power, creative in the widest sense and dynamic, which lies latent in each human being, and which is directly related to the spirit, or* atman. *The plunge into the depths of consciousness—a subjective action which is the essence of absorption (*dhyana*) and marks a step further than thinking—with mind completely stilled and in a poised, receptive state of awareness, results in* revelation. *Such revelation or inner seeing may take the form of vision, of sudden flashes and realisations of great truths otherwise left unconceived, or of communion with denizens of another dimension of life, or their manifestation; it expresses itself finally, at the mental level, through what is poorly translated as magic formula, rather a cryptic or shorthand transcript . . . by means of the right combination of sound, rhythm and image values, expressive of cosmic mysteries.*[18]

Miller further characterizes the Vedic *brahman* as invocation and evocation, "an active participation, by means of mental energy and spiritual insight, in the divine process."[19] As the Vedic seers pray: "Invigorate our meditations, invigorate our visionary insights" (*Rig-Veda* VIII.35.16). They speak of "yoking" (*yunjate*) the mind and the visionary insights. This is indeed the essence of Vedic Yoga. Miller goes on to explain Vedic meditation in three aspects, which she labels "mantric meditation," "visual meditation," and "absorption into the heart" respectively. These are not separate types of exercise but overlapping features of Vedic meditation practice.

The ultimate purpose of Vedic meditation is, as one hymn of the *Rig-Veda* (VI.17.3) puts it, to "manifest the Sun." The sun has since ancient times been a symbol of higher consciousness, or enlightenment, the Self (the *atman* of Vedanta). In the *Vedas*, to realize this inner sun is to *become* the Light of lights, the Godhead beyond all deities, the supreme Reality. Once the sun is understood as the essential Self, all the secrets of the Vedic Yoga begin to unfold, not as some primitive Shamanism but as Vedantic philosophy couched in mantric symbols.[20]

8. *Mantra recitation*: The word *mantra* stems from the verbal root *man*, meaning "to think, ponder." The suffix *tra* indicates instrumentality. Thus mantra is that which cultivates deep thought, which develops the mind. Mantras are sacred utterances of numinous power and wisdom, which are repeated in various ways to direct the mental energies toward higher realities and especially to the singular (*eka*) Being at the apex or the heart of creation.

The entire collection of hymns known as the *Vedas* is mantric in nature. Hence it is not surprising that many of the most important mantras of later Hinduism—but also of Buddhism and Jainism—should be found in the *Rig-Veda* itself. For example, Buddhist and Hindu Tantric texts begin many chants with the sacred syllable *om* and end them with *svaha*, which is the prime Vedic mantra used when placing offerings into the sacred fire. The syllable om is not mentioned in the *Rig-Veda*, possibly because it was deemed too sacred to be spoken out loud. Interestingly enough, also no graphic representation of om has so far been found in the excavated Indus towns. Even in some of the early post-Vedic scriptures, this sacred mantra is referred to only indirectly as the *pranava* (humming sound) or *udgitha* (upward song). In one Rig-Vedic hymn (I.164.39), cited on page 184, we may have an oblique reference to the sacred syllable om. At any rate, om is first named or written out in such Vedic scriptures as the *Shukla-Yajur-Veda* (I.1).

Mantra-Yoga is an integral part of the Vedic approach to spiritual realization.

> *The fathers found the hidden Light. With mantras of truth they generated the dawn [of true knowledge].* (*Rig-Veda* VII.76.4)

The fathers here are the spiritual fathers—the great seers and sages of the human race—not merely family ancestors. Elsewhere in the *Rig-Veda* (I.67.2), it is stated that the Divine can be discovered in the "hidden place" by chanting the *mantras* that the sages have fashioned in the heart. The "hidden place" is the innermost chamber of the heart, or the heart's spiritual counterpart. As in later times, the notion of the heart as the seat of the Divine plays an important role in the *Vedas*.

In the *Rig-Veda* (I.164.45), as in later scriptures, four levels of sacred utterance, or mantra, are recognized. Only the outermost level is accessible to the ordinary mind, while the others are opened only by mystical apprehension. The sacred word is often personified as the Goddess Sarasvati. In the *Atharva-Veda* (XIX.71), she is called the "Mother of the *Vedas*," who grants life, vitality, creativity, and the splendor of spiritual wisdom.

Another important notion of Vedic Mantra-Yoga is captured in the term *nama*, meaning "name" and referring to the various names given to the Divine by the Vedic sages.

> *The seers meditated the original name of the Cow. They discovered the three times seven supreme [names] of the Mother.* (*Rig-Veda* IV.1.16)

The Cow symbolizes the Divine Mother or cosmic feminine energy that nourishes and supports all creation, what later came to be called *prakriti* or *shakti*. To this day, Hindus treat cows with great reverence, though many are not aware of the archaic Vedic origins of this custom.

This divine word or name is identified with the sacred syllable *om*, which is said to be the quintessence of the *Vedas*. Thus Classical Yoga, as expounded by Patanjali in the *Yoga-Sutra*, knows om as the symbol of the Lord, who is the primordial teacher of Yoga.

9. *Breath control*: Several Vedic deities are intimately associated with the wind, air, breath, or life force, variously referred to as *prana*, *vata*, and *vayu*. This is clearly so in the case of Indra, the foremost of the Vedic Gods, who is coupled with God Vayu in several chants. In one Rig-Vedic hymn (VII.91.4), the worshipping sages invoke Indra-Vayu, inviting him to join their sacred assembly and drink with them the mind-expanding soma draft. In fact, Indra-Vayu gets the first and best part of the ambrosial juice.

From a yogic perspective, the soma liquid represents the pure residue of the sage's experience when the doors of perception are cleansed. Indra-Vayu symbolizes the purified life-force that wells up within the sage's tranquil mind, giving him or her spiritual vigor and physical stamina.

In other hymns, God Vayu is invoked as the bestower of life. As Sri Aurobindo explained:

> *Vayu is the Lord of Life. By the ancient Mystics life was considered to be a great force pervading all material existence and the condition of all its activities. It is this idea that was formulated later on in the conception of the Prana, the universal breath of life.*[21]

Aurobindo went on to explain that whereas Vayu was venerated as the master of life energy, Indra was the master of life itself, who ruled over the mind. The coupling of their names shows that the seers understood the close connection between mental activity and psychosomatic energy and its most visible expression, the breath. They could be said to stand for inner and outer action respectively, both of which are necessary for spiritual work to succeed.

The Vedic ritual proceeds by means of mind (meditation), speech (mantra recitation), and breath (*pranayama*). The practice of controlled inhalation, exhalation, and breath retention in ritual contexts is well-established by the time of the earliest *Brahmanas*, nearly four thousand years ago. For instance, the *Jaiminiya-Brahmana* (III.3.1) instructs the priests not to breathe during the recitation of the *gayatrimantra*. The *Baudhayana-Dharma-Sutra* (IV.1.24) states that magical heat (*tapas*) can be generated by holding the breath. The *Kaushitaki-Brahmana* (II.5) speaks of breath control as the internal fire sacrifice (*agni-hotra*).

In the *Atharva-Veda* (XV.15-18), which antedates the *Brahmanas*, the various categories of the *prana*, or "wind/breath/life force," are mentioned. This classification was undoubtedly not merely theoretical but had practical applications, as do similar schemas in the later Yoga tradition, especially the Hatha-Yoga branch.

10. *Posture*: As Mircea Eliade, one of the great twentieth-century historians of religion, has shown, Yoga is based on the principle of reversal: The *yogin* seeks to do the exact opposite of the ordinary worldling.[22] Thus he endeavors to stop his mind, hold his breath, abstain from food, shun social contact, arrest his semen (through chastity) and, not least, remain motionless in the body—all in order to inhibit the flux of time itself by lifting his consciousness into the infinite, immortal dimension of the Divine. In the case of Bhakti-Yoga and Karma-Yoga, this principle of reversal can be seen in the cultivation of selfless love and service, neither of which characterize the behavior of the ordinary individual, who tends to be driven by egotism and the profit motive. The Tantric scriptures even have a name for this principle of reversal: *pratikula*, meaning literally "counter-bank," that is, going against the stream.

Asana, which means "seat" or "posture," is the most outward aspect of the yogic work of reversing the ordinary flow of life. It should therefore not surprise us to find evidence for the existence of this limb of the yogic path in Vedic times. Many of the soapstone seals of the Indus-Sarasvati civilization, which, as we have argued in this book is essentially Vedic, show figures seated in various sacerdotal postures, including the famous Pashupati seal, depicting Shiva, Lord of the Beast.

The *Vedas* themselves do not mention specific Yoga postures, or *asanas*, but neither does Patanjali in his *Yoga-Sutra*, which was composed several thousand years later. In one aphorism (II.46), Patanjali merely specifies that posture should be steady and comfortable. This does not mean that such postures were not known, but that they would have been part of a more specific, oral, instruction. The proliferation of yogic postures as known today was the product of the inventiveness of the masters of Hatha-Yoga, which enjoyed increasing popularity after 1000 A.D., though it was probably based upon older traditions.

Vedic Spirituality and the Hindu Tradition

Hinduism is a stupendously complex phenomenon. It could be said that there are more religions within Hinduism than outside of it. Hinduism has never discarded or excluded anything, giving each teaching its particular niche within an ever-expanding framework of ideas, beliefs, and practices. In this way, Hinduism has been able to assimilate alien ideas and practices without forgoing its own fundamental teachings. The more it has changed, the more it has remained the same.

FIG. 39. *A contemporary representation of God Shiva.*

One way in which change has occurred within India's religious culture is in the gradual eclipse of particular deities and the emergence into prominence of other Gods and Goddesses. Thus the great Vedic deities Indra, Agni, Soma, and Surya were superseded by the great Hindu deities Shiva, Vishnu, Devi, and the elephantine Ganesha. It has been suggested that this change was the result of a resurgence of pre-Vedic non-Aryan traditions. But this is not borne out by the archaeological record. Otherwise one would expect these later deities to somehow be associated with the Sarasvati region and its mythology, which is not the case. Rather, Gods like Shiva and Vishnu could be said to reflect the heritage of the Ganges-Yamuna era of Puranic times, while the classic Vedic deities reflect the Indus-Sarasvati phase.

For example, God Shiva, who is often regarded as the main pre-Vedic or indigenous Indic deity, is in Hindu mythology the deity associated with the Ganges River, which descends on his head. Shiva's sacred city is Benares (Kashi), which lies on the banks of the Ganges, not the Indus or Sarasvati. By contrast, the principal Vedic God Indra, who in many respects resembles Shiva, distinctly relates to the Sarasvati River. The connection of the later deities of Hinduism with the Ganges River shows their later origin, at the time when the Vedic culture shifted its center to the east after the Sarasvati went dry.

The rise to prominence of such deities as Shiva and Vishnu has traditionally been understood as a development within the Vedic tradition itself, and not as the assimilation of non-Aryan deities. Given the long history of India's civilization, these changes can be expected. No outside influence need be invoked to account for the appearance of these popular Hindu deities and the religious practices associated with them. They are crystallizations of theological-mystical imagery present already in the *Rig-Veda* (which incidentally has five hymns dedicated to Vishnu).

This does not mean, of course, that there was no outside influence at all upon the Vedic tradition, but whatever foreign elements were absorbed by the culture of early India, they did not change the core features of the Vedic heritage. This recognition brings immediate order and simplicity to the mass of historical facts. We no longer have to postulate a mysterious pre-Vedic tradition that was somehow lost or obscured, only to resurface here and there in subsequent times. In addition, we do not need to interpret the Vedic tradition as being substantially at variance from later Hinduism, the two being separated by a strange and inexplicable rupture. Rather, we can look upon India's spiritual heritage as a consistent cultural system, which happens to be the oldest surviving civilization in the world.

Chapter 11

The Birth of Science in Ritual

Scientific Abstraction and Sacred Lore

OUR WORD "SCIENCE" STEMS FROM THE LATIN *SCIENTIA*, which is itself derived from *scire* meaning "to know" and "to discern." Science is thus the pursuit of knowledge. In our outward-looking civilization this has come to mean primarily the search for knowledge of how the external world works and how we can learn to manipulate it better. This understanding of science is rather limited, and it fails to take into account knowledge that is accessible through introspection and higher states of awareness as cultivated in the spiritual traditions. When we glance into the past, we find that the creators of ancient cosmologies relied greatly on these other forms of knowledge. Today we often tend to dismiss their knowledge systems, or worldviews, as mere myth. In doing so, we fail to acknowledge that in our push for objective knowledge we too utilize intellectual modes that are not always strictly rational, as has been shown by philosophers like Michael Polanyi and Paul Feyerabend.[1] In the preface to his four-volume history of science, John Desmond Bernal makes this germane statement: "Science, in one aspect, is ordered technique; in another, it is rationalized mythology."[2]

When we consider the evolution of science, we can sketch a process that starts with counting. The ability to count is basic to all knowledge systems and human societies. This counting skill, combined with the capacity for simple observation, revealed to archaic humanity certain fundamental regularities in Nature, notably the seasons as well as solar and lunar cycles. The more intelligent observers of the past then formulated in their heads a predictive model, which we now call a calendar. According to Alexander Marshack, the marks on a forty-thousand-year-old rib bone found at Ishango near the headwaters of the Nile represent the earliest calendrical notations.[3] Microscopic analysis showed that the incisions on the bone had been made at different times by different tools. Marshack—a gifted writer rather than a scientist—speculated that what were previously thought to be mere decorative or hunting marks are in fact markings recording a periodic event, specifically the Moon's phases. In support of his hypothesis, Marshack pointed to recent carving-stick calendars kept on the Nicobar islands in the Andaman Sea, which belong to India. There is nothing intrinsically wrong with the assumption that Paleolithic humanity should have been able to count or to observe the Moon's periodicity. However, it challenges current scientific notions about the level of cultural sophistication at that time, and therefore Marshack's proposition has remained controversial.

Whatever we may think about Marshack's hypothesis and the computing skills of Paleolithic humanity, there can be little doubt that the emergence of agriculture in the Neolithic age was dependent on knowledge of the calendar, which allowed the ancients to determine the right time for planting and harvesting crops. We can envision that this naturally led to a more detailed mathematical analysis of the movements of the Sun, Moon, and planets. Moreover, trade requires bookkeeping, and commerce was apparently as important to our Neolithic ancestors as it is to us today. Hence it should not be surprising that arithmetic was known in a complex civilization such as that of ancient India, which had both a thriving agriculture and far-flung trade.

Of course, mathematics and science are more than mere counting. Mathematics involves the discovery of abstract general rules, such as the Pythagorean theorem, which captures the fact that the square of the longest side of a right-angled triangle equals the sum of the squares of the other two sides. Geometry and physics likewise call for generalization beyond the empirical.

Science in this sense did not flower in all ancient civilizations, but we do find it present in the Indus/Sarasvati civilization. Some historians even have suggested that the birth of science was triggered by Vedic philosophy and ritual.[4] The Vedic worldview acknowledges that there is an intimate relationship beween the cosmic, the terrestrial, and the spiritual, which is expressed in terms of equivalences. The idea of equivalence, which is fundamental to what has been called initiatic science, is that the universe is an interconnected system—a notion that has made a comeback through the findings and interpretations of nuclear physics and modern cosmology.

A related idea is that the macrocosm is mirrored in the microcosm and that the study of the large can reveal secrets about the small. Discontented with the limitations of quantum physics, the British avant-garde physicist David Bohm formulated his model of the implicate (enfolded) order.[5] According to this model, the world we see is the manifestation of a deeper, hidden dimension of reality in which everything is contained and interlinked. Bohm gave this deeper reality the name "holomovement" to indicate that it is an all-inclusive dynamic process. Thus an elementary particle is not elementary or fundamental at all but merely a name given to a particular aspect of the holomovement. Little wonder that his work is widely thought to build a bridge between contemporary science and traditional wisdom.

Ancient humanity appears to have been extremely sensitive to correspondences or equivalences in Nature. The regularity of celestial phenomena, of the tides, and not least of biological rhythms—all must have provided a powerful rationale for this holistic cosmology. What we might dismiss as pure coincidence, our forebears would take as a sign of the beautiful interwovenness of all things. Therefore they noticed correspondences and also imbued them with special meaning. For instance, the Ayurvedic savants made the astonishing discovery that the number of bones in the human body equals the number of days in the year. They arrived at this number by counting the 308 bones of a newborn, 32 teeth, and 20 nails. They took this as a confirmation of their basic belief that the human being is a mirror image of the cosmos. In the *Rig-Veda* (X.90), the cosmos is likened to an enormous man (*purusha*). Conversely, the human individual is a representation of that cosmic giant. In today's scientific language, we would say that "the body enfolds not only the mind but also in some sense the entire material universe."[6] Without this understanding, we cannot hope to understand the *Rig-Veda* and the esoteric traditions built upon its worldview.

Sacrificial Ritual and Astronomy

Vedic cosmology evolved in conjunction with a complex system of sacrificial ritualism. Sacrifice was understood as a means of preserving the cosmic order on the human level by utilizing equivalences existing between the individual person and the macrocosmic reality. We may see in the Vedic sacrifice a form of technology exploiting the equivalences or correspondences in Nature. In the sacrificial ritual, the Vedic priests remembered the original self-sacrifice of the cosmic giant owing to which the cosmos came into existence. Thus the sacrifice involved in bringing forth the explicate order of reality from the implicate order is essentially the same sacrifice that must be performed by the human being wishing to trace the way back from the explicate order to the implicate order—from the phenomenal world to the realm of immortality, luminosity, and sheer bliss.

Many early agricultural societies understood this in a literal sense—as human sacrifice. But in Vedic times, a metaphoric interpretation was in place: The sacrificer had to endure the hardship of the ritual in order to consciously connect with the hidden dimension, the implicate order, of the Ultimate Reality, the nameless One, which was yet named in various ways. The thread leading to that One was to be found within oneself, though only through the agency of the properly executed external ritual. Only later on, at the time of the *Upanishads*, was the ritual fully interiorized, being performed as a Yoga of inward concentration and contemplation. However, elements of this inner ritual can be met with already in the preceding period.

For the asceticism (*tapas*) connected with the Vedic ritualism demanded utmost mental focusing, will power, and self-transcendence. The Vedic sage, as much as the later yogin, had to undergo the ordeal of inner transformation. But whereas the former availed himself of the supportive framework of the sacrificial ritualism, the latter relied largely, though by no means exclusively, on the codified path of meditative introversion.

When we examine the various Vedic rituals, we are struck again and again by the pervasiveness of the cosmological principle of equivalence. Thus, in one of the most important of these sacrificial rituals—the *agni-cayana* or "heaping up the fire"—the sky and the earth were represented by square and round altars respectively. The square arrangement of the sky altar was derived from the four cardinal directions, while the roundness of the earth altar represented the globe. During the ritual, the round altar was made symbolically equivalent to the square altar, which posed the problem of squaring a circle. This and other similar symbolic issues led to basic mathematical and geometrical questions.

Incidentally, the sky and earth altars were correlated with the male and female gender respectively. Sexual symbolism is pervasive in the Vedic religion. Thus the *adhvaryu* priest was deemed male while the *neshtri* priest, who was typically associated with the Goddesses, represented the female gender. The Vedic texts speak of the "copulation" between the chants and the prose formulas, the former being considered feminine and the latter masculine. There are numerous "couplings" (*mithuni-karana*) of this type in the *Vedas* and the subsequent ritual literature. It is in this Vedic custom that we must look for the seeds of the metaphysics of medieval Tantrism, which views the cosmos as the product of Shiva's and Shakti's divine embrace (*maithuna*).[7]

The emphasis on knowledge in the Vedic worldview naturally also caused the ancients to pursue astronomy. Indeed, there are numerous astronomical references in the *Vedas*, and the planets and stars have a special importance in the Vedic rituals. The principal deity of the Vedic ritualism was God Agni, who was understood as a personification of time. More specifically, Agni represented the year, and the twelve-day agni-cayana ritual commemorated the ideal year of 360 days. This astronomical preoccupation is also reflected in the architecture of the Indus cities, for the streets and monumental buildings are aligned according to the cardinal directions. The human world was made to conform to the divine world.

Until recently, when one of the present authors (Subhash Kak) discovered the presence of a code in the design of the Vedic altars, no proof had been available that the ancient Indic civilization possessed any scientific knowledge. In fact, most scholars have regarded the Vedic civilization as pre-scientific—a term that is widely used to suggest the subordination of knowledge to myth and ritual. Yet, even before the discovery of the Vedic astronomical code, this widespread opinion was clearly contradicted by the facts. As the renowned Dutch scholar Jan Gonda observed:

> *Many places [in the Vedic literature] attest to what may be called a pre-scientific interest in, and study of, the world and to attempts at systematizing the knowledge resulting from this study. Much attention is paid to chronology and the calendar . . . astronomy, cosmology and cosmogony. This scientific concern is wholly determined by man's ritual and religious interests and constitutes an integral part of one and the same harmonious view of life and the world. This does not however exclude the occurrence of references to a certain knowledge of anatomy, embryology, and medical practice. Nor did some linguistic facts—as far as they were utilizable for ritual purposes—escape the authors' notice.*[8]

The astronomical basis of the fire altars as well as the discovery of an altar code in the organization of the material of the *Rig-Veda* confirm the need for a new understanding of the origins of science and astronomy. The genealogies of the *Puranas* as well as astronomical references in the Vedic scriptures take us back to events in the fourth millennium B.C. and earlier, as we have already noted.[9] This considerably pushes back the date for the earliest beginnings of science in the broader sense of the term, as the systematic observation and study of phenomena. The emergence of rational science is generally associated with the ancient Greeks, who are hailed as the early masters of mathematics and especially geometry. The Vedic evidence obliges us to reconsider this assessment.

The *Rig-Veda* is a fascinating and unique record of ancient science four thousand and more years ago. As we have discovered, the number of syllables and the verses of the *Rig-Veda* are layed out according to an astronomical plan. The *Rig-Veda* could be called a verbal counterpart to the monumental structures of Stonehenge, which served astronomical computations. However, this famous archaeological site in England is thought to have been constructed in the period from 1900 B.C. to 1600 B.C., long after the composition of the *Rig-Veda*. Also, whereas Stonehenge is badly damaged, the *Rig-Veda* is considered by all scholars to be in a state of near perfect preservation. Finally, words are more eloquent than even the most imposing stone monument. And the words preserved in the Rig-Vedic hymnody are most thoughtful and poetically skillful utterances by seers whose vision penetrated deeply into the nature of existence. They also happen to be the oldest recorded words of which we have knowledge. In its overall plan, the *Rig-Veda* is an altar fashioned from hymns rather than bricks. Its internal organization contains important cosmological information, which gives us a unique glimpse into the Vedic way of thinking. The following section, which may be somewhat difficult to follow, shows just how sophisticated the Vedic intellectuals—the sages and seers—were.

Fire Altars and Heavenly Mathematics

The Vedic rituals were generally performed at an altar, built with a specific number of bricks that had not only ritualistic but astronomical and calendrical equivalences. Thus the altar design was based on numbers that reconciled the lunar and solar years. The solar year is slightly longer than 365 days, whereas the lunar year fractionally exceeds 354 days. Reckoning the seasons with either of these calendars creates considerable problems. Since the Vedic rites were seasonal and meant to mark the passage of time, a workable calendar had to be formulated. The ideal year of 360 days was found most suitable. Other ancient civilizations, notably the Maya, reached the same conclusion.

The fire altars were meant to symbolize the universe at large, and the important agni-cayana rite involved three types of altars, which respectively represented the earth, the atmosphere (or mid-region), and the sky (or Heaven). The sky altar was constructed in five layers of bricks. The sky was taken to stand for the universe as a whole, including the atmosphere and the earth. The first layer represented the earth, the third the atmosphere, and the fifth the sky. The second layer symbolized the joining of the earth and the atmosphere, whereas the fourth layer stood for the joining of the atmosphere and the sky. This altar was most often symbolically represented in the shape of a falcon or a tortoise, but could be constructed in several other forms as well.

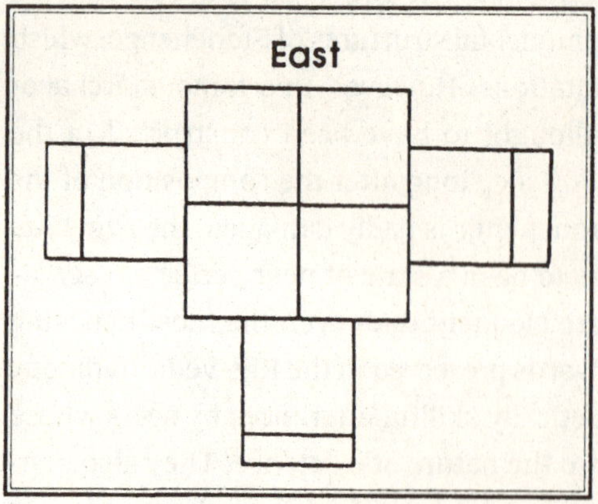

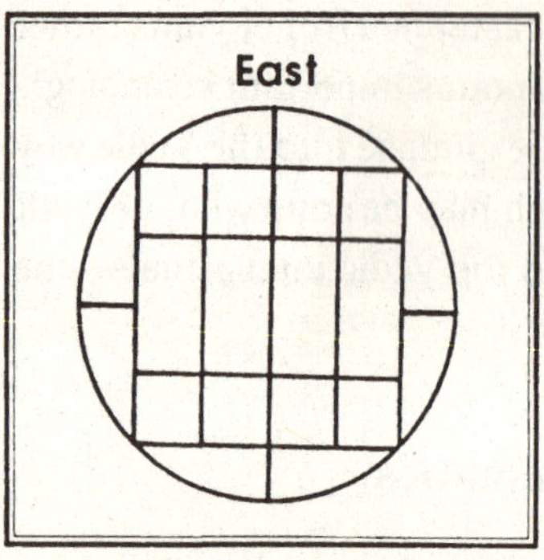

FIG. 40 *(top). Basic form of the Vedic fire altar.* FIG. 41 *(above). Round variant of the Vedic fire altar.*

The altars were built in a sequence corresponding to ninety-five years, with the size being increased every year by a certain amount. The amount of the increase represented the extra days needed to make the lunar year equal to the solar year. At the completion of this sequence, after the necessary number of intercalary months had been added to the lunar years, the ancients obtained an excellent synchronization of the lunar and solar years.

An intercalation cycle of ninety-five years hints at a knowledge of the length of the tropical year being equal to 365.24675 days, which would be a surprisingly accurate figure for that early time of more than five thousand years ago. Such knowledge could only be based on a centuries-long tradition of astute astronomical observation. The number of days in the year were mapped into altars of different designs, using bricks of various shapes but of fixed size. This raised problems of mapping equal areas of various shapes, such as a circle into a square. The necessary intercalation was expressed in the altar design. Solutions to these practical problems required the development of mathematics, algebra, and geometry.

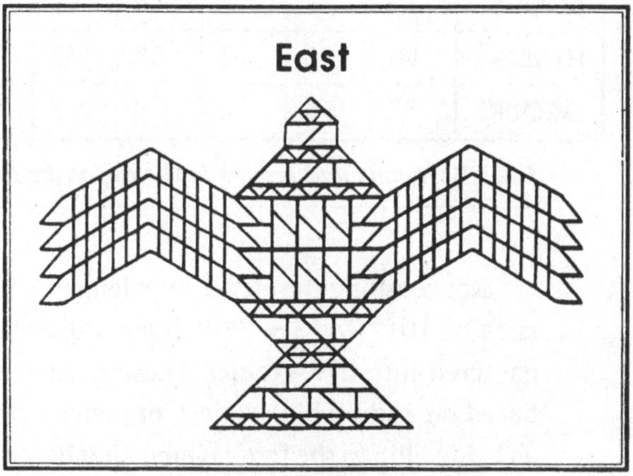

FIG. 42. *Bird variant of the Vedic fire altar.*

The fire altars were surrounded by 360 enclosing stones; of these, 21 were around the earth altar, 78 around the atmosphere altar, and 261 around the sky altar. In other words, the earth, the atmosphere, and the sky were given the symbolic value of 21, 78, and 261 respectively. Since the cosmos was thought to include the atmosphere and the sky, the two principal cosmological numbers were 21 and 339 (78 + 261).

When we turn to the *Rig-Veda*, we find from the total number of syllables that this text was itself taken to represent a symbolic altar. Thus the number of syllables in the *Rig-Veda* is supposed to add up to the number of *muhurtas* (1 day = 30 *muhurtas*) in forty years, which is 432,000. The same number of syllables were alloted to the *Yajur-Veda* and the *Sama-Veda* conjointly, thus yielding a total of 864,000 syllables for the three principal *Vedas*. In reality, however, the syllable count for the *Rig-Veda* is somewhat less because certain syllables are meant to be left unspoken.

The verse count of the *Rig-Veda* (excluding the eleven supplemental hymns) can be viewed as the number of "sky" days in forty years (or 261 x 40 = 10,440). Again, the verse count of all four *Vedas* is 261 x 78 = 20,358. Even the *actual* Rig-Vedic syllabic count of 397,265 can be obtained from these astronomical numbers.

BOOKS	1	2	3	4	5	6	7	8	9	10
HYMNS	191	43	62	58	87	75	104	92	114	191
GROUPS	15	5	4	11	7	5	12	18	7	132

TABLE 3. *Hymns and groups in the Rig-Vedic books.*

Not counting the eleven supplemental hymns, the *Rig-Veda* consists of 1017 (or 3 x 339) hymns distributed over 10 books and gathered into 216 groups. These groups are the natural divisions based on authorship, subject, or meter. When we treat the *Rig-Veda* as being akin to the five-layered altar described above, we obtain the following picture:

191	114
104	92
87	75
62	58
43	191

TABLE 4. *Rig-Vedic altar of books.*

As the diagram shows, we can represent the *Rig-Veda* as a five-layered altar with two books to each layer. For our proposed parallel between the construction of the fire altars and the internal organization of the *Rig-Veda* to hold, we would expect the first two Rig-Vedic books to correspond to the atmosphere intermediate between the earth and the sky. This is indeed the case. The number of hymns in the first two books (43 + 191) is 234. When we multiply the symbolic value of the atmosphere (78) by three, corresponding to the tripartite cosmology of the *Vedas*, this yields a total of 234, which is exactly the number of hymns in these two books.

Further astronomical values are obtained when the number of hymns of the various books are considered. For example, the first four books contain 354 hymns, which corresponds to the length of the lunar year (the period between twelve new moons). Similarly, the total number of hymns in the middle four books (four to seven) is 324, which equals the *nakshatra* (constellation) year of 12 x 27 days. When this is multiplied by a close approximation of pi, we arrive at 1017, which corresponds to the number of hymns in the entire Rig-Vedic collection (excluding eleven supplemental hymns).

The decipherment of the Rig-Vedic code has shown that, remarkably, the Vedic poet-mathematicians had discovered the astronomical significance of the numbers 108 and 339.[10] The number 108, which is one-half the number of hymn groups, as listed in Table 3, is roughly the average distance between the Sun and Earth in terms of solar diameters. It is also the average distance between the Moon and Earth in terms of lunar diameters. These values can be obtained by simple measurements with the naked eye. For example, if a pole of a certain height were to be separated from the observer by a distance that is 108 times this height, its angular size would be exactly equal to that of the Sun or the Moon.

The second number—339—is simply the number of solar disks it takes to measure the Sun's path across the sky during equinox: pi x 108 = circa 339. That the *Rig-Veda* should reflect the Sun steps during the equinox is very fitting in light of the special role of the Rig-Vedic hymns in the spring equinox celebrations. The above discovery also would seem to explain why 108 beads are used in Hindu rosaries. A full round on the rosary represents a symbolic journey from the earth to the sky.

We must note here that the actual—rather than the ideal—Vedic year was reckoned as consisting of 366 days. This allowed for easy calculation, because northern India has a unique six-season climate; thus each season can conveniently be assigned sixty-one days. The year of 366 days was divided into two equal parts of 183 days, one part representing the deities (or light) and the other representing their counterpart (darkness). This symbolization was also understood to stand for the northern and southern courses of the Sun. It appears that the ancients sought to reconcile the 339 steps of the Sun with the symbolic value 183 (representing the deities) by postulating a value of 78 for the atmosphere, since 339 = 183 + 2 x 78.

That this proposed interpretation of the numbers 108 and 339 is not based on mere coincidence is borne out by additional evidence. For instance, significant validation can be found in the number of solar steps for the winter and summer solstices, which also can be derived from the code. The solar steps would be 339 on the day of the equinox and would vary relative to the solstices when the days are shorter or longer. The two numbers in question are 296 and 382.[11] They yield a ratio of 1.29 between them, which can be regarded as the ratio between the longest to the shortest day from which the latitude of the place of the composition of the hymns, or the code, can be obtained. Significantly, this ratio corresponds to the latitude of the lower Sarasvati valleys, which textual evidence confirms was the region of the composition of the hymns! Later Indic astronomy used as its prime meridian the city of Ujjain, which is of a similar latitude.

The Planets and the Gods

There can be no doubt that the Vedic Indians studied the movement of the Sun and the Moon very carefully. It seems unlikely, therefore, that they would have failed to notice the movement of the planets as well. The *Rig-Veda* speaks of the thirty-four "lights," which are the twenty-seven lunar constellations, the five planets, and the Sun and the Moon.[12] There is also mention of "seven suns," comprising the Sun, the Moon, and the five planets. The *Atharva-Veda* mentions the planets along with the lunar nodes (*rahu*), which suggests that the Vedic priests were able to predict eclipses.

According to Hindu mythology, the twenty-seven constellations (*nakshatra*) through which the Moon passes are the Moon God's wives. Rohini (in Taurus) is his favorite spouse. In the *Taittiriya-Samhita* (II.3.5), belonging to the *Yajur-Veda*, the Moon God is said to have thirty-three wives, which undoubtedly are the twenty-seven constellations, the Sun, and the five planets closest to the Sun. Validating this idea, a hymn of the *Rig-Veda* (X.85) celebrates the marriage of the Moon God with the Sun Goddess. The Vedic people observed the Moon's transit through various constellations and the planets involved. As the fastest moving heavenly body, the Moon was considered to be activating or impregnating the constellations and the planets with which it became conjoined. The Sun and the planets were seen as having a similar activating role. In this regard, the *Rig-Veda* (I.105.10) speaks of the five bulls who reside in Heaven, which are none other than the planets. All this irrefutably indicates the antiquity of astronomical observation in India.

Information about the planets can be in terms of sidereal or synodic periods or both. Sidereal periods are computed with reference to stars, corresponding to the period in which a planet circles around the Sun, whereas synodic periods relate to successive conjunctions. Thus the synodic period of the Moon is the interval between successive full moons. Naked-eye astronomy is sufficient to compute both types of periodicity. The sidereal periods for Mercury, Venus, Mars, Jupiter, and Saturn have traditionally been calculated as being 87, 225, 687, 4,332, and 10,760 days respectively. These numbers are quite accurate. The sidereal periods can be obtained by multiplying smaller numbers as shown here.

$$87 = 87 \times 1 \text{ (Mercury)}$$
$$225 = 58 + 75 + 92 = 75 \times 3 \text{ (Venus)}$$
$$687 = 191 \times 3 + 114 \approx 43 \times 16 \text{ (Mars)}$$
$$4{,}332 \approx 62 \times 70 \approx 58 \times 75 \text{ (Jupiter)}$$
$$10{,}760 \approx 104 \times 104 \approx 92 \times 117 \text{ (Saturn)}$$

Factors from each of these equations appear as the number of hymns per book (*mandala*). The arrangement of the Rig-Vedic books also yields the synodic periods in days and *tithis*. A *tithi* was reckoned as a 360th part of the lunar year. Since the lunar year is slightly more than 354 days, a tithi is somewhat shorter than a day. The use of the tithi, which cannot be observed but must be calculated, in itself indicates sophisticated astronomical knowledge. In this connection we should note that the total number of deities given in the *Rig-Veda*—namely 3339—strongly suggests the tithi measurement. There are 371 tithis in a year of 365 plus days, and when we multiply this figure by 9 we arrive at 3339. The 3339 Vedic Gods and Goddesses thus represent a ninefold division of the year measured by tithis.

By adding the hymn counts of the ten books of the *Rig-Veda* in different combinations, we obtain numbers that are factors of the sidereal periods and the five synodic periods reckoned in days as well as in tithis. The probability of this happening by chance is about one in a million. Hence whoever arranged the *Rig-Veda* encoded into it not only obvious numbers like the lunar year but also hidden numbers of great astronomical significance. This is an achievement unparalleled in that early era.

This Vedic accomplishment is surely as astonishing as the astrogeometrical code of the Great Pyramid. As the Egyptian-born engineer Robert G. Bauval has shown in his intriguing book *The Orion Mystery*, the northern shaft of the King's Chamber of the Cheops pyramid was aligned with Alpha Draconis in around 2450 B.C., whereas the southern shaft was aimed at Zeta Orionis at that time.[13] In addition, the northern shaft of the Queen's Chamber pointed at the star Kochab in Ursa Minor.

Bauval firmly believes that the ancient Egyptians knew about the curious astronomical phenomenon of the precession (caused by Earth's slight tilt) and that the three pyramids of the Giza plateau capture the secret of the precessional return in solid stone. Other researchers, notably J. B. Sellers and Schwaller de Lubicz, have expressed a similar view.[14] This represents a significant departure from conventional scholarly wisdom, which credits the Greeks—in particular Hipparchus of Alexandria of second century B.C.—with the discovery of the precession of the equinoxes.

Vedic and Hindu Astronomy

The Vedic sacrifices required precise astronomical knowledge and a calendar based upon it. Full- and new-moon sacrifices occurred every month, and those for the Moon when half full were sometimes marked as well. There also were annual sacrifices based upon the solstices and the seasons. The months were determined astronomically by the particular constellation (*nakshatra*) in which the full moon occurred during the month. Thus astronomy was one of the fundamental sciences of the Vedic Indus-Sarasvati civilization.

How did the science of astronomy arise in ancient India? The encyclopedia-like *Puranas* credit the legendary figure of Pururavas, one of the earliest Vedic kings, with the division of the one fire into the three fires that are the basis of the Vedic ritual. He is said to have learned this secret from the *gandharvas*, a group of angel-like beings. The *Rig-Veda* (X.95) contains a mythological conversation between Pururavas and the water nymph Urvashi, from which we gather that he had previously violated Urvashi, who was pregnant with his son. Consumed with passion but failing to win Urvashi back by his pleading, the king finally threatens, in a veiled way, to commit suicide. This might explain his curious name, which means "he who roars much."[15] One can conclude from the Puranic references and the genealogical seniority of Pururavas that the fire ritual was a part of the Vedic religion from the earliest times.

We may further speculate that the planetary periods were determined toward the end of the Rig-Vedic age and incorporated into the code. It is possible that as this astronomical knowledge became more widespread, its encoding in the inner structure of the *Rig-Veda* was gradually forgotten.

The astronomical code of the Vedic altars and of the *Rig-Veda* refutes the prevalent supposition that observational astronomy began in Babylon during the middle of the first millennium B.C. The fact that the earliest Vedic ritual was astronomical is attested to by textual references in the *Rig-Veda* itself.

It is generally accepted that the references to the Vedic deities Mitra, Varuna, Indra, and the Nasatyas in the Hittite-Mitanni treaty of the second millennium B.C. refer to the Indo-Aryans rather than the Iranians. It appears that the Indic element existed in southwestern Asia by the beginning of the second millennium. In light of the geological and archaeological evidence, which shows a time of troubles for the Indic civilization along the Indus and Sarasvati Rivers around 1900 B.C., we can now postulate an exodus of peoples from India. We can further surmise that this westward migration was in all probability accompanied by a corresponding flow of traditional knowledge from India to the Middle East. This exported knowledge would have included the astronomy of the fire altars and the planetary period values of the *Rig-Veda*. Yet, we must add, it is also possible that Vedic groups were present in southwestern Asia at an earlier period, forming offshoots or colonies of the Indus-Sarasvati civilization before the great disaster struck.

We know for certain that there was a continuing interaction between India and Babylon in subsequent centuries. This is clearly mirrored in certain interesting parallels between their respective astronomies. Earlier in this chapter, we mentioned that the ratio between the longest and the shortest period of daylight changed from 1.29 to 1.5, which implies a shift in astronomical observation from the Sarasvati valleys to northwestern India. The latter value can be found in the *Vedanga-Jyotisha*, a manual of Vedic astronomy, which mentions the winter solstice at the beginning of the constellation Dhanishtha (23° 20' Capricorn) and the summer solstice in the middle of Ashlesha (23° 20' Cancer). This configuration corresponds to about 1400 B.C. Interestingly, we find the same ratio of 1.5 in the Babylonian texts of the first millennium B.C., even though the earliest Babylonian texts spoke of a ratio of 2.0, which more accurately reflects a region much farther north.

The other significant parallel is that the Babylonian texts use a linear zig-zag function to determine the length of daylight in intermediate months, which is already present in the Rig-Vedic model. It is, moreover, weighty evidence that the Babylonians also used the notion of tithi, referring to it simply as "day," as was often done in India as well. One might speculate that Vedic astronomy was taken over by the Babylonians and was built upon further during the flowering that took place in Babylonia around 700 B.C.

Classical Hindu astronomy arose after the close interaction between the Indians and the Greeks subsequent to the invasion of India by Alexander the Great (323 B.C.). The existence of an indigenous tradition of astronomical observation and theorizing, as shown by the Rig-Vedic code, helps explain the puzzling fact that classical Hindu astronomy diverges in many ways from the Greek astronomical legacy. The existence of the Rig-Vedic code itself suggests that the mathematical framework for the planetary motions was very old by the time the influence of the Greek heritage made itself felt in India.

The development outlined here is consistent with what has been proposed for the rise of Indian mathematics and geometry.[16] Furthermore, our present arguments confirm the prescient remarks by the American scholar Ebenezer Burgess, who, over a century ago, noted that the shared aspects of the astronomies of India, Babylonia, and Greece appear to stem from India.[17]

The discovery of the Rig-Vedic code has opened important doors of understanding for us. Since the code appears to be many layered, and we have so far deciphered only the top layer, we may wonder what further secrets about ancient observational astronomy still lie hidden beneath it.

Qualitative Science: Astrology

The Vedic insight that the cosmos is reflected in the terrestrial and the human realms led, among other things, to the development of astrology. In fact, in ancient times, astrology and astronomy did not form separate disciplines but simply were aspects of the same comprehensive cosmology. According to the astrological view, the planets and stars are not merely physical bodies or quantities of matter whirling in space but qualities of both cosmological and psychological import. Their movement and patterned relationship to one another are thought to have a significant parallel in the lives of individuals and nations. Various Vedic deities were assigned rulership over the constellations, and their influence was thought to be activated by the movement of the heavenly bodies through the constellations, affecting both the psyche and destiny (karma) of living beings.

Astrology is traditionally considered to be effective not because of any actual physical influence of the planets or stars upon the human individual or collectivity, but because of the preestablished harmony between macrocosm and microcosm. In other words, astrology is deemed an expression of the inherent generative mechanism of Nature, which we can grasp, to some extent, through the theory of correspondences cr equivalences.

Ayurveda and Yoga

The notion of equivalence, which is fundamental to Indic astronomy and astrology, also underlies ancient India's medical system, or Ayurveda. The compound *ayur-veda* means literally "life science." Ayurveda has often been called a naturopathic system of medicine. That it is much more is evident from the fact that the practitioners of this medicine were also skilled surgeons, capable of plastic surgery on the face and other parts of the body. Already at the time of the *Rig-Veda* (I.116.15), surgeons seem to have been able to deal with battle wounds and fit amputees with artificial metal limbs. "In this respect," as A. L. Basham commented, "Indian surgery remained ahead of European until the 18th century, when the surgeons of the East India Company were not ashamed to learn the art of rhinoplasty from the Indians."[18]

The vast body of knowledge to which the term *ayur-veda* refers is sometimes considered a fifth *Veda*. The earliest expression of Ayurvedic knowledge can be found in the *Atharva-Veda*, one of the four hymnodies forming the Vedic sacred canon. From there a long but still obscure line of development led to the great medical compendiums of the post-Christian era, the *Caraka-Samhita* (150 A.D.) and the *Sushruta-Samhita* (350 A.D.). The latter work is attributed to the physician and sage Sushruta, who appears to have lived in the early sixth century B.C. and thus may have been a contemporary of Gautama, the founder of Buddhism.

The doctors of Ayurvedic medicine, which is still practiced today, regarded a healthy or wholesome (*hita*) life as consisting in the proper balance of body, mind, and emotions. In determining what is wholesome, the Ayurvedic authorities took into account not only the present life but also future lives, or embodiments. They acknowledged the need for self-preservation, happiness, and a benign postmortem existence as basic to a wholesome life. Unless a person was severely afflicted by karmas from wrongful thoughts and actions, he or she was thought to be destined for a long life of a hundred years. Contrary to other systems of thought, the Ayurvedic schools contended that proper medical care could prolong an individual's life even when adverse karmic conditions prevailed, providing the karma was not produced by truly heinous transgressions of the moral order (such as homicide). Thus the Ayurvedic physicians rejected the theory of total determinism, allowing the human will (and of course medicine) a measure of freedom to interfere with the karmic process.

According to the Ayurvedic system, the mind is composed of the fundamental qualities or constituents of Nature—*sattva*, *rajas*, and *tamas*. Sattva is the principle of lucidity and purity, rajas the principle of dynamism, and tamas the principle of inertia or darkness. Mental instability is the result of an imbalance between these three factors. When they are balanced, the sattva component is in a state of great purity, which releases the inner intelligence or wisdom. The main cause of illness is held to be the obstruction of this native intelligence (*prajna-aparadha*).

Paralleling this triadic deep structure of the mind are the three humors of the body—*vata*, *pitta*, and *kapha*. They are often rendered as "wind," "gall," and "phlegm" respectively, though these translations are rather inadequate. In this theory of the triple humors (*tri-dosha*), the three bodily components roughly correspond to the elements of air, fire, and water. These, in turn, are associated with the three principal Vedic deities Indra (for vata/wind), Agni (for pitta/fire), and Soma (for kapha/water).

Incidentally, Plato proposed a similar theory in which health was based on a correct relationship between the three elements of *pneuma* (representing wind), *chole* (or "gall," representing fire), and *phlegma* (which is a manifestation of the water element). As the French Indologist Jean Filliozat noted, the tri-dosha theory is of Vedic origin:

> *As these* doṣas, *and especially the association between the gall and the fire are already known in the Vedic literature, the* tridosa *theory cannot have been borrowed in India from Plato. On the contrary, as during the Persian domination on Greek Asian Countries and on a part of India, scientific intercourses have been easy, an influence of the Ayurvedic theories on those described by Plato is quite probable. In any*

way, we have several direct references in the Hippocratic Collection to the borrowing of some Indian drugs and Indian medical formulas in Greece. In the period of the expansion of Indian culture toward Central Asia and China, and toward Indo-China and Indonesia beyond the seas, Indian Ayurvedic medicine has been one of the main matters of export, along with astronomy, religions and arts.[19]

In symmetry with the five-layered Vedic altar, the ancient sages considered the body to be composed of the five material elements, generally listed as earth, water, fire, air, and ether. A Balinese illustration of the brain, drawn according to Ayurvedic ideas, shows a traditional representation of the terrestrial equivalences of cosmological or astronomical facts. Thus we find the cosmic mountain, Mount Meru, in the middle of the brain, representing a symbolic axis of brain functions that corresponds to the axis connecting Earth's center with the center of the universe at large. Mount Meru has been equated, on the physical plane, with the pyramid-shaped Mount Kailas in western Tibet.

Similarly, the Milky Way is a macrocosmic analogue of the terrestrial Sarasvati and Ganges Rivers. Within the human body, it has its parallel in the nerve pathways called *nadis*. These nadis, which serves as conduits for the life force, are of great importance in Yoga. The yogins seek to control the flow of the vital energy in these conduits, since this gives them control over the higher nerve centers of the brain and thus over the mind.

Following the Vedic theory of macrocosmic/microcosmic equivalence, the scriptures of Hatha-Yoga speak of an inner or psychosomatic sun and moon. The former is located at the level of the solar plexus, while the latter is said to be situated in the head. Central to the Hatha-Yogic process is the synchronization, or harmonization, of these two internal luminaries. According to an esoteric explanation, the word *hatha* (ordinarily meaning "force") is composed of the syllable *ha*, standing for the solar force, and the syllable *tha*, representing the lunar force in the human body. Yoga is the union of these two fundamental principles.

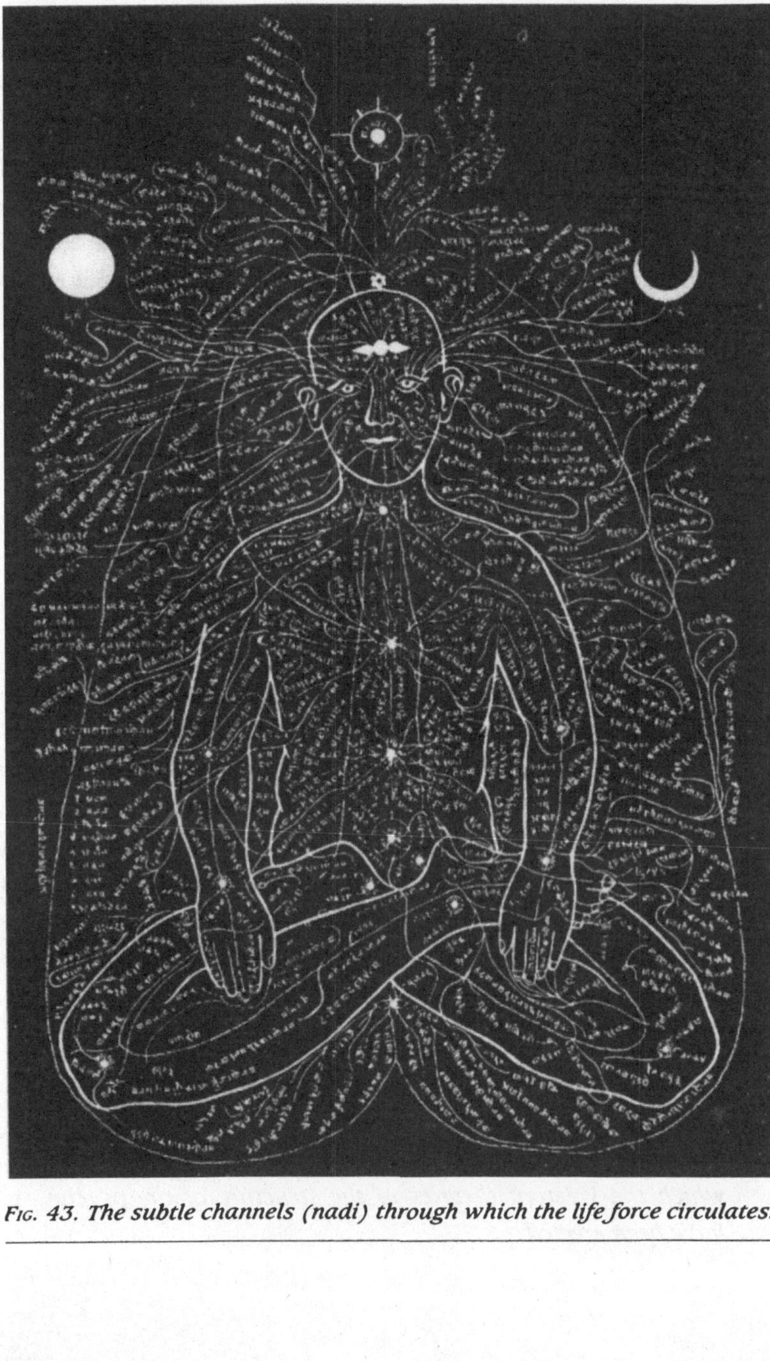

Fig. 43. The subtle channels (nadi) through which the life force circulates.

This yogic notion of internal polarization has its modern counterpart in the medical concept of hemispheric specialization, which was discovered in the 1930s, though it began to be more widely researched only in the 1960s.[20] According to this model of the brain, certain mental activities tend to be associated with the left cerebral hemisphere, while others are more specific to the right side of the cortex. Writing two decades before this discovery, purely on the basis of yogic experience and theory, Sri Aurobindo made this pertinent observation:

> *The intellect is an organ composed of several groups of functions, divisible into two important classes, the functions and faculties of the right hand, the functions and faculties of the left. The faculties of the right hand are comprehensive, creative, and synthetic; the faculties of the left hand critical and analytic. . . . The left limits itself to ascertained truth, the right grasps that which is still elusive or unascertained. Both are essential to the completeness of the human reason.*[21]

The medical understanding of the natural polarization of the human mind may well represent ancient scientific knowledge, arrived at through deep introspection and personal meditative experimentation. The same approach, for instance, underlies much of what Patanjali states in his *Yoga-Sutra* about the nature of consciousness and the possibility of supersensory knowledge. The yogins, India's psychonauts, anticipated many of the insights of contemporary psychology, and their practical knowledge of the higher reaches of the human mind remains unmatched in the world of modern science. As Mircea Eliade observed:

> *The psychological and parapsychological experience of the East in general and of yoga in particular is unchallengeably more extensive and more organized than the experience on which the Western theories of the structure of the psyche have been erected. . . .*[22]

Knowledge from the Vedic Perspective

What is the method of science? Briefly stated, the scientist isolates a phenomenon, observes cause-effect relationships, and then describes the phenomenon in terms of its components. But before scientific observation can begin, it is essential to assume that the world is knowable and that it follows natural laws. The Vedic sages made precisely this declaration.

The Vedic theory of knowledge is based on a belief in the interconnectedness and unity of the whole universe. As mentioned before, according to the *Vedas*, the cosmos (*adhideva*), the individual living being (*adhibhuta*), and the Spirit (*adhyatma*) are intimately connected. It was for this reason that the *Vedas* were meant to be interpreted in three ways. Thus the *Vedas* speak of the seers in the sky as stars, on Earth as sages, and in the head as cognitive centers. Likewise, the Vedic texts know of the Ganges of the sky (the Milky Way), the Ganges River on our planet, and the Ganges of neural pathways of the brain. These mysteries of the universe were communicated to the people through the theater of ritual. As we have seen, cosmological knowledge was encoded in the design of the altars and in the Vedic ritual itself.

The Vedic rishis appear to have thought very deeply about the limits of logic and science, and they were the first to recognize that straight logic cannot answer all questions. They realized that scientific knowledge inevitably includes paradoxes, because reality is inherently larger than the language or languages by which we endeavor to describe it. Yajnavalkya, the famous seer of the *Brihadaranyaka-Upanishad* (IV.2.2), expressed this insight very well, if poetically, when he said: "The Gods are fond of the invisible (*paroksha*) and dislike the visible." The invisible here is the vast realm of existence that transcends the senses and the mind.

The seers of the *Rig-Veda* addressed the great mysteries of existence and tried to shed light on them without, however, dissecting them intellectually to the point where they vanish and lose their psychological efficacy. Rather, the Vedic seers allowed their thoughts to gently revolve around the mysterious, leaving it intact, while at the same time communicating its essence. They were masters of paradox. Hence we must not read the *Rig-Veda* superficially. Otherwise we will find ourselves in the same state of perplexity that befalls our mind when, for instance, we take the quantum-mechanical principle of complementarity literally: An electron is sometimes a wave and at other times a particle. This principle makes sense only when we resort to a metaphoric interpretation.

The Vedic tradition has long understood the difficulty of capturing reality through the net of language. Hence it has always emphasized intuitive insight and the search for deeper meaning behind language. Thus, the Vedic texts are not about anthropomorphic Gods and Goddesses competing with each other, for each deity *is* every other deity; in reality, they are merely metaphors for certain universal principles or psychocosmic agencies.

The *Vedas* are to be read not with the closed mind of dogmatism but with a questioning attitude. To ask questions is the first step in the discovery of meaning. The Vedic system enjoins the use of questioning and reasoning, which is a clear sign of its scientific orientation, in the broad sense explained above.

The Beginnings of a Unified Science in the *Vedas*

The Vedic hymns repeatedly proclaim a unity that lies beyond all categories of opposition, such as being and nonbeing, death and immortality, knowledge and ignorance. This radical oneness is inexplicable and, by implication, can only be "seen" in an elevated state of mystical awareness. The differentiated aspects of this oneness are our everyday distinct categories—from trees to people to the star-studded sky.

That ultimate singularity (*eka*) is conceived as a creative reservoir or potentiality. Creation proceeds by means of the paradoxical process of sacrifice. The Sanskrit word *yajna*, usually translated as "sacrifice," has several connotations, including "creation through transcendence," which is the meaning most appropriate to the philosophical hymns of the *Vedas*. The whole universe is conceived as a sacrificial altar out of which the world's potentialities emerge into actuality. According to the Vedic seers, the properly attuned mind can comprehend the nature of this creative process that extends from the microcosm to the macrocosm.

In a famous hymn of the *Rig-Veda* (X.90), the ultimate creative singularity is envisioned as a macranthropos or giant man, called *purusha*. This primordial superbeing is described as having "a thousand heads, a thousand eyes, a thousand feet." The purusha pervades the world and transcends it by "ten fingers." Only one quarter of the macranthropos can be found in the realm of creation, while three quarters are said to be immortal in the heavenly domain.

Through the purusha's self-sacrifice the world was created. His mind is said to have given rise to the Moon; his eyes to the Sun; his breath to the air element; his navel to the midspace; his head to the sky; his feet to the earth; and so on. Even the structure of ancient India's society was thought to have been preordained by this self-sacrifice, since the purusha's mouth gave rise to the brahmin estate; his arms to the warrior estate; his thighs to the people at large; and his feet to the servile estate.[23]

The symbolic representation of the universe in the shape of the Cosmic Man found expression in a distinctive approach to architecture, sculpture, and literature. The purpose of all human creation was not only to preserve the unity of the macranthropos but also to recapitulate the purusha's original creative sacrifice that produced the cosmos itself. More than that, all human activity—whether sacred or secular (which is really a modern distinction)—was to be modelled on the Cosmic Man. The very purpose of life was to know the great mystery of existence, which is the mystery of the purusha.

Vedic Psychology

The Theory of Pure Awareness

The pivot of Vedic psychology is the notion of the transcendental unitary Self, or *atman*, which is pure awareness. Later Hindu tradition speaks of it as the witness (*sakshin*). Mircea Eliade remarked about this idea that it is "one of India's greatest discoveries," which must not be disregarded by Western thinkers.[24] The Self, which is also called *purusha*, is the ultimate core of the human being. It is nonlocal and atemporal, constituting the singular and irreducible *individuum* underlying each human personality. It represents the dimension of freedom and unalloyed bliss, transcending all mental and physical phenomena, which are inherently limited. Thus the Self, or Spirit, is the ultimate Singularity hidden behind all things. This notion stands in stark contrast to Western philosophical thought, which treats awareness or consciousness as an attribute of the mind which, in turn, is considered a product of the brain's neural activity.

If awareness is transcendental and singular, the question arises of how the mental processes in diverse brains are possible. Here Vedic tradition offers an ingenious answer. It explains our ordinary consciousness—as opposed to the transcendental awareness—as a cerebral phenomenon. In this it agrees with modern neurophysiology. However, the Vedic tradition makes the further claim that the mental processes are continuously apperceived by the Self and that the Self's presence in the background of the mind is sufficient to give our mental processes the appearance of being independently conscious.

Part of this illusion of the mind's independent consciousness is the ego sense ("I," "me," "mine"), which so powerfully dictates the flow of ordinary life. The ego sense is also referred to as the empirical self or psyche (*jïva*), as opposed to the transcendental Self. It is this empirical self that is transcended in the moment of enlightenment, when one awakens to the all-inclusive identity of the *atman* and ceases to identify with a particular body-mind.

The relationship between the Self and the mind is typically compared to the relationship between a source of light and a mirror: Acting as a mirror, the human mind has no light of its own but merely reflects the light (or awareness) of the self-luminous Self, just as it reflects the objects presented to it via the senses. The philosophical schools of Hinduism have paid considerable attention to the problem of how the transcendental Self can possibly have any interaction at all with the immanent body-mind. They invented a variety of possible solutions to the problem. However, in the final analysis, all these theories contain paradoxes that leave the logical mind unsatisfied and demand of us that we go beyond linear thought.

Nor are the explanations offered by the philosophers of the various schools intended to be ultimately satisfying answers. Their purpose is more modest, namely to guide the inquirer into an intuitive appreciation of the reality behind the logical system. Logic and argument have fulfilled their function when they have successfully pointed the way to direct realization. In other words, all schools of Hindu philosophy purport to be paths to spiritual liberation.

In addition to the monumental paradox of the relationship between Self and the finite body-mind, we also encounter various paradoxes when we try to describe physical reality, as the Vedic philosophers discovered long ago. They noted, for instance, that if matter is divisible, each atom must be pointlike because otherwise it would be further divisible. But how can pointlike atoms generate gross matter, which is of a certain size? Some Vedic philosophers reasoned that space is neither continuous nor discontinuous. If it were continuous, its points could not be isolated and enumerated. On the other hand, if it were discontinuous, we would have the problem of how objects could move across the discontinuity? A popular way of expressing these difficulties was to talk about the riddle of being and becoming. The basic question here is: How does an entity change its form and become another? This kind of sophisticated speculation is attested to already for the *Rig-Veda*.[25]

The Vedic Model of the Mind

The postulation of an ultimate unity behind the multiplicity of the universe made it natural for the ancient Indic sages to take up the study of the mind. After all, the mind does not automatically give us this knowledge of unity. If anything, it appears to contain a mechanism that actively occludes the Self. The Vedic model of the mind is best epitomized by the famous chariot metaphor found in such Sanskrit works as the *Katha-Upanishad* and the *Bhagavad-Gita*. Here a person is compared to a chariot that is pulled in different directions by the horses yoked to it; the unruly horses represent

FIG. 44. *The chariot represents the body in a metaphor widely used in the Yoga and Vedanta literature.*

the senses in their undisciplined state. The driver holding the reins is the mind, and next to the driver/mind stands the charioteer, representing the Self, which is pure awareness and perfect unity.

As these ancient texts explain, the purpose of Yoga is to restrain the senses/horses and make them compliant with the driver's will. Modern parlance reflects something of this task in the expression "Hold your horses!" The driver has to be disciplined enough to receive and execute properly the directions of the charioteer, the master of the chariot. In other words, the mind has to open itself to the Self's light. This, the ancient sages assure us, is perfectly possible through the key yogic practices of meditation and concentration.

The Five Sheaths

In an attempt to understand the relationship between the transcendental Self and the psychophysiological structures of the individual human being, the Vedic thinkers elaborated a model that makes use of the principle of hierarchy. According to this model, which was first fully expressed in the *Taittiriya-Upanishad* (II.2-5) some three thousand years ago, the self-luminous Spirit, or atman, is encased by five layers. These are known as the five sheaths (*kosha*), representing progressively lower levels of vibratory existence. In descending order, they are:

Blissful sheath (*ananda-maya-kosha*)
Intellectual sheath (*vijnana-maya-kosha*)
Mental sheath (*mano-maya-kosha*)
Energetic sheath (*prana-maya-kosha*)
Physical sheath (*anna-maya-kosha*)

Beyond and obscured by these layers, and yet forming their very essence, is the Self (atman or purusha).

The top three sheaths are often grouped together and collectively called the mind. The mental sheath is concerned with the "lower" mental functions, which process the input from the five senses to form perceptions out of the raw data provided by sense organs. This level of mental activity is commonly captured in the Sanskrit term *manas* (from the verbal root *man*, meaning "to think"). The *manas* is the sensory-motor mind, which thrives on the material it gathers from the senses of hearing, touch, sight, taste, and smell.

The intellectual sheath is related to "higher" mental functions, such as discernment and cognition in states of mystical awareness. These higher functions are often expressed in the term *buddhi*, which can mean simply "cognition" but also "intellect" and "wisdom." The buddhi further transforms the material already converted by the lower mind from the sensory impressions. This is the organ of philosophical thought and metaphysical intuition. It is also the seat of the human will, by which we orient our life toward either unreflective bodily experience or enhanced awareness and spiritual realization.

The blissful sheath is accessible only through ecstatic states or in deep sleep, when bliss (*ananda*) is experienced. This sheath is closest to the luminous Self, and acts like a final thin veil before the truth. In many schools of Hinduism, the Self is itself said to be blissful, but this bliss is unconditional, exceeding both the body and the mind.

According to Vedic teachings, inserted between the threefold mental sheath and the material body is the energetic sheath. This is a template of concentrated life force (prana), which, on the physical level, corresponds to the nerve impulses. Prana, in its universal aspect, underlies all physical *and* mental processes. But in this schema, it stands specifically for the field of energy that penetrates and surrounds the physical body and has variously been styled "astral body," "etheric double," and "plasma body." It is the medium of exchange in the whole psychophysiological system.

This Vedic model has exercised a great influence over much subsequent psychological thought in India. It is important to realize that the various frameworks developed by the early and later Indic authorities all stand in the service of practical spirituality. To reiterate, they are not mere academic analyses but an integral part of the effort by sages and mystic explorers to map out a practical path to Self-realization.

The Hierarchy of Psychophysiological Functions: The Cakras

Since a person's state of mind is mediated by the psychosomatic energy, or prana, the ancients paid intense attention to the study of the energetic template. They discovered that prana is not evenly distributed in the pranic sheath enveloping the material body. Rather it forms several vortices or funnels that seem to be actual connecting points between the etheric field and the nervous system of the physical body. These vortices are widely called *cakras* (also spelled *chakras* in some English books), which literally means "wheels." Often they are also referred to as *padmas*, or lotuses, because in appearance they somewhat resemble the lotus flower.

The Hindu tradition recognizes seven such primary focal points of the prana, which correspond to major nerve plexuses in the physical body and are analogous to the seven primary lights of the external universe. The *Rig-Veda* frequently speaks of seven worlds, seven rivers, seven sages, seven wisdoms, seven pranas, and so on. While the *Rig-Veda* does not specifically mention the cakras, it is quite possible that the Vedic sages knew of these seven pranic vortices. At any rate, the model of seven energy wheels is thoroughly Vedic.

The lowest vortex, called "root-prop wheel" (*muladhara-cakra*), is located at a place corresponding to the base of the spinal column. The next pranic center, enigmatically called the "self-standing wheel" (*svadhishthana-cakra*), is a few inches above the reproductive organs. The third vortex, called "jewelled city wheel" (*manipura-cakra*), is at the solar plexus. The "wheel of the unstruck sound" (*anahata-cakra*) is in the heart region. The fifth vortex, known as the "purity wheel" (*vishuddhi-cakra*), is at the throat. Between the eyebrows and possibly located at the brain core is the "command wheel" (*ajna-cakra*). At the crown of the head (fontanelle) is the "thousand-spoked wheel" (*sahasrara-cakra*).

By stimulating these cakras through breath control, concentration, and other techniques, the ancients endeavored to cultivate not only paranormal abilities (extensions of our ordinary sensory functions) but also mystical states of consciousness. Above all, by activating the topmost pranic vortex, the sages and yogins have always aspired to piercing through all the layers or sheaths of the body-mind in order to realize the transcendental Self, or spiritual Singularity. According to an esoteric teaching transmitted in the *Upanishads*, it is also the center at the crown of the head through which the sage seeks to consciously exit at the hour of death. On the cosmological level of explanation, this represents an ascent to the top of Mount Meru, or the pole star. Esoterically, the pole star is the pinhole in the roof of our symbolic universe through which we can escape into the implicate order of the invisible reality. The Vedic sages were as concerned about the way in which they exited the world as how they conducted their life while living in it. They did not fear death, because in their intuitions they had acquired knowledge of the deathless realm of Being, but they respected it. For them, the emergency of death meant emergence into the invisible domain.

Evolution from the Vedic Perspective

The idea of evolution is integral to the Vedic theory of knowledge, which regards all of Nature as a manifestation of the Self. According to this evolutionary understanding, the higher animals are endowed with greater cognitive abilities, and thus are capable of mirroring more faithfully the more subtle or sublime dimensions of the universe.

The Vedic understanding of evolution is not at odds with the Darwinian theory of evolution, though it has a different focus. The urge to evolve into higher forms is taken to be inherent in nature. The movement from inanimate to progressively higher forms of life is clearly articulated in the system of Samkhya, which recognizes twenty-four principles of existence—from the material elements to the psychic or mental faculties to the transcendental matrix out of which all dimensions and objects of Nature evolve. Samkhya emerged as a full-fledged philosophical system after the time of the Buddha. However, many of its principal ideas can be found in the early Upanishadic literature of three thousand and more years ago. Some scholars have even suggested that certain hymns of the *Rig-Veda* (notably X.90 and X.129) contain the seeds of the later cosmological ideas.

At the mythological level, ancient India's evolutionary ideas are most strikingly expressed in the Puranic model of God Vishnu's various incarnations. These are thought to have progressed from the form of a fish, tortoise, boar, man-lion, and dwarf to that of a human being. The first human form in this evolutionary sequence was Parashu Rama or "Rama with the Axe," whom some writers have identified as an anonymous teacher of Paleolithic humanity. Next came Rama, the hero of the *Ramayana* epic, who was followed by Krishna, the divine mentor of Prince Arjuna in the *Mahabharata* epic, more particularly the *Bhagavad-Gita*.

In modern times, the Bengali seer-philosopher Sri Aurobindo made a conscious attempt to connect the spiritually oriented Vedic evolutionism with the Darwinian evolutionary theory. He expressed the ancient Vedic point of view well when he wrote:

> *We speak of the evolution of Life in Matter, the evolution of Mind in Matter; but evolution is a word which merely states the phenomenon without explaining it. For there seems to be no reason why Life should evolve out of material elements or Mind out of living form, unless we accept the Vedantic solution that Life is already involved in Matter and Mind in Life because in essence Matter is a form of veiled Life, Life a form of veiled Consciousness. And then there seems to be little*

objection to a farther step in the series and the admission that mental consciousness may itself be only a form and a veil of higher states which are beyond Mind. In that case, the unconquerable impulse of man towards God, Light, Bliss, Freedom, Immortality presents itself in its right place in the chain as simply the imperative impulse by which Nature is seeking to evolve beyond Mind. . . .[26]

In sum, the Vedic thinkers evolved a system of analysis within a consistent metaphoric framework, which was supported not only by mystical vision but by skillful ratiocination. By postulating interconnections and similarities across Nature, they were able to use logic to reach extremely subtle conclusions about diverse aspects of reality. It appears that they were the first to create a science that went beyond mere observation in order to obtain a comprehensive understanding of the workings of the universe. This science was largely based on a quantitative and qualitative model of astronomy, which was applied both to the physical cosmos and the human mind.

A remarkable demonstration of the elegant and economic approach of the Vedic scientific method, as formulated in ancient India, is the influential Sanskrit grammar of Panini, which is one of the jewels of Indic thought. Panini, who probably lived in the fourth century B.C., succeeded in describing, in the tersest fashion imaginable, the complex structure of the Sanskrit language in four thousand rules. As A. L. Basham noted in his book *The Wonder That Was India*:

Though its fame is much restricted by its specialized nature, there is no doubt that Panini's grammar is one of the greatest intellectual achievements of any ancient civilization, and the most detailed and scientific grammar composed before the 19th century in any part of the world.[27]

Panini was able to draw on the expertise of a long line of grammarians preceding him. While we do not know how far back grammatical experts were pondering the Sanskrit language, a love for language and analysis is evident already in the *Rig-Veda*. Such careful attention to language presupposes a high level of self-reflection and critical intellectual ability, which also is implied by the Vedic thinkers' intensive preoccupation with astronomy, mathematics, and other scientific disciplines. We can expect the same sophistication in the area of spirituality, which is precisely what we are trying to convey in this book.

CHAPTER 12

Vedic Myths and Their Astronomical Basis

Stars, Science, and Myth

IN THE PRECEDING CHAPTERS WE REPEATEDLY REferred to the astronomical information contained in the *Vedas* and, among other things, have mentioned how the Vedic references to astronomical positions can be used to determine the dates of the hymns. In this chapter we will examine the astronomical basis of Vedic and Hindu mythology so that we can better understand how such knowledge was obtained and what its greater implications might be.

From our modern perspective that contrasts the sacred with the secular, we can barely appreciate that the ancient world did not artificially divorce spiritual wisdom from scientific knowledge, or myth and ritual from astronomy and calendrics. The worldview of the bearers of the early Indic civilization formed an organic whole. It was a comprehensive cosmology within which there were no watertight compartments of knowledge but various areas of understanding with permeable boundaries. These diverse areas were held together by the fact that all knowledge had one and the same purpose, namely to provide existential meaning and guidance so that the cosmic order (*rita*), the divine mandate, could be fully respected through consonant action on the human level.

Today knowledge seldom has this life-enhancing function, and perhaps because of the compartmentalization of modern knowledge, most people's self-understanding is quite defective. According to some guesstimates, every year around one hundred billion new bits of information are created. This massive growth in knowledge notwithstanding, science has so far proven lamentably incapable of guiding us to wholeness. It emphasizes analysis at the expense of synthesis, and in its radical skepticism and pronounced materialistic orientation has undermined the knowledge system that forms the bedrock of our religious heritage. Even though the religious worldview, as it informed the minds and hearts of our forebears in the Middle Ages, had great shortcomings, it did provide a compass that allowed people to live with faith and to escape the canker of meaninglessness and alienation. Nevertheless, new paradigms of science, such as those of quantum mechanics and complexity theory, do attempt to address the question of wholeness. They keep alive the debate within scientific circles about the relationship between fact and value, or empirical data and meaning. It is not surprising that these more integral paradigms are closest in spirit to the Vedic vision.

If we want to comprehend the Vedic hymns, we must suspend our peculiar psychological malaise and epistemological narrowness. We must adopt a "soft" approach, remaining open to the various intersecting levels of discourse in them. For instance, on one level the deities are spiritual beings with whom mystical communion is possible and whose benign presence is invoked to shape a person's life on Earth. On another level, the deities are forces associated with Nature's spectacles, such as light, darkness, fire, wind, water, earth, dawn, and not least fertility. On a third level, the Gods and Goddesses of the Vedic pantheon are related to psychological aspects of the human being, such as brightness, somberness, anger, creativity, or love. On a fourth level, the deities are in some contexts associated with or representing the mighty forces of the celestial vault, such as the two luminaries, the planets, and the stars and stellar configurations. Put differently, the Vedic deities are universal archetypes of great flexibility. They were called upon to explain or render meaningful both internal and external phenomena, which were understood as being part of the same all-embracing continuum.

Astronomy and mathematics were crucially important to the ancients, as scholars are beginning to realize. Recent work on this aspect of antiquity—which has been given the label "archaeoastronomy"—has brought about a veritable revolution in our understanding of the religious symbolism and rituals of past civilizations. Today we barely look up at the night sky and when we do, we scarcely are able to identify the visible planets, stars, and constellations. Surprisingly few people are aware of the fact that, like the Moon, the stars too traverse the celestial vault. Fewer still know that at the two equinoxes the rising Sun seems to hover for a while on the horizon, or that the constellation of the Ursa Minor (Little Bear) revolving around the pole star in exactly twenty-four hours makes a perfect nocturnal clock.

Astronomy was not born from idle curiosity. Rather the ancients looked to the heavens for guidance. Knowledge of the luminaries, including the stars, was vital to their existence. By the stars merchants navigated safely across the oceans and deserts, and farmers planted their precious crops at the right time to guarantee a harvest of plenty. Most importantly, the regularities in the sky provided the key to sacred time and space. The behavior of Sun, Moon, planets, and stars was of decisive importance for the ritual calendar.

The ancients believed that the celestial processes governed human destiny. This sense of correlation between heaven and earth was later epitomized in Hermes Trismegistus' famous esoteric axiom "As above, so below." It was the task of the religious specialists to study the heavenly patterns so that the rituals would faithfully reflect the divine order. More than that, the celestial geometry served the ancients as an archetype for their sacred buildings—altars, temples, and sacred cities.

The British astronomer Gerald S. Hawkins has demonstrated that Stonehenge is a giant three-dimensional stone computer, erected at the beginning of the third millennium B.C., that permitted the precise calculation of the solar solstices and equinoxes as well as extreme positions of the moon.[1]

In 1961, the American archaeologist Warren L. Wittry discovered an assemblage of large pits in southern Illinois, known as the

Cahokia's Sun Circle, which has been called the largest earth pyramid.[2] Apparently the pits once contained tall posts by means of which the Sun's movement in the sky was tracked. Of unknown age, the Sun Circle presumably served a similar function to Stonehenge.

The Great Pyramid in Egypt, which is generally ascribed to the pharaoh Cheops but which is possibly much older, has been shown to embody sophisticated astronomical knowledge. The sides of this colossal stone structure, consisting of more than 2.3 million limestone blocks and weighing nearly 6 million tons, are precisely oriented toward true north and south or east and west. The deviation is between 2 and 2.5 minutes.

Much of Egyptian astronomy and symbolism revolved around the star Sirius, which was known as Sothis. Sirius in the constellation Canis Major is the brightest star in the night sky, and was particularly associated with Isis. The Egyptians eagerly watched for its heliacal rising, which at that early time coincided with the annual flooding of the Nile, bringing bounty to the country. The heliacal rising is the appearance of a star on the horizon prior to sunrise. For the Egyptians, the heliacal rising of Sirius heralded the beginning of a new year. However, over the centuries, the heliacal rising of Sirius shifted from a day near the summer solstice to the middle of August, thus becoming increasingly out of sync with the yearly inundation.

The Mayan stepped pyramid at Chichen Itza in the Yucatan Peninsula was constructed—around 1000 A.D.—in such a manner that at sunset on the days of the spring and fall equinoxes, the interplay of light and shadow on the ninety-one stairs creates the effect of a large undulating snake descending the stairway. The wavelike effect terminates at a large serpent head sculptured at the base of the stairway. The snake was a principal religious symbol for the Maya, representing the sky. The Mayan word *chan* denotes both "snake" and "sky." The striking equinoctial phenomenon at Chichen Itza, which was rediscovered only in the 1980s, presupposes a combination of astronomical, mathematical, and architectural skills. Another fascinating effect, which was discovered recently, is that on the day of the winter solstice the Sun can be seen to climb the northern stairway of the same pyramid.

As scholars are beginning to appreciate, the ancient Maya were keen stargazers who kept astoundingly accurate astronomical tables. They also were extraordinarily skillful timekeepers, working with no fewer than five calendars. Their preferred object of astronomical study and religious veneration was Venus.

We could pile example upon example from around the world to show both the high regard in which the star-studded sky was held in remote antiquity and the considerable astronomical knowledge the ancients accumulated over millennia. The situation was much the same in ancient India. From the Vedic literature we know that the entire sacrificial ritualism of the Indic/Vedic tradition is based on cosmological and astronomical correlations.[3] In this chapter, we will be looking at Vedic mythology from an astronomical perspective. We intend to show the intimate connection between Vedic myths, rituals, and astronomy.

Similar Myths, Different Cultures

The decipherment of the scriptures of the lost civilizations of the ancient world has revealed intriguing parallels between the mythologies of the Indic, Greek, and Roman civilizations. What is more, the ancients were aware of these parallels. Thus when Alexander made his brief incursion into northern India in 326 B.C., the Greeks were surprised to discover that the two most popular Indic deities were similar to their own Herakles and Dionysos. It is now believed that these parallel Gods were Krishna and Shiva respectively. Both Herakles and Krishna were dark-skinned deities. Each killed a monster—Hydra was slain by Herakles and the demon Kaliya by Krishna. Both enjoyed sexual relations with many maidens—nymphs in the one case and cowherdesses (*gopi*) in the other. Dionysos and Shiva were conceived as powerful divine beings of great mystery and paradox, who moved at the fringes of the celestial elite. Because of their liminal position, they felt free to show humans the way to mystical union with the deities and the ultimate Reality.

The ancient Greeks fancifully assumed that the wine-bibbing Dionysos had visited and conquered India accompanied by his wild entourage of Maenads and Satyrs. According to Diodorus, Dionysos's expedition to India took two years, after which he returned to Boeotia, riding on an elephant to celebrate his alleged victory. However, the direction of the flow of religious ideas appears to have been in the opposite direction—from India to Greece and other Mediterranean countries. As the French indologist Alain Daniélou observed:

> *We have no texts explaining the rites and ceremonial of the Dionysiac mysteries in the Greco-Etrusco-Roman world, although there are allusions which can often be clarified with the aid of Indian texts . . . By studying Shivaite rites [from India], the only ones which have continued down to our own times, the real practices of the Dionysiac rites and "mysteries" may be reconstructed.*[4]

As we might expect, there are important differences in the stories about Krishna and Herakles on the one hand, and Shiva and Dionysos on the other. Yet, the learned men accompanying Emperor Alexander—and later the ambassador Megasthenes—recognized that the similarities outweighed the differences, which were due to the separate cultural contexts. They also recognized that behind the multitude of Gods and Goddesses, as symbols for various aspects of Nature, lay the same belief in a single, fundamental Reality.

The ease with which deities with different names in geographically separated cultures were accepted as being identical indicates that the ancients knew that names in themselves did not define their Gods and Goddesses, but rather that it was their attributes that were significant.

We now know that myths in far-removed cultures can have many shared themes. This may be due to a common cultural origin in the distant past, or the commonality of human experience, or possibly also the internal archetypal logic of mythmaking. But we must not overlook a fourth possibility, which is that of cross-fertilization through contact between cultures, especially by way of trade or military conquest.

As we have stated previously, the ancient world was culturally far more interconnected than has been assumed. In particular, we have made a strong case for ancient India's extensive maritime experience. The Norwegian explorer Thor Heyerdahl demonstrated the technological feasibility of sea journeys in antiquity. Among other things, he sailed a reed boat down the Tigris to the mouth of the Indus. From there he headed southwest toward the African coast, though he could just as easily have gone on to sail to the tip of the Indian peninsula and beyond to the Maldive islands. For this is exactly what northern India's merchants did four thousand and more years ago. In his book *The Maldive Mystery*, Heyerdahl reports on his discovery of Harappan artifacts on the islands south of the Indian peninsula, which clearly demonstrate the seafaring enthusiasm and skill of the Indus-Sarasvati sailors.[5]

The ships from India carried not only cargo of much-sought-after spices, exquisite cotton, precious gold, and other rare metals, as well as exotic timber and animals, but also people who held all manners of ideas and beliefs and practiced all kinds of religious rituals. It seems reasonable to assume that these seafarers were as important an influence on other cultures as the luxury goods they came to deliver. Perhaps, in not a few cases, the ideas they brought across the ocean with them had a more penetrating and long-lasting effect.

We can imagine, for example, that when the merchants and learned travelers from India shared with their hosts in foreign countries some of their astronomical knowledge they peppered their accounts with the telling of relevant legends and myths.

Some of the earliest astronomical lore is found encoded in myths.

Myths and the Starry Sky

When we consider the astronomical element in myths, we discover that Varuna (India), Ouranos (Greece), and Osiris (Egypt) are identical in fundamental ways. All three deities were born to the Great Mother Goddesses and typically represent the night sky. More specifically, they symbolize the constellation of Orion, and their myths refer to the vernal equinox in that constellation, corresponding to the era of the seventh to the fifth millennium B.C., which is roughly the age of Gemini. The ancients appear to have been aware of the precession of the vernal equinox, and they sought to do justice to it by translating Orion's mythology into the symbolic language of the era of Taurus and later the era of Aries.

Thus, according to Egyptian mythology, Osiris was killed by his hostile brother Seth (Ursa Major), and, in Indic mythology, Tvashtri Dyauspita and Prajapati were killed by their youngest son, namely Indra or Rudra (Sirius). Prajapati's death at the hands of Rudra marks the passage of the vernal equinox from Orion (or zodiacal Gemini) to Taurus. The old *Aitareya-Brahmana* relates the latter story of how Prajapati, the lord of the year, is punished for being in love with his own daughter Rohini (the star Aldebaran in Taurus), by having his head cut off by Rudra. This is a further explanation that the year had shifted from Orion to Rohini—a transition that occurred after 4000 B.C. The story of Dyaus and Indra refers to a still earlier age.

The idea of the equinoctial precession is also expressed in one of the best known myths of India, which is the churning of the primordial milk ocean, as graphically described in the *Mahabharata* epic (I.17-19). In this myth, which seems to be hinted at in the *Rig-Veda* (X.136.7) already, the churning symbolizes the precessional shift of Earth's position in regard to the stars. Here is a brief paraphrase of this popular myth.

At the end of a world age, the deities and the demons united to churn the cosmic ocean in order to win the draft of immortality (*amrita*) hidden in its depths. Using Mount Mandara, the cosmic mountain, as the churning stick and the Serpent King Vasuki as a rope, the two parties set the giant mountain in motion. From their efforts, the foaming mass first yielded milk, next the Moon, and then the Sun. These were followed by the magical *kaustubha* gem and the cosmic elephant Airavata.

As they churned on, the world ocean produced the *kalakuta* poison, which promptly enveloped the entire universe. In order to prevent the world's total extinction, God Shiva came to the rescue, holding the poison in his throat by the power of a sacred chant. It discolored his throat permanently, whence he is called the blue-throated God. At the request of the Creator-God Brahma, Shiva swallowed the poison to eliminate its threat forever.

The churning continued, and at long last a white vessel containing the precious nectar of immortality emerged. Instantly, the demons seized the vessel, but before they could drink its priceless fluid and achieve immortality, God Narayana (Vishnu) intervened. Assuming the beautiful form of Mohini, enchantress of illusion, he approached the host of demons. They were so bewitched by Mohini's appearance that they willingly handed her the vessel. She immediately gave the nectar to the deities, who drank it and thus secured eternal life for themselves.

When we decode this myth from an astronomical viewpoint, we find that the primordial milk ocean is none other than our Milky Way. The deities represent the stars of the northern sky, whereas the demons symbolize the stars of the southern celestial hemisphere. The rope is the zodiacal serpent, which determines the Sun's course through the constellations of the ecliptic. Mount Mandara (or Mount Meru) is both the world axis and the Earth axis. The turning of this axis determines not only the microcosmic day and year but also the macrocosmic event of what is called the Zodiacal Year. The Zodiacal Year has traditionally been fixed at 25,920 years, which is one full cycle of the shifting of the Sun's equinoctial passage from one constellation to the next every Zodiacal Month, extending over 2160 years. Shiva's swallowing of the poison establishes the stable order that prevents the breakdown of the cosmic clockwork. He thus embodies the archaic Vedic notion of universal harmony (*rita*).

In their quest for harmony, the ancients looked for perfect order in the heavenly vault. They deemed any irregularity, such as the sudden appearance of comets, as inauspicious and threatening. The phenomenon of the precession must have seemed to them a phenomenon lying midway between harmony and chaos, certainly holding a great secret. They regarded the switch of the equinoctial point from one constellation to the next as a major change, heralding significant consequences on the microcosmic level—that is, on the level of human life on Earth. As above, so below.

Indeed, when we examine the symbolism of past cultures belonging to different equinoctial eras, we find a corresponding fascinating shift of emphasis from the motif of the cosmic twins (in the

Gemini era) to the bull (in the Taurus era), to the ram (in the Aries era), and then to the fish (in the Pisces era). In each era, the astronomers-astrologers-priests seem to have created new imagery for ancient truths, pouring, so to speak, old wine into new wine skins.

The annual celestial circuit of the Sun is due to the motion of Earth in its orbit around the Sun. From Earth it appears that the Sun is moving in relation to the background of stars. This circuit is called the ecliptic. The constellations of stars that fall along it are known as the zodiac.

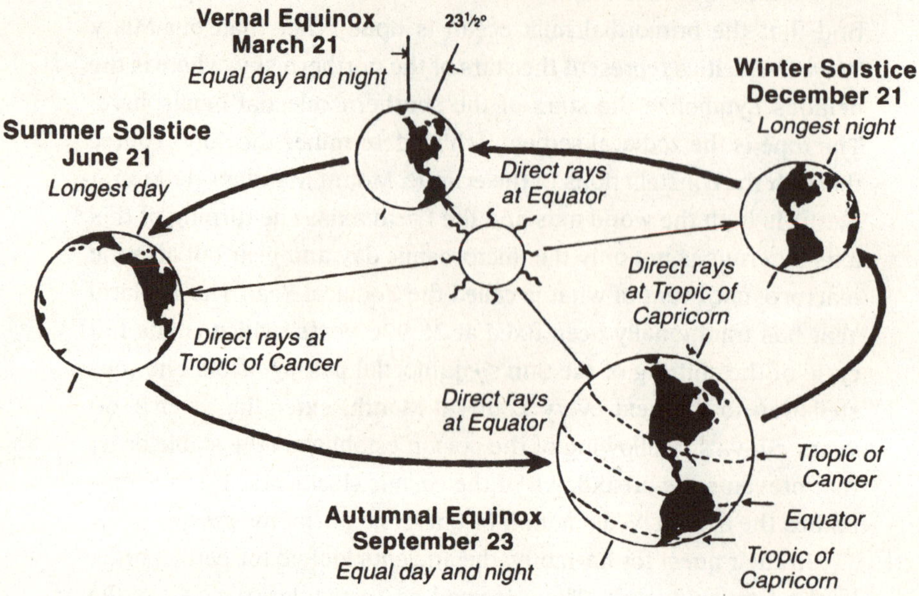

FIG. 45. *A diagram showing the position of the Earth relative to the Sun throughout the year in the* Northern Hemisphere *and the resultant dates of solstices and equinoxes. The discovery of the precession ranks among the most significant discoveries of the ancient world.*

The Earth's axis of rotation is tipped at an angle of 23.5 degrees with respect to the direction of its orbital motion around the Sun. This is what causes the changing seasons because the length of the day keeps on varying. The longest and the shortest days, also called summer and winter solstices, occur roughly near the 21st of June and the 21st of December. The date of a solstice (literally "sun still") can be marked by noting that on that day the Sun appears to linger at the same extreme at noon. During the summer solstice the shadow cast by a vertical stick at noon is the shortest, whereas at the winter solstice it is the longest. This is one way in which these two dates were fixed in ancient India.

The days on which daytime and nighttime are equal are called equinoxes (literally "equal nights"). The two equinoxes, vernal in spring and autumnal in fall, mark the halfway point between summer and autumn. The equinoxes occur at the two intersections of the celestial equator and the ecliptic.

Long ago, the stars began to be used as a means of calibrating the calendar. Some groups of stars dominate the winter nights and others the summer nights. Thus astronomers would look for the first or last appearance of a striking group of stars like the Pleiades. Another calibration could be done with respect to a star's heliacal (presunrise) appearance. As mentioned before, the heliacal rising of Sirius (Dog Star) was extremely important to the Egyptians, who calibrated their calendar according to it.

Due to the precession, the elongated axis of Earth does not always point to the same fixed star. Polaris (alpha Ursae Minoris) is the pole star now, but around 3000 B.C. it was alpha Draconis, which was later followed by beta Ursae Minoris; twelve thousand years from now it will be Vega. The equinoxes and the solstices shift with respect to the background stars.

More than a hundred years ago, the Hindu scholar Bal Gangadhar Tilak argued in his controversial book *The Orion* that a great deal of mythological narrative is a symbolic description of the changing orientation of Earth against the background of the stars.[6] More recently, Georgio de Santillana and Hertha von Dechend have put forward the same idea in their exceptional work *Hamlet's Mill.*[7]

The precession of the polar axis leads to a precession of the equinoxes and solstices. The equinoxes move along the ecliptic in a direction opposite to the annual course of the Sun, shifting from Cancer (circa 8000-6000 B.C.) to Gemini (circa 6000-4000 B.C.) to Taurus (circa 4000-2000 B.C.) to Aries (circa 2000-0 B.C.) to Pisces (circa

0-2000 A.D.), rather than the reverse. The next equinoctial constellation will be Aquarius, the sign of the Water Bearer.

In Vedic times, Earth was pictured—that is, abstractly represented—as a plane going through the celestial equator. In this view, the equator divides the zodiac into two halves: the northern band of the zodiac, reaching from the vernal to the autumnal equinox, represents dry land; the southern band of the zodiac represents the cosmic waters below. The four corners of the world are the zodiacal constellations rising heliacally at both the equinoxes and the solstices. The central frame of the cosmos is represented by the world axis (called *skambha*), which pierces through all layers of the multistory universe. As the *Atharva-Veda* (X.7.35) states:

> *The skambha sustains both heaven and earth here; the skambha sustains the mid-region between them; the skambha sustains the six wide directions; the skambha entered this whole world.*

In ancient India, the stellar constellations were mapped out into twenty-seven or twenty-eight lunar constellations or mansions (*nakshatra*). While the Moon spends about a day in each of these mansions, the Sun traverses each constellation in the course of about 13⅓ days.

De Santillana and von Dechend have plausibly argued that the Vedic God Agni, who is said to be born in the "highest sky" and who had three other Agnis precede him, represents the heliacal rising of Sirius at the vernal equinox. There is overwhelming evidence, as these two scholars have noted, that Agni and Soma ("lord of the world poles") represent the equinoctial colures (the two great circles of the celestial sphere which intersect each other at the poles). They particularly pointed to the so-called Shunahshepa hymns of the first book of the *Rig-Veda*, identifying Shunahshepa as Cynosoura, "Dog's Tail," that is, Ursa Minor.

Vedic mythology introduces Shunahshepa as the adopted son of the sage Vishvamitra, who represents one of the stars of Ursa Major. This appears to point to a noteworthy conjunction of two stars. Shunahshepa is the second of three brothers, who are given names that also mean "dog's tail." This suggests that, astronomically speaking, Shunahshepa stands for the star Delta in Ursa Minor.

There is a well-known myth in the *Purana* literature in which Agni fathers Skanda on Krittikas (Pleiades). Since the Krittikas are a group of six stars, Skanda is shown to have six heads. In later Hindu mythology, the fire God Agni is replaced by Shiva, who, like the Vedic God Rudra, is identified with the star Sirius, the brightest star in the sky. Rudra-Shiva's most ancient astronomical significance is that of the Dog Star, or what Stella Kramrisch put it, "the hound of heaven, gnashing his formidably bright teeth."[8] The *Rig-Veda* (VII.55.2) tells the story of the sage Vasishtha, who, casting a spell, commanded the God to stop gnashing his teeth at him and to fall asleep instead.

Subsequently, when the the vernal equinox was located in Rohini, Sirius-Rudra-Shiva became known as the star Mriga-Vyadha, the antelope hunter. The antelope was none other than the Creator-God Prajapati who died, pierced by Rudra's arrow. Prajapati can be equated with the star alpha in Taurus, also known as Aldebaran, which is a bright, orange-hued star.

It is clear from the various versions of this ancient myth that Prajapati in some way collaborated in his murder, and, according to some accounts, even committed suicide. For the Vedic people, as well as their Hindu descendants, he embodied the ideal of self-sacrifice. Early on, then, Prajapati represented both the year (symbol of continual change) and the sacrificial altar.

The timeless love story of Goddess Radha and her beloved Krishna can similarly be understood from an astronomical perspective. Krishna is a deity of the spring season, and Radha is related to the constellations Vishakha (Radha) and Anuradha, which mark the beginning of Scorpio in the heavens. The full moon in these two constellations would have marked the vernal equinox in the period from about 3000-1000 B.C.

In the Vedic literature, Indra is associated with "bounty" or "success" (*radhas*) and is called the "lord of success" (*radhas-pati*). The *Mahabharata* epic speaks of the rivalry between Indra and Vishnu/Krishna and how Vishnu claimed Indra's spouse Shri. In the *Atharva-*

Veda (XIX.7.3), the word *radha* is used in regard to the two stars called *vishakha*. Indra is called a "planetherd" or cowherd (*gopa*) and is paired with a vishakha. The two vishakhas are paired with Indra and Agni, who are praised as the two best cowherds. In building the *agni-cayana* fire altar, the layers of bricks which are taken to be pairs of feminine constellations, the vishakhas, are coupled with the masculine deities Indra and Agni. Thus an astronomical theme underlies the details of the altar designs.

The Secret Language of Myth

Myths, as we have tried to show, can contain important astronomical codes. But to understand their secret language more fully, we must also pay close attention to the names of Gods and Goddesses, in addition to the symbolic motifs and imagery associated with them.

Consider, for example, the representation of Vishnu as Narayana during the interval between two phases of creation. Why is Narayana shown resting on the back of the Serpent-King Shesha? If we want to understand this image, we must remember that, according to Hindu cosmology, the universe was created out of the primeval waters, which we have equated with the Milky Way. In an attempt to give Nature's potential an anthropomorphic face, ancient India's mythmakers pictured Vishnu (All-Pervader) as resting on an immovable primordial rock. This is exactly what the word *naga* means, which is applied to the serpent God Shesha. The word is traditionally split into *na* (not) and *ga* (to go). As such it can refer to the cosmic mountain or cosmic tree at the center of cosmic existence.

However, the word *naga*—with a long middle *a*—also stands for "snake." In the present context, it refers to the cosmic sky serpent, which we also know from pharaonic Egypt and the Mayan civilization. Another name of Shesha, the cosmic serpent, is Ananta, meaning "He who is infinite," because he is thought to encircle the whole of creation.

The word *shesha* means "residue," referring here to that which is left behind when all creation is absorbed back into the primordial soup. It is this infinite serpent residue that Vishnu, as Narayana, uses for his couch during the sleep of the universe and all its creatures. Narayana, the God whose abode is in the waters, is often depicted with a thousand heads, which may refer to the traditional teaching that a thousand world ages correspond to a single day in the life of the Creator-God Brahma. The image, as Sukumari Bhattacharya proposed, may also have suggested itself to the ancients when watching the waves of the ocean rolling toward the shore, which "look like a myriad-hooded serpent."[9]

Since medieval times, Brahma has been regarded as the creator, Vishnu as the preserver or sustainer, and Shiva as the destroyer of the universe. But in the sacred Hindu literature, Vishnu is just as often venerated as the all-pervading being who is also the Primordial Man and the firstborn of creation, having neither beginning nor end. Thus Vishnu is taken as the sole source of the universe, who is active in all three phases: creation, preservation, and dissolution. Precisely the same role is assigned to Shiva (Benevolent) and Shakti (Power)—the masculine and feminine principles—by their devotees.

When we consider the figure of Shiva, we find that many of the myths about this popular deity are intended to highlight the paradoxical aspects of existence. However, there also are other stories that have a clear astronomical purport, as in the case of Prajapati's death at the hands of Rudra-Shiva.

The Goddess Ganga can stand either for the river Ganges or the Milky Way, which is a portion of our spiral galaxy and which resembles a sparkling river that stretches across the sky. Ganga is clearly equated with the Milky Way in the *Vishnu-Purana*, which has been dated to the early Christian era but contains much older material.

In her embodiment as the river, Ganga has her source in the nail of the great toe of Vishnu's left foot, and Dhruva (Polaris) receives and sustains her day and night devoutly on his head. For this reason, the Seven Sages (the stars of Ursa Major) constantly practice austerities in Ganga's waters, wreathing their braided locks with her waves. The lunar orb, encompassed by her accumulated current, derives augmented luster from this contact. Falling from on high, as she issues from the Moon, Ganga alights on the summit of Meru (the world mountain in the north), and thence flows to the four quarters of Earth for its purification. The place where the river proceeds is the third division of the celestial regions, which is the seat of Vishnu.

Stars and Calendars

As elsewhere in the world, myth and ritual were integral aspects of the same worldview. The stories about the deities, often encoding astronomical knowledge, were not told for mere edification. They provided the backbone for the ritual enactment of the cosmic order on the human level. Thus, not surprisingly, India's temple architecture also reflects the cosmic vision mirrored in the great myths of the Indic civilization. The temple represents the universe or the Primordial Man (purusha). The various parts of the temple are named after body parts. The two sides are the hands (*hasta*), a pillar is a foot (*pada*), and the top of the temple is the crown of the head (*shikhara*). The innermost sanctum of the temple is the "womb-house" (*garbha-griha*). In another conceptualization, the *garbha-griha* is the cosmic pillar (*skambha*), and the devotees are like the stars who, by natural law, must revolve around it. There is a parallel in the Hindu *puja* ritual, in which the devotee moves the lamp around the picture or image of the object of worship.

FIG. 46. *South Indian temple—a miniature model of the universe.*

According to the *Brihat-Samhita*, generally dated to the fourth century A.D. but relying on much older ideas, the temple must reflect the cosmic order. The Hindu architects accomplished this by drawing a square grid of ninety-one equal squares. The central nine squares are the domain of the Creator-God Brahma. Surrounding squares are thought to represent the Sun and the Moon, as well as the planets and the guardians of the directions. Sometimes the ideal grid for temple construction contains the drawing of the Primordial Man in such a way that all the ninety-one squares are filled by the body.[10] In temple architecture, we have the fruitful union of astronomy/astrology and mathematics, as well as myth and symbolism. A common Sanskrit word for "temple" is *vimana*, which means "that which is well-measured." The temple proportions have to conform to the Hindu standards of harmony, so that the sacred building truly reflects the sacred order of the cosmos.

The Vedic people not only sought to bring the celestial harmony down to Earth by creating a sacred space for themselves but also by sacralizing the flow of time. Stella Kramrisch made these insightful observations:

> *The "time" of Prajapati, or Prajapati as Time, allowed itself to be laid out spatially in a work of architecture. The time of Śiva flowed into the movement of the limbs of Śiva, the lord of the dance. Works of sculpture and architecture demonstrate each in its own form the time of which they are the symbols. The building of the Vedic altar, by the accompanying words of the sacred rite of architecture, is self-explanatory. Symbolically, time, the time of the seasons, was built into the altar. The form of the altar comprised time, conceived as it were in terms of space.*[11]

For the Vedic sages, all time was sacred time. Predictably, the calendars they devised to bring order to the temporal flow, were informed by the heavenly order revealed through astronomical observation. Significantly, in some regions of India, a calendar of 2700-year cycles, known as the Saptarshi calendar, is still in use.[12] In Kashmir its starting point has been fixed to 3076 B.C. This appears to be India's oldest calendar. It derives its name from the seven (*sapta*) seers (*rishi*), equated with the seven principal stars of Ursa Major.

According to the very old *Shatapatha-Brahmana*, the Seven Sages were married to the Krittikas. The Greeks knew this constellation as

Pleiades, the Seven Sisters: Alcyone, Atlas, Electra, Maia, Merope, Taygete, and Pleione. This celestial marriage sounds strange to modern ears, but the *Puranas* offer a plausible explanation. According to Puranic lore, the Seven Sages spend one century in each lunar constellation. This explanation implies a reckoning in terms of one hundred years. Since there are twenty-seven lunar constellations, the full cycle is 2700 years. It appears that the tradition of twenty-eight nakshatras came later. Attempts to reconcile old events to the two different reckoning schemes based on the differing constellation counts led to the two different traditions regarding the date of the great war chronicled in the *Mahabharata*. One tradition places the war in 3137 B.C., the other in 2449 B.C. However, both dates may be somewhat too early.

Writing about two thousand years ago, Greek historians Pliny and Arrian, who based themselves on the reports from the ambassadors at the Maurya courts, mentioned that the native historical tradition of India knew of 154 kings, ruling over a period of 6,450 years. When we reconstruct this tradition, it appears that during Mauryan times the calendar was taken to commence in 6676 B.C. This epoch is exactly 3,600 years before the beginning of the current Saptarshi era. Because 360 years were counted as one divine year, it appears that at the end of a divine decade a new cycle—the current Saptarshi era—was thought to have begun. This knowledge, like so much else, was forgotten during India's chaotic Middle Ages.

Traditional India knows three other famous calendars: the Kaliyuga (beginning in 3102 B.C.), Vikrama (beginning in 58 B.C.), and Shaka (beginning in 78 A.D.). According to Hindu tradition, the famous Bharata battle, around which the countless stories of the *Mahabharata* are woven, took place thirty-five years before the beginning of the *kaliyuga*, or Dark Age. This era is thought to commence with the death of Krishna, the divine teacher of Prince Arjuna. According to another school of thought, the battle between the Kuru and the Pandava tribes was fought in 2449 B.C. This is apparently supported in the *Puranas*. A third view, expressed in the *Puranas*, assumes that a total of 1,050 years elapsed between the time of Parikshit (Arjuna's grandson) and Mahapadma Nanda's rule. If correct, this would place the war around 1500 B.C. Whatever the actual date may have been for this massive conflict between the Kurus and Pandavas, which is said to have lasted eighteen days, it is established that it took place at the end of the Vedic age.

Because of the incompatibility between these three chronological traditions, many scholars believe that the Kaliyuga calendar was devised after the Maurya dynasty (322 B.C. to 185 B.C.). However, we must note that the idea of world ages (*yuga*) itself occurs as early as the *Atharva-Veda* and the word is certainly mentioned in the *Rig-Veda* (I.115.2) already, although scholars are divided over its precise meaning. The most plausible explanation is that the Saptarshi calendar was the old reckoning system and the reckoning in terms of twenty-eight constellations was put forward later. This second scheme then was made the basis of the Kaliyuga calendar. The antiquity of the Saptarshi era is indicated by its mention in the *Shatapatha-Brahmana*, which is around four thousand years old. In view of this, it makes sense to base the earliest history of India on the Saptarshi calendar.

Ever since the time of German philosopher G. W. F. Hegel (1770-1831), Indic civilization has been characterized as being thoroughly unhistorical, or lacking proper historiography.[13] The chronologies of the encyclopedic *Puranas* have, with few exceptions, been summarily dismissed as imaginative fabrications.[14] It is true that the genealogical lists of the *Puranas* are riddled with problems, but so are the dynastic chronologies of Egypt and Sumer. While we must not look for flawless accuracy over what amounts to an incredibly long period of four thousand years or more, we cannot fail to observe that the Indic literature provides a historical record far more complete than any record we have for the rest of the ancient world. By and large, scholars have passed judgment on this issue without having studied the literature in any appreciable detail. Those who did delve into the *Puranas*, have come away with a greater appreciation of India's chronicling ability. Thus the Canadian Sanskritist R. Morton Smith observed that "the *Puranas* preserve good historical tradition."[15] This, too, is part of the promising reevaluation of ancient India's civilization underway today.

As we are correcting our picture of antiquity, and of the early Indic civilization in particular, we find that the highest aspirations and the deepest concerns of the ancients still speak to us, and in a way *for us*, today. We discover in their symbols, myths, and rituals a world pregnant with meaning—a world that belongs to our common human heritage. Myths and mythmaking are fundamental to being human. As the American psychiatrist Rollo May wrote in his last book:

> *Myths are our self-interpretation of our inner selves in relation to the outside world. They are narrations by which our society is unified. Myths are essential to the process of keeping our souls alive and bringing us new meaning in a difficult and often meaningless world.*[16]

The revivified encounter with the past through archaeology, history, and a host of other disciplines, is at the same time a fresh encounter with the implicate order of our own psyche. For, as Carl Gustav Jung and Joseph Campbell among others have shown, the past is still effectively present in us.[17] We may deny the living dimension of myth within our own being, but we cannot thereby eliminate myth itself. For to do so would be to eliminate the psyche itself. If anything, the rationalist effort to demythologize everything is part of a new mythology that is destructive rather than animating and constructive. We of today live in the shadow of our own repressed past and denied potential for spiritual greatness. A new, open-eyed encounter with the wisdom of the ancients can put us in touch with our own psychic reality. And, as Jung discerned, the psyche "is the world's pivot."[18] For behind the psyche looms the infinite uncharted domain of the implicate order as such, which the ancients called the Spirit.

CHAPTER 13

India and the West

Ex Oriente Lux

"WE OF THE OCCIDENT ARE ABOUT TO ARRIVE AT A crossroads that was reached by the thinkers of India some seven hundred years before Christ. This is the real reason why we become both vexed and stimulated, uneasy yet interested, when confronted with the concepts and images of Oriental wisdom."[1] The German Indologist Heinrich Zimmer made this observation half a century ago. In the meantime we *have* arrived at the crossroads, and our interest in the spiritual heritage of the East has unquestionably become more pronounced, as we are facing the challenge of an emerging global civilization.

What we need to realize is that the East, in particular India, has long exerted an influence on the cultural evolution of the West. Therefore our present-day interest in India does not occur in a vacuum but is backed by a long history of more or less tacit contact with that great civilization.

There is no question of India's impact on classical Greek thought, which, together with the Judeo-Christian heritage, is commonly acknowledged as one of the pillars of our Western civilization. Europe always looked to India as the great supplier of spices, cotton, and gems, as well as the land of mysteries and spirituality. In his classic work *Lectures on the Philosophy of History*, first published in 1837, G. W. F. Hegel put it this way:

> *. . . India as a land of desire formed an essential element in general history. Since the earliest times, all nations have directed their desires and wishes to gaining access to the treasures of this land of marvels, the most costly treasures of Nature on earth—pearls, diamonds, perfumes, rose essences, lions, elephants, etc.—but also treasures of wisdom. The way by which these treasures have passed to the West has at all times been a matter of world-historical importance bound up with the fate of nations.*[2]

In antiquity, India was indeed a seemingly inexhaustible treasure trove for the Mediterranean world, including the Persians and Arabs. Ever since the days of Socrates and before, the Greeks were engaged in vigorous trade with India, with goods—and ideas—mainly flowing from India westward. The mystery cults of Dionysos and Orpheus, which vied with the Homeric religion, were known to have their origin outside Greece, in the East. Some scholars have pointed to India as their source. The influence of Orphic ideas on Plato is well known, and, in turn, Plato's overwhelming influence on subsequent thought needs no explanation.

Relying on the authority of Aristoxenus (circa 300 B.C.), the church historian Eusebius, who lived in the fourth century A.D., recollected that Socrates once encountered a "gymnosophist," a wise man from India. The sage asked Socrates to explain to him the business of philosophy. When the great philosopher told him that it was the study of human life, the Indic sage burst out laughing, saying that such a study is futile without reference to the Divine. For him, obviously, philosophy was not merely a rational enterprise but shot through with spiritual concerns. He may have done Socrates an injustice, but the fact that such an encounter is thought to have taken place is itself instructive.

The Greeks, who thought highly of their own intellectual achievements, occasionally conceded to looking upon the Egyptians as their mentors, while the Egyptians clearly regarded them as children whom they taught. In the period from 500 B.C. to 200 A.D., Egypt was a veritable melting pot, and we know that a perhaps not insignificant cultural impetus came from India. As Sir Flinders Petrie first pointed out, there was an Indic colony in the Egyptian city of Memphis by 500 B.C., and there could easily have been other similar colonies elsewhere at that time and earlier.

Later it was Alexandria that not only housed the most extensive library in the ancient world but also served as an important meeting place between East and West. The Buddhist *Jatakas* speak of Indic merchants *and* thinkers voyaging to Alexandria. It has sometimes been suggested that the Therapeutae of Alexandria were of Buddhist origin or at least were strongly influenced by Buddhism. A similar suggestion has been made in regard to the Essenes. The link between the Essenes and primitive Christianity has been firmly established by the Dead Sea Scrolls discovered at Qumran in Palestine in 1947. The messianic figure of the True Teacher spoken of in the scrolls foreshadowed the figure of Jesus, as we can grasp it from the gospels.

The Essene-Buddhist connection is reinforced by another fact. In the tenth century A.D., a Middle Eastern work entitled *Barlaam and Josaphat* gained great popularity, especially among the Cathars. It was translated into several languages. Scholars are agreed that the book relates the ill-concealed story of Gautama the Buddha, though with a Christian slant. While the early history of *Barlaam and Josaphat* is obscure, the name Josaphat is related to the names Joseph and Asaph, which were linked with the True Teacher of the Essenes.

But let us return to the Greeks. In this connection we must remember that no less a philosopher than Pythagoras—apparently the first to use the word *philosophia*—was initiated into the great mysteries at the banks of the Nile. According to his biographer Iamblichus, Pythagoras spent twenty-two years in Egypt, traveling from temple to temple, where he was well received by the priests and magi, and a further twelve years in Babylonia. We cannot rule out that in the course of his travels he also came in contact with thinkers and sages from India, who had found their way to Egypt and Mesopotamia early on. Certainly his teaching, with its emphasis on mathematics, geometry, music, dietary restrictions, and the belief in reincarnation, has many points in common with India's heritage. In his book *Pythagoras und die Inder* (Pythagoras and the

Indians), published in 1884, the German scholar Ludwig von Schroeder argued that Pythagoras had been influenced by the Samkhya school of thought, the most prominent branch of Indic philosophy next to Vedanta.[3]

Pythagoras, who lived in the sixth century B.C., was undoubtedly one of the earliest catalysts, perhaps even the greatest, in this process of cultural osmosis between the East and the West. The role of Pythagoreanism in the development of Greek culture can hardly be overestimated.

The vital connection between India and Europe was tightened when the thirty-year-old Alexander the Great, who was as much a romantic as he was a conqueror, marched with his troops into northern India in 326 B.C. Disregarding Aristotle's advice to treat the conquered "barbarians" like animals, he instead upheld the ideal of universal brotherhood and encouraged intermarriage with the natives of India. This young cosmpolitan was the principal architect of the Hellenistic culture on which Rome modeled itself.

Megasthenes, the ambassador of Seleucus Nicator at the court of the famous Indic ruler Candragupta, left us a description of ascetics—whom he called gymnosophists—living with utmost simplicity in the mountains or in quiet groves outside the cities. Megasthenes, who was at the court from 302 B.C. to 291 B.C., distinguished between brahmins and what he called *sarmanas* (Sanskrit: *shramanas*), the latter being both Hindu and non-Hindu (Buddhist, Jaina) ascetics. The Buddhist scriptures include a well-known work in the Pali language, the *Milinda-Panha*, that records a philosophical conversation between the Greco-Indic ruler Menander, who reigned in Kabul around 150 B.C., and the Buddhist monk Nagasena.

The cultural enclave created by the Greek rulers of Bactria (modern Afghanistan), who conquered parts of northern India in the second century B.C. in the wake of Alexander's invasion, remained peripheral to traditional Hinduism and before long was absorbed into the social fabric of India. However, Alexander's conquest established, or rather reestablished, the passageway to Europe. The British historian Vincent A. Smith conservatively appraised the impact of Alexander's invasion as follows:

> *The Greek influence never penetrated deeply [into the Indic civilization] . . . On the other hand, the West learned something from India in consequence of the communications opened up by Alexander's adventure. Our knowledge of the facts is so scanty and fragmentary that it is difficult to make any positive assertions with confidence, but it is safe to say that the influence of Buddhist ideas on Christian doctrine may be traced in the Gnostic forms of Christianity, if not elsewhere. The notions of Indian philosophy and religion which filtered into the Roman empire flowed through channels opened by Alexander.*[4]

We may detect India's influence in the teachings of the Roman Stoics, such as Seneca (a teacher of Nero), and emperor Marcus Aurelius. The emperor's book *Meditations* still makes for thought-provoking reading today and elicits in the student of India's wisdom echoes of the *Upanishads* and the *Bhagavad-Gita*. To furnish only one brief example, Marcus Aurelius wrote:

> *Take pleasure in one thing and rest in it, in passing from one social act to another social act, thinking of God.* (VI.7)[5]

Does this not strongly call to mind the Karma-Yoga, or Yoga of self-transcending action, taught by the divine Krishna to his human protégé, Prince Arjuna?

Furthermore, there is the possible influence of Indic thought on Neoplatonism. We know from Porphyry's *Vita Plotini* that his teacher, Plotinus, was fascinated with India's spiritual philosophies and even made an attempt to travel to India to learn them firsthand. However, wanting to secure the Hellenic purity of Plotinus's teachings, several generations of classical scholars have vehemently denied any Eastern elements in Neoplatonism. Yet parallels between Neoplatonism and Indic metaphysics abound and call for an explanation.[6]

There is also the added possibility that Plotinus's own teacher, the Alexandrian Ammonius Sakkas, might have been an initiate of Buddhism. The epithet *Sakkas*, generally said to mean "sack carrier," also has been interpreted as the Latinized form of the Sanskrit *shakya*, this being a common designation of the Buddha and his followers.

With the rise of the Roman Empire, the Romans achieved a political and economic unification that was unparalleled in the ancient West. But it was precisely this unification that also opened the doors to numerous foreign cultural elements, notably the Eastern mystery religions, such as Pythagoreanism, the cult of Cybele and Attis, Isis religion, Mithraism, and then also Christianity. It was through these cultural imports that, among other things, Indic beliefs and practices found their way deeper into Europe.

The collapse of the Roman Empire had many causes, but one of them was the reliance of the Romans on the contributions of their conquered territories. Since the Roman citizens were voracious consumers, they managed to create a massive trade deficit in regard to India, which was too far away to succumb to the Roman legions and whose goods and treasures therefore had to be purchased at great expense. As we have pointed out on several occasions, the flow of material goods involves people, and people are not merely carriers of valued commodities but also of philosophical ideas, religious beliefs, and ritual practices. These were the hidden cost of the trade between cultures so vastly different as the Indic and the Roman.

The Muslim Connection

European trade with India continued into the Middle Ages and was invigorated as a result of the crusades, beginning in 1096 A.D. and lasting several centuries. The official purpose of the crusades was to win back Jerusalem from Muslim hands, but other motives, not least economic considerations, played no small role as well.

As the Islamic world expanded and grew in strength it proved a formidable barrier between Europe and India. Yet, it was not altogether impenetrable, for Indic cultural elements continued to migrate to the West via the Arabic language. Thus the above-mentioned Buddhist legend of Barlaam and Josaphat was first retold after the Sanskrit sources in Arabic. Likewise the fables of Bidpai were, unbeknownst to the large number of people who enjoyed hearing them, chiefly derived from India's *Pancatantra*. This famous collection of legends was translated or paraphrased not only into any number of Indic tongues but also various Middle Eastern and European languages. The *Pancatantra* was also a strong source for Aesop's fables, which delighted the Greeks as they do the modern English reader.

Christianity periodically remembered its own early history, according to which St. Thomas successfully preached the gospel of his twin brother Jesus in India. Most scholars regard this as pure legend and believe that the Thomas remembered in India was a merchant who came several centuries after Jesus' own time. However, there is an ancient Christian community in the South Indian states of Kerala. In 884 A.D., according to the Anglo-Saxon Chronicle, King Alfred sent an envoy to India bearing offerings for St. Thomas's tomb. In the twelfth century A.D., Christendom became fascinated with the legend of Prester John, who supposedly ruled "the Indies," which was the medieval name for India. The legend fired crusaders and treasure-seeking adventurers with the hope that once they broke through the Muslim bloc they would find a thoroughly Christian empire. When they finally discovered Abyssinia/Ethiopia, they thought they had found the mythical Prester John in the Christian emperor ruling then. Many believed that he was a descendant of the Queen of Sheba and that he knew where the Ark of the Covenant was to be found that had been missing since the destruction of the Temple in Jerusalem during Solomon's reign. Mainly what the legend of Prester John shows is the tremendous fantasy and nostalgia surrounding faraway India in the mind of Europeans during that era.

In the meantime the Muslim civilization surpassed its European rival during the Middle Ages—surprisingly, in part because it embraced "pagan" learning whereas the Christianized West bluntly rejected it. However, as the renowned American historian Harry Elmer Barnes noted, Muslim science and scholarship were "not so much original or indigenous as a synthesis and exposition of the science and philosophy of Greece, India, and the East."[7] With the ascendancy of the city of Baghdad, Muslim translators were sponsored by the aristocracy and the wealthy to translate both Greek and Hindu works into Arabic. Later the Muslim-ruled cities of Cairo (in Egypt) and Cordova and Seville (both located in what is now Spain) became great centers of learning, where the flame of knowledge was kept alive while much of Europe was plunged into intellectual darkness.

The Muslims were eager astronomers and mathematicians, and much of their knowledge stemmed from India—including the so-called Arabic numerals. It was also from India that they adopted the decimal system and the numeral zero. That they also were fond of studying India's philosophical systems can be seen in the Arabic renditions of Patanjali's *Yoga-Sutra* (called *Kitab Patanjal*) by al-Biruni (973-1048 A.D.). He also wrote a monograph on Indic culture, the *Kitab al-Hind*, which, however, never achieved the prominence of Iranshahri's less original work on comparative religion, written around the same time. The encounter with the Arab and Persian world proved fertile for the Europeans, and contributed to the cultural upswing that we call the Renaissance.

The disruption of trade with India as a result of the Turkish conquest of the Byzantine Empire, marked by the fall of Constantinople in 1453 A.D., forced the European merchants to search for a new trade route to India—by sea. This directly led to Columbus's discovery of the new world, the land of the so-called American Indians. As is well known, Columbus had set out to sail for India in quest of great fortune, but ended up in the New World in 1492 A.D.

It was the Portuguese captain Vasco da Gama who, six years later, rediscovered India for the Europeans. He was unaware that had it not been for internal political intrigues in the ruling Ming dynasty of China, he might not have had such an easy time establishing trade posts on the subcontinent. For until 1433 A.D., China had been a formidable maritime force, which had reached Ceylon (Sri Lanka) and the gates of the Persian Gulf. But once the reckless Portuguese and his immediate successors had disposed of the Arabs, who had inferior ships and guns, they remained unopposed until the French arrived on the scene in the seventeenth century.

Finally, in the mid-eighteenth century, both the Portuguese and the French forfeited their trade advantage in India through Britain's naval supremacy. The British accomplished what none of the preceding European powers had been able to accomplish, namely to consolidate its mercantile interests by assuming political control in the form of the British Raj. Not until 1947 did India achieve independence, not least through the unorthodox efforts and charismatic leadership of Mahatma Gandhi.

The Rediscovery of India's Heritage in Modern Times

Whatever harm the British Raj caused in India, and the harm done was substantial, it indirectly led to some positive developments, notably the scholarly exploration of the multiple facets of Hinduism. This intellectual encounter, in turn, fertilized popular Western culture with the rich pollen of Indic thought and culture. The renowned British Sanskrit scholar Arthur A. Macdonell summarized the situation well when he said:

> *Since the Renaissance there has been no event of such world-wide significance in the history of culture as the discovery of Sanskrit literature in the latter part of the eighteenth century.*[8]

From a study of India's legal system, which is inseparable from the philosophical and spiritual assumptions of Hinduism, the British discovered dimension upon dimension of the vast Sanskrit and vernacular literature. Although the first translations of Indic texts into European languages were undertaken by Christian missionaries in the sixteenth century, the new discipline of Sanskrit scholarship can be said to have started with Charles Wilkins. At the behest of Warren Hastings, who established the British Raj, Wilkins studied with pundits at Benares. In 1785 he published the first translation of the *Bhagavad-Gita*, Hinduism's most popular philosophical and religious work. He also translated several literary works from the Sanskrit and compiled a Sanskrit grammar.

The first great Western Sanskrit scholar was Sir William Jones, a supreme court judge with a passion for Indic, Arabic, and Persian poetry. In addition to translating the pre-Christian law book of Manu, the *Manu-Smriti*, he firmly established the linguistic connection between Sanskrit and European languages such as Greek, Latin, and

German. The German version of his English rendering of the famous Sanskrit drama *Shakuntala* by Kalidasa (circa 350 A.D.) enchanted the two famous German poets and literati Goethe and Herder.

The founder of Indic philology was Henry Thomas Colebrooke, who also was the first to provide more detailed information about the *Vedas* than had hitherto been available. His countryman Alexander Hamilton likewise learned Sanskrit from India's pundits and taught the German poet Friedrich von Schlegel, one of the leaders of the Romantic movement. His brother August Wilhelm von Schlegel became the first Sanskrit scholar in Germany.

In France the foundations for the new discipline were vigorously laid by scholars like A. L. Chézy and Eugène Burnouf. Soon the emerging translations won a small but appreciative circle of readers. In particular the first rendering of the *Upanishads*, the most esoteric portion of the Vedic literature, gained considerable attention and praise. This was despite the fact that it was a Latin rendition of a flawed Persian translation of the Sanskrit original. Upon reading Anquetil Duperron's work, published under the title *Oupnek'hat*, Arthur Schopenhauer declared the *Upanishads* to be the "product of the highest human wisdom." As L. S. S. O'Malley observed:

> *The wisdom found in Sanskrit works was greeted with something like reverential awe. Thus the French philosopher Victor Cousin, speaking of the poetical and philosophical movements of the East, and above all, those of India, which were, he said, beginning to spread in Europe, declared that they contained so many truths, and such profound truths, that he was constrained to bend the knee before the genius of the East and to see in that cradle of the human race the native land of the highest philosophy.*[9]

In the nineteenth century the galaxy of Indic scholars included men like Friedrich Rosen (the first to translate a portion of the *Rig-Veda*), Max Müller (who prepared a critical edition of the *Rig-Veda* and founded comparative mythology), Otto Böhtlingk (compiler of the St. Petersburg Sanskrit dictionary), Albrecht Weber (who wrote the first comprehensive history of Indic literature), Paul Deussen (a philosopher who pioneered the study of Vedanta), T. W. Rhys Davids (Buddhist scholar and founder of the Pali Text Society).

The interlude of German Romanticism in the study of India is especially interesting. That the Romantics did indeed romanticize India is evident from Friedrich von Schlegel's book *Über die Sprache und Weisheit der Inder* (On the Language and Wisdom of the Indians), published in 1808. This work, which has been quite influential, is prone to what has been styled "mythicizing enthusiasm."[10] Remarkably, in the same year that Schlegel's work appeared in print, he converted to Catholicism, and subsequently he appears to have lost interest in the subject of India's philosophical thought.

Echoes of the Romantic movement can be found in the work of Max Müller, who admitted to having derived an important stimulus from the movement. Though remaining committed to his Christian roots, Müller was a lifelong champion of Indic culture. Swami Vivekananda, who visited the aged German savant in his home in England, said of him: "What love does he bear towards India! I wish I had a hundredth part of that love for my own motherland!"[11] Toward the end of his life Müller wrote:

> *We all come from the East—all that we value most has come to us from the East, and in going to the East . . . everybody ought to feel that he is going to his 'old home,' full of memories, if only he can read them.*[12]

Müller died at the dawn of the twentieth century, and to our ears his words have an almost prophetic ring, because two generations later the Beat generation discovered their Eastern roots through the medium of Zen. The Japanese Zen master and scholar D. T. Suzuki came to America around 1950 and almost single-handedly inaugurated the intellectual, "cocktail-party" interest in Zen. This was followed in the late 1960s by a more practical interest, which in due course led Americans to the literatures and teachers of Mahayana Buddhism and then Tibetan Vajrayana. Buddhism in America, though deriving primarily from Japan and Tibet, is an indirect gift from India, the homeland of Gautama the Buddha.

Others who tried to break away from mainstream American culture received their initiation into Eastern and especially India's spirituality through the writings of Emerson and Thoreau, who had provided the American "Transcendentalist" counterpart to German Romanticism. They also poured over the ever-ecstatic and ever-eclectic Walt Whitman who had thoroughly embraced Eastern wisdom, and they religiously studied Hermann Hesse's *Siddharta*, turned on to the poetry of their contemporaries Jack Kerouac, Allen Ginsberg, and Gary Snyder, and to the music of Zen-inspired John Cage.

As for Hinduism, it made its presence first powerfully felt at the Parliament of Religions held in Chicago in 1893, where Swami Vivekananda was a towering figure. He can be said to have initiated the modern missionary Hinduism, which has brought a ceaseless stream of gurus from India. In the early part of the twentieth century, the Theosophical Society (founded in 1875) played an important catalytic role in this process, not least by its extensive publishing program featuring translations of key Vedanta and Yoga scriptures. The Society also groomed Krishnamurti, who later became an incredibly successful speaker under his own banner.

The influence of Hindu Yoga continued with various teachers who, like Paramahansa Yogananda, had made their home in the West. Yogananda lived in the United States for thirty-two years until his death in 1952, after having taught yogic philosophy, meditation, breath control, and other similar techniques to tens of thousands of Westerners.

In the late 1960s, the Transcendental Meditation movement captured the imagination of the spiritually hungry, largely because the Beatles, the Rolling Stones, and other pop heroes had gone to the movement's founder, Maharishi Mahesh Yogi, for initiation into mantra meditation.

Today hundreds of thousands of Europeans and Americans are reading Eastern classics—notably the *Bhagavad-Gita* and *Upanishads*—which are available as mass market paperbacks for ready consumption. An estimated four million Americans are practicing physical exercises derived from or described as Yoga. Although most Westerners are mainly interested in the calisthenic aspect of Hatha-Yoga, they can hardly escape being exposed to some of the notions behind the exercises and to Indic metaphysical beliefs like karma and reincarnation in general. Many thousands are regular meditators, following one system or another.

When we look closely at the maelstrom that we call our postmodern civilization, we find not only breakdown but also many constructive efforts that derive their impetus or inspiration from Eastern sources. In his daring and sweeping reconstruction of the West's cultural history, Richard Tarnas speaks of a revitalization of Western religion not only by its own plurality of viewpoints but also as a result of the influx of Eastern spirituality.[13] He sees us possibly moving toward a climactic overarching synthesis.

The insights of India's great sages and spiritual virtuosos, as we have seen, have found their way into the writings of some of the finest and most influential minds of the modern West—from Schopenhauer, Bergson, and Goethe to writers like Heine, Tolstoy, Thoreau, Emerson, Whitman, Hesse, Zweig, Rolland, Forster, Huxley, Coleridge, Shelley, Wordsworth, Blake, Yeats, and Eliot. The combined effect of these great figures of Western literature upon the general public is inestimable. To varying degrees they have through their creative work served as conduits for those values, ideas, and ideals that have inspired India's branch of humanity.

Outside the worlds of literature and philosophy India also is exerting an increasing influence on those avant-garde circles in which the models for the "new science" are being hatched. In particular, scientists and philosophers concerned with the wider implications of quantum physics have been impressed with traditional cosmological ideas found in the sacred literature of Hinduism. Thus the Vedic sages and philosophers speak of the central role of consciousness in understanding reality; modern scientists have reached the same conclusion. For example, Erwin Schrödinger, the Austrian physicist who was one of the creators of quantum mechanics, believed that the problem of determinism and free will could be resolved only in the Vedic framework of a single universal consciousness of which our individual consciousnesses are fragments.[14] However, the full implications of the Vedic insights to the creation of a science of consciousness are yet to be worked out.

Western psychologists, too, are beginning to accept that India has much to teach them. Through his psychiatric studies Sigmund Freud opened up the nonrational dimension of the human psyche for investigation—a dimension that has been studied in extreme detail in India for several thousand years. Freud's pupil Carl Gustav Jung further broadened the psychological frame of reference, leading to a better appreciation of the fact that the subconscious or unconscious is not merely a dumping ground for unprocessed material from the ordinary waking consciousness but also the fertile soil for paranormal and higher mystical experiences. This insight is not novel but merely a rediscovery, for the higher cognitive capacities of the human being have been the forté of countless generations of India's psychonauts. As Jung himself admitted in his book *Modern Man in Search of a Soul*:

> *Our studies of sexual life, originating in Vienna and in England, are matched or surpassed by Hindu teachings on this subject . . . Psychoanalysis itself and the lines of thought to which it gives rise—surely a distinctly Western development—are only a beginner's attempt compared to what is an immemorial art in the East.*[15]

There is nothing we wish to add to this judgment, which comes not only from one of the great psychologists of our time but also one of the most perceptive and learned scholars the modern West has produced.

The Indo-Europeans Again

So far we have talked about the migration of commodities, ideas, and practices from east to west. But perhaps our enduring Western fascination with India has deeper roots. For we must not forget that we have much in common with our Indic cousins. As we have noted in previous chapters, India's non-Dravidian languages—notably Sanskrit—all belong to the same branch of the tree of languages as reconstructed by comparative philologists. We also have pointed out here and there that we share with India's civilization many basic beliefs and practices, as comparative mythology and the history of religion have made evident.

Albanian, Armenian, Baltic (i.e., Lithuanian, Lettish), Celtic (i.e., Scots Gaelic, Irish Gaelic, Welsh, Breton, Cornish), Danish, Dutch, English, Flemish, French, German, Greek, Icelandic, Italian (and Latin), Norwegian, Portuguese, Rumanian, Slavonic (i.e., Bulgarian, Croatian, Czech, Macedonian, Polish, Russian, Serbian, Slovak, Slovene, Ukranian), Spanish, and Swedish—all belong to the same linguistic group whose speakers have long been distributed throughout Europe. The only exceptions to this Indo-European presence in Europe are Basque, Finnish, Hungarian, Lapp, Ostyak, Samoyed, Turkish, and the dead Etruscan language, all of which have comparatively few speakers.

These diverse languages are thought to have derived from a common ancestral language, which scholars have dubbed "Proto-Indo-European." Although there is no one-on-one relationship between language and culture, speakers of the same language often tend to have other cultural features in common as well. Thus the Proto-Indo-European speakers are supposed to have been agriculturalists and pastoralists who brought their economic skills along with them when they migrated from their original homeland.

According to archaeologist Colin Renfrew, the Proto-Indo-Europeans were settled in Anatolia (modern Turkey) as long ago as the eighth or even tenth millennium B.C. Other scholars favor the Ukraine and the third millennium B.C., though it is difficult to squeeze the available evidence into this model. The regions of Northwest India and Central Asia also have been proposed as the Proto-Indo-European homeland, and this scholarly opinion favors an early date similar to Renfrew's.

At one point, for reasons not yet fully understood, the Proto-Indo-European tribes began to split up and migrate (with their various dialects) into different directions. Some went toward the east and ended up founding the Aryan/Vedic civilization of India, giving rise to the multitude of Indo-European tongues spoken on the subcontinent today. Those journeying toward Europe created their own linguistic, cultural, and ethnic enclaves, gradually giving birth to the pluralistic Europe of modern times. As the Indo-European speakers grew in number and importance, the earlier non-Indo-European languages of Europe were, with only a few exceptions, progressively replaced and lost. In turn, the various Proto-Indo-European dialects crystallized into separate languages.

Scholars have endeavored to reconstruct the Proto-Indo-European language, just as they have attempted to identify the exact period and homeland of the Proto-Indo-European speakers. But all these efforts are highly speculative, and a variety of solutions have been proposed. We consider the model proposed by Colin Renfrew to have the greatest plausibility so far, though it stands in need of some modification, because the Indo-Europeanization process seems to have taken place over a period of several thousand years, as a result of numerous migrations.[16]

Common Ground

Apart from a shared *Ur*-language, the Indo-European speakers also have much else in common, not least their cosmology as expressed in myths, as we have already pointed out. This is not the place to furnish a detailed account of the similarities in social structure and belief systems between the Indic peoples and their European cousins; however, we do want to provide at least one striking illustration—the Gundestrup cauldron—to show how geographically remote cultures, namely the Indic and the Celtic, can astonish us with their similarities.

In 1891, peat cutters working in a peat bog near the Danish hamlet of Gundestrup found a large silver bowl containing seven decorated plates that, together with one missing plate, had once formed the sides of a massive cauldron. The pictorial representations on the plates are scenes of battles and heroic encounters between bearded deities or priests and beasts, and they also include a bare-breasted Goddess and a horned figure seated in a Yoga-like posture, holding a snake in one hand and surrounded by animals of the wild.

Art historian Timothy Taylor, who analyzed the plates, concluded that the Gundestrup cauldron fits none of the archaeological preconceptions that have been applied to it so far. Although the style resembles Celtic art, Taylor speculated that the fine work had likely been executed by Thracian silversmiths around 150 B.C. It is not clear how the cauldron, which is twenty-seven inches in diameter, came to be in Denmark. But Taylor conjectured "that an intrusive Celtic tribe called the Scordisci had commissioned the cauldron from native Thracian silversmiths and that Germanic looters had then carried it off."[17] In trying to place this artifact in its proper context, he concluded that in those days the boundaries between cultures were far more fluid than they are now and also that "religious beliefs may have been flexible and multifaceted."

Taylor further suggested that the craftsmen who created the cauldron very probably constituted a caste—or, as we prefer, a guild—who "moved outside settled societies."[18] These guilds, moreover, followed a certain artistic canon, laid down long ago, which is the reason why the Gundestrup cauldron includes imagery that has a strong resemblance with imagery found on one of the soapstone seals of the Indus-Sarasvati civilization. The artifact in question is the well-known seal that has generally been taken to depict God Shiva Pashupati, the Lord of Beasts, made more than two thousand years before the cauldron was created.

The notion of artistic guilds at the cultural margins is intriguing and matches what we know of musicians, singers, and performance artists in the ancient world. Such artistic guilds would certainly have taken pride in carefully preserving the traditional imagery handed down from father to son. At the same time, however, it seems reasonable to assume that these migrant artists would also have made artistic concessions to the surrounding culture, or executed commissioned work. In their interaction with the larger culture, marginal groups tend to develop strong survival mechanisms, as is illustrated by the Gypsies, who are known to have originated in India. Romani, the language of the Gypsies, is fairly close to Sanskrit, and many of their customs can be traced back to the Indic culture as well. While the Gypsies have always drawn close boundaries around their own culture, they have developed skills—from music and dancing to bartering—that allowed them to survive in their migrations through various cultural locales.

The Gundestrup cauldron, as Taylor affirmed, could well have

FIG. 47. *The symbolism of the finely crafted Gundestrup cauldron connects Europe with the East.*

been created by non-Celtic artists for a Celtic sponsor. In this case, they would very likely have drawn on Celtic mythology, using a Celtic style but, perhaps, mixing in artistic elements from their own inherited canon, created long ago and undoubtedly modified in the course of many generations. At any rate, the Thracian artists had to ensure that their Celtic sponsor would resonate with their creation. Perhaps they would not have been able to accomplish this had they themselves not been primed by the same symbolic world, which is that of the Proto-Indo-Europeans. In other words, both the Thracian artists and the Celtic sponsor drew from the same well of archetypal symbolism within their subconscious—symbolism that allowed for the inclusion of an old artistic motif such as the horned figure surrounded by animals, which we know from the early Indic civilization.

In a similar vein, we would like to suggest that many Westerners today are able to enthusiastically respond to India's wisdom precisely because they carry deep within themselves something of the archetypal symbolism that marks the Vedic or Hindu spirituality. Jung once observed with some concern that "while we are overpowering the Orient from without, it may be fastening its hold upon us from within."[19] But Jung's worry seems misplaced because, in light of the foregoing discussion, we could say that by turning toward India, we simply are looking for our own roots.

In this case, the lesson is perhaps the same as that learned by one Rabbi Eisik, son of Jekel, a pious man in Cracow, who is told in a dream that he should travel to the distant city of Prague where he would find a treasure buried beneath the main bridge.[20] Eisik tries to ignore the dream but after it recurred twice, he sets out for Prague.

There he discovers that the bridge is guarded day and night. He befriends one of the sentries and even reveals his mission to him. To his surprise, the soldier tells him that he too has had a dream in which he was told to travel to Cracow where he would find a treasure in the house of a certain Eisik, son of Jekel. He explains that he had given no thought to it since half of Cracow's Jewish population bore the name Eisik and the other that of Jekel.

Eisik rushes back to Cracow, digs under his house, and indeed finds a marvelous treasure.

Our search for India's spirituality and the Indic roots of our Western civilization is a little bit like Rabbi Eisik's journey to Prague. We must venture forth to discover that the truth has been with us all along. We have never been without India, which, as we have shown, has exerted a steady influence on the Western world. But, as the adage says, travel broadens the mind. Our quest, we hope, will enrich and mature us, uncovering those unshakable verities of wisdom that are the marrow of India's civilization as much as our own.

CHAPTER 14

The Vedas *and Perennial Wisdom*

Taking Stock

OUR REEXAMINATION OF THE EARLY HISTORY OF INDIA, THE land of the sages and seer-bards, has led to a view of ancient times that is radically different from textbook versions. This revised history even challenges our ideas about humanity and ultimately about the reality we live in. How we view history is, after all, a reflection of how we see ourselves. This is not merely a dry academic issue but a matter that goes to the very root by which we give value to things: Our vision of the past is shaped by, and in turn shapes, our vision of the present. It is the very bedrock of our cosmology—those complex and comprehensive images that we carry around in our heads and by which we decide what is true or false and right or wrong.

Having completed our reappraisal of ancient India and its rich spiritual heritage, we are now able, and indeed obliged, to question the foundations of our present civilization. How advanced or enlightened really is our current postindustrial civilization? Is the mainstream view of the genesis of human civilization correct, limited, or fundamentally wrong? Are we moving in a positive direction toward a better world, or are we in danger of destroying ourselves because the prime values of our society are out of sync with the laws of life?

As the American sociologist Peter Berger pointed out, we moderns are afflicted with a false sense of superiority.[1] We tend to feel superior to whatever and whomever has preceded us. This is captured in the idea of progress, which has governed Western thought for the past two hundred years. Yet, as Berger and others have noted, the price for all this progress has been a growing sense of dislocation or "homelessness." Our homelessness is not merely social but metaphysical: We are ill at ease in the world at large. "This has produced an anguish all its own," observed Berger.[2]

Carl Gustav Jung stated that "modern man has suffered an almost fatal shock, psychologically speaking, and as a result has fallen into profound uncertainty."[3] This confusion is evident in the countless problems that vex our world, some of which are seemingly insurmountable, such as the unabated devastation of our environment caused by a runaway technology whose only purpose appears to be to stimulate the consumption of goods.

Though part of the world is enjoying unparalleled material abundance, the majority of humanity is still forced to live at a subsistence level. In fact, a hundred million people are starving to death every year. Advances in the swift dissemination of information and mass-media entertainment, generated by our bored and sensation-hungry society, have served to make people around the world more discontent, restless, and disturbed. The psychological health of the so-called developed world has frequently been called into question, and its dis-ease is rapidly spreading over the entire planet.

Today human unhappiness seems more pronounced than ever, not least because we have severed the organic root that connects the individual to the family and to the Earth itself. The individual feels lost and abandoned, and frustration all too often vents itself in violence of one kind or another. Moral corruption is present in all domains of society—especially in the political arena where integrity and rectitude as well as sound judgment are most urgent requirements.

Religious traditions are faltering under the onslaught of secularism, cynicism, and a general hopelessness. Those that thrive tend to cater to fundamentalism and fanaticism. We certainly do not appear to be any closer to the Divine, or spiritual reality, than our ancestors were in previous ages. In fact, our estrangement from the sacred dimension is more complete than would have been possible in the ancient world.

Manifestly, there is much for us to question and change about the current state of affairs. Yet it would be wrong to say that there have been no positive developments at all, or that there are no glimmers of hope on the horizon.

One of the greatest and undoubtedly most far-reaching advances has been that of the knowledge and communication industry: Today an unparalleled expansion of information is occurring, which has thrown many of us into confusion, but which also has brought us numerous practical benefits. Above all, it has reduced the barriers that exist between human beings. Through the mass media—which are the Earth's evolving nervous system—we are in touch with the most remote parts of our planet. In an instant we can learn of the problems and sorrows as well as the triumphs and joys of people far removed from our own society and culture. The present-day communication revolution is effectively bringing humanity together, though there are still many who oppose this powerful trend. Unfortunately, the mass media as yet fail to appreciate their true potential, preferring instead to reduce their communications to the lowest common denominator.

If science and technology have triggered a multitude of problems, they are also helping us to free ourselves from the limiting concepts of nation, race, religion, and culture that previously divided humankind. We can no longer see ourselves in merely local terms but must acknowledge the greater world in which we live. Truth can no longer be seen as the property or prerogative of one group or another. We must realize that knowledge is universal and must not be claimed by special interest groups to further their own limited goals. Today we can recognize knowledge as a powerful evolutionary instrument that belongs to humanity as a whole.

Our contemporary problems of overpopulation, pollution, ozone depletion, dwindling of natural resources, threat of nuclear war, terrorism, and so forth are global problems and require that we tackle them together. Many of us—individuals and nations—are still trying to resist this globalization process, but it is inevitable if we are to survive as a species. No one country or belief system can solve these problems independently. What happens on the other side of the world can profoundly affect us where we live. It is increasingly becoming apparent that the only solution to the present world crisis is to build a global civilization, which requires a clearly articulated view of one humanity.

Knowledge Beyond Information

History has truly become world history. For the local history of a town, state, or nation has a significance exceeding its limited circumference. This fact has recently been symbolically captured in the quantum-physical experiment, conducted in 1982 at the Institute of Optics in Paris, which demonstrated that a photon can instantaneously change its angle of polarization in synchrony with its photon twin. Some researchers, like the British physicist Paul Davis, inferred from this that this kind of nonlocal connectedness is a general property of Nature.

Thus what we do locally has an impact on the whole world. To put it dramatically but correctly, our every breath and thought have cosmic consequences. Hence we must assume profound responsibility for our personal, political, and economic actions.

Moreover, the view of history of a single group has repercussions for all others. Thus we can no longer regard the Western European view of world history as universal, any more than we can regard European culture and customs as comprehensive of all of humanity or as representing all the best within it. We must acknowledge the contribution to world history and world thought that has been made by the Hindus, Maya, American Indians, Brazilian forest tribes, black South Africans, and other "minority" or traditional groups. Their voice is our voice. To create a global culture we must recognize our global heritage.

This also means that we have to come to grips with the Eastern spiritual roots of Western humanity. Whatever our Western civilization may have inherited from the non-Indo-European populations of Europe and the Americas, its most powerful spiritual tap roots clearly are to be found in the East. The old saying *ex oriente lux* ("From the

East, light") is no platitude, for civilization's torch, especially the core sacred tradition of perennial wisdom, has been handed down from the eastern hemisphere.

According to *The World Almanac 1994*, there are over one billion Christians in Europe and the two Americas. There are over sixteen million Muslims, over eight million Jews, more than three million Hindus, a little over one million Buddhists, more than one million Baha'is, half a million Sikhs, 250,000 Chinese folk religionists, 30,000 Confucianists, 23,000 Jains, and 2,000 Shintoists in Europe and the two Americas. Let us recall that Christianity, an offshoot of Judaism, began as a small spiritual countergroup in Jerusalem. With the exception of the million or so adherents of Native American religions, all the other religious traditions likewise had their birthplace in the Eastern hemisphere. The Middle-Eastern creations of Judaism and Christianity, which largely have given our civilization its present shape, were, as we have noted, influenced by ideas stemming from countries farther east, especially India.

Of all these Eastern traditions, by far the oldest continuous religious heritage is, without question, that of Hinduism. Thus, the *Rig-Veda* gives us a view of a pristine spiritual tradition from which we can derive understanding and inspiration.

Many of us are troubled by the present course of civilization and are probing for ways out of the looming crisis. We must therefore ask about the nature of knowledge. What is knowledge? What is it that we are seeking to know? Are we content merely to know the names and numbers that explain the outer world, or are we seeking knowledge of a deeper reality? Are we satisfied with knowledge bound by time and space, or are we looking for eternal Truth?

Evidently, on a personal level, we are not content merely to know ourselves or each other in terms of names and numbers, as biochemical processes, or as social statistics. We are looking for a deeper meaning and awareness than the factual mind can produce.

This is where the perennial wisdom, as long ago encoded in the *Rig-Veda*, is highly pertinent. According to the Vedic view there are two levels of knowledge: the knowledge of the practical world of name, form, and appearance; and the knowledge of the ultimate, nameless, formless, infinite, and eternal Reality. There are certain fundamental questions that we all ask at some point in our lives. What is the Divine? What in us. if anything, transcends death? What is the origin of the cosmos? Such questions cannot be answered by a knowledge that relies solely on name and form or time and space.

While modern science has advanced far in the first type of knowledge, we do not appear any closer to answering the fundamental existential questions. Yet it is precisely the role of ancient teachings like the *Vedas* to offer profound answers to the ultimate questions of life. There can be little doubt that ancient humanity was more concerned with spiritual realities than we are. This does not mean that our ancestors formulated those questions in the same way that we might today. A symbolic or reverential language, such as contained in the *Vedas*, may pose questions and give answers by way of an offering, adoration, or worship. In fact, all worship and prayer can be regarded as means of accessing the fundamental Reality that transcends ordinary ways of knowing. Worship and prayer entail the recognition that our ordinary instrument of knowledge is insufficient and that we must somehow open ourselves up to, or humble ourselves before, a greater reality and intelligence.

Today we are in need of a philosophy, science, and spirituality that are deep and broad enough to accommodate the emerging global civilization. In releasing our grip on merely local expressions of mind and culture, we inevitably are led back to considering, as did our ancestors, the infinite, eternal, impartite Reality. The reason for this is that only in that which has no boundaries can there be the ground for integrating all the diverse aspects of human creativity.

This brings us face to face with the need to create a global spirituality that transcends all parochial religious modes of knowledge and experience. Yet, how can we create such an encompassing spirituality? Clearly, we cannot create it out of nothing. Just as any new human language, such as Esperanto, is built step by step upon existing foundations, we must draw upon all those resources that we as a whole species have already created. As Carl Gustav Jung noted, "Man is never helped in his suffering by what he thinks for himself, but only by revelations of a wisdom greater than his own. It is this which lifts him out of his distress."[4] This insight has more than personal relevance; it holds true of us collectively as well.

The *Vedas* are the earliest available expression of the perennial philosophy, or universal spirituality. Their revelatory knowledge contains depths that, in the words of Raimundo Panikkar, "still resound in the heart of modern Man."[5] Panikkar, a Roman Catholic priest and professor of religious studies, is one of the most appreciative interpreters of the *Vedas*. In his book *The Vedic Experience*, we find the following passage that fittingly describes our present endeavor as well:

> *[T]he Vedic experience introduces nothing alien to modern Man, but helps him to realize his own life and emphasizes an often neglected aspect of his own being. In this sense the* Vedas *occupy a privileged position in the crystallized culture of Man. They are neither primitive nor modern. Not being primitive, they present a depth, a critical awareness, and a sophistication not shown by many other ancient cultures. Not being modern, they exhale a fragrance and present an appeal that the merely modern does not possess.*[6]

The Light of Perennial Wisdom

There are many spiritual teachings and traditions upon whose experience and wisdom we can call in our effort to create a global spiritual "science" that steps beyond the limitations inherent in specific paths but that also does not seek to merely replace them or diminish their practical significance and value for spiritual seekers.

In order to develop such a global spirituality we must look into all the many traditional paths and must not reject anything useful that might be contained in any one of them. Ours is a plural world, and henceforth presumably will always be so. What we must overcome is the fragmentation of humanity and knowledge into disparate parts between which communication flows too sparingly, too haphazardly, or not at all.

It would appear that none of the world's extant traditions are as old and comprehensive as the Vedic-Hindu tradition. It is so embracing that it seems to contain all the different approaches to the Divine, or ultimate Reality, found in the other traditions. Every spiritual means—from simple devotional surrender to complex visualization to postural variation—has been systematically explored in this great tradition.

As historian Stanley Wolpert put it, "India is a Civilization predicated upon faith."[7] That is to say, spirituality has been the bedrock of India's multifaceted culture during the past eight thousand and more years. This long experience with the sacred dimension is crystallized in the unbelievable wealth of wisdom and metaphysical understanding in the diverse schools of Hindu philosophy. The early nineteenth-century German philosopher and poet Friedrich von Schlegel was so impressed with Indic spirituality that he declared:

> *When one considers the sublime disposition underlying the truly universal education [of traditional India] . . . then what is or has been called religion in Europe seems to us to be scarcely deserving of that name. And one feels compelled to advise those who wish to witness religion to travel to India for that purpose. . . .*[8]

The Hindu sages have turned every aspect of human culture—including art, drama, music, medicine, astronomy, and language—into a tool of spiritual awakening and realization. To get to the origin and core of the Vedic tradition is therefore crucial to any endeavor in generating a global spiritual tradition today. This does not mean, of course, that a new global tradition will be Vedic or that it should be called Vedic. What it means, instead, is that it must come to grips with the essential spirituality at the heart of the *Vedas* if it aspires to be integrated and of relevance to humanity in the imminent third millennium.

The *Vedas* embody what has been referred to as the perennial philosophy at its purest and noblest. The phrase "perennial philosophy"—corresponding to the Hindu notion of an "eternal teaching" (*sanatana-dharma*)—was apparently coined in the seventeenth century by the German philosopher Leibniz, who used the Latin phrase *philosophia perennis*. It was made popular in modern times by the British novelist Aldous Huxley. In his book *The Perennial Philosophy*, he explained:

> *[The perennial philosophy is] the metaphysic that recognises a divine Reality substantial to the world of things and lives and minds; the psychology that finds in the soul something similar to, or even identical with, divine Reality; the ethic that places man's final end in the knowledge of the immanent and transcendent Ground of all being.*[9]

Unlike academic philosophy, the perennial philosophy is founded in spiritual practice and moral discipline, leading to a personal experiential realization of the ultimate Reality. As Huxley noted, the practitioners of this philosophy are the saints, sages, and enlightened beings of the various cultures on Earth.

The American philosopher and historian of religion Huston Smith also has spoken of the perennial philosophy as the "primordial tradition."[10] "Perennial" and "primordial" both capture the fact that this approach seeks to tune into an aspect of humanness that transcends personal style and cultural fashion. The words also, in a way, suggest that this approach has been an integral part of human culture since the beginnings of civilized humanity.

This perennial *philosophia* ("love of wisdom") revolves around a few focal issues: the singularity of truth, the supreme value of diversity, and the sacredness of existence and of the human individual. Today, from the vantage point of our present place in the unraveling drama of evolution on this planet, we can add a fourth feature: the homogeneity of humankind and its history on this planet.

The Singularity of Truth

"Truth," says the heroine in Shakespeare's *Measure for Measure*, "is truth / To the end of reckoning." In this the great bard echoes Plato who called truth "durable." Truth is enduring because it is singular, complete in itself. Yet, for some modern philosophers, truth is little more than an abstract proposition that is self-consistent or that corresponds to the facts, while for the ordinary individual it is "all relative." Relative to what? we might ask. Speaking from within the primordial tradition, the answer has to be: relative to the ego's momentary desires. But the truth of the ego with its fitful passions is not the truth that fills perennial philosophers with awe or stirs them to higher aspiration.

We have won through to the recognition that there is only one science—that the laws of science do not change relative to our varying opinions or beliefs, cultures, or customs. Although scientific paradigms change, and with them scientific explanations, there is a fundamental pool of understanding that remains intact. Thus whether fire burns is not a matter of social habit or personal judgment but a fact of life to be recognized and understood. Scientists strive to comprehend the laws of nature through reason and experiment. The proof of a scientific theory is independent of the country, culture, customs, or personal background of the scientist.

Similarly, there is only one Truth, one Reality, to be discovered by humanity. There is not a distinct God, or Truth, for each of the world's religions, any more than there is a different Sun or Moon for astronomers of various nations.

To discover that ultimate spiritual Truth, we must approach it with the same rigor that a scientist applies to his or her experiments. In Western civilization, science and religion have become opposed and conflicting forces. To simplify somewhat, science emphasizes reason and experiment, whereas religion bases itself on faith and dogma. At first, religious authority sought to suppress the scientific enterprise, holding the threat of excommunication over the heads of the bold adventurers of this new way of acquiring knowledge. Where the Church failed to intimidate scientists with the threat of excommunication, it often resorted to imprisonment, torture, and execution. But scientists would not be silenced.

In their turn, scientists often felt the need to disprove religion, regarding religion as mere fantasy or wish fulfillment and religious states as mental derangements. Thus a bitter enmity between religion (the clerical establishment) and science was created—an enmity that has by no means been overcome today. However, there are now more and more thoughtful people who consider the old dichotomy between religion and science as false and unconstructive. They prefer to look at these two approaches to reality as complementary.

This approach corresponds to the view of the perennial philosophy. Thus, according to the Vedic tradition, science and religion are not only compatible but essentially identical, because both endeavor to know the truth. We can formulate the Vedic view as follows: Religion must be founded on reason and experience. It should not be contrary to natural law and should be part of a way of objectively understanding the inner or higher truth of the human being and the universe. Likewise science must address the ultimate issues of life and death and not merely concern itself with transient matters. It must not merely turn its eye upon the outer world but also look into the inner world of consciousness. It also must be a way of linking up (*religio*) with the cosmic and infinite reality through deep, unbiased consideration.

The challenge today is to harmonize science and religion, which gives birth to a spiritually sensitive science that combines the objective approach of science to inner realities with the sacred reverence of religion toward the outer world. Such a new science calls for a methodology of introspection that provides direct experiential access to the inner reality.

We propose that the *Vedas* contain the rudiments of such an integral spiritual science, which we must reclaim for ourselves. An important aspect of this task is to translate the Vedic understanding into modern concepts and make it relevant to our contemporary situation.

Unity and Diversity

If the notion of unity is a focal point of the perennial philosophy, so is the idea of diversity. We need both concepts to adequately understand life. Not surprisingly, both play an important role in science and religion as well.

Of late, the interplay between unity and diversity has been brought to our attention nowhere more strikingly than in the young discipline of ecology. We are rediscovering that life is a web of interconnected and ultimately inseparable individualities. Unity and diversity are equally essential to the business of living.

Our own human individuality is not a separate affair. On the contrary, as we are fast relearning, our individual existence is interdependent on all the other myriad forms that evolution has spawned. We must recover the sense of kinship with all other beings and things that was fundamental to the culture of our early ancestors and that is still felt deeply by many members of tribal societies.

Accepting that there is an underlying unity to life does not mean that we must ignore diversity or deny the uniqueness of each individual. Unity must not be turned into an ideological stereotype that is used to suppress variety. On the other hand, diversity should not become divisiveness that is destructive of unity.

In the context of religious life, too, both unity and diversity must be safeguarded. The world's predominant religions have yet to nurture a sense of unity with other religious traditions. Simultaneously, they still have to recognize the need for diversity in religious beliefs and practices.

Western ideas about religion have been defined mainly in terms of monotheism, or the belief in a single (male) God who has issued a code of behavior—the Word of God (as embodied in the Ten Commandments and other Middle-Eastern teachings)—that must be followed by all who want to be saved.

It is this revealed morality that is used as the standard for judging all religious traditions. In their more orthodox formulations, Christianity, Judaism, and Islam all claim uniqueness and exclusiveness. To be saved one must be a Christian, a Jew, or a Muslim. All others are considered mistaken and condemned. However, while there is only one Truth, or Reality, there is no one religious group that owns or dispenses Truth. Similarly, there is no one scientific or political group that has an exclusive on reality itself.

The primordial tradition, as preserved in the *Vedas*, recognizes that there is only one Truth, the supreme Spirit, which cannot be limited to any particular name, form, or personality. This Being is inherent in all things and yet transcends them. In its immanent aspect it is found even in a clump of dirt, in suffering and disease, and in evil. In its transcendental aspect, one cannot even call it God, as commonly understood, because it exists prior to all form, including that of the Creator. All the forces of nature are its functions and appearances, and yet it infinitely overflows them.

This view is not limited to the people of ancient India. We find the same fundamental idea expressed in the traditional religions of many cultures, including those that are labeled "primitive." For instance, the Australian aborigines speak of the original Dreamtime in terms reminiscent of the homogeneity of the Source before all creation. The Native American Indians know of the Great Spirit. The ancient Chinese celebrated the One Being as the *tao* or "way."

The ancient Egyptians recognized a pantheon of deities, the *neters*, who were really functional aspects of the one divine Light. A similar situation prevailed among the ancient Greeks, the Germanic people, and many tribal societies in Africa, the Far East, and South America. Thus, in the first century A.D., the Roman historian Tacitus described the Germans of his era as worshiping the nameless Power by calling upon their various deities.

Belief in a single Reality need not be at odds with the recognition that there are many deities, both male and female, since they can be considered as manifestations of that universal Being. Even a more liberal view of Western monotheistic religion resolves itself in this direction, with the various angels and archangels being analogous to the various Gods and Goddesses of so-called polytheistic traditions.

The Vedic view respects both identity and differentiation, both monism and creative diversity, which are seen as complementary sides of a reality that is both singular and infinite. This has frequently been interpreted as either polytheism or pantheism, though these labels are far too simplistic. In the Vedic view, there is no one God or Goddess for all humanity, but there is one Reality, or Truth, for all beings. There is one way to that Truth, yet it comprises within itself many diverse approaches, possibly as many as there are human individuals who seek to realize that sacred Singularity.

The Vedic view reflects the actual universe in which we live. There is not just one kind of food for all humanity, just one type of body for all individuals, or only a single language or form of art. At the same time, behind all our differences, we share certain commonalities of biological, psychological, and mental makeup, as well as an identical spiritual potential. Above all, we are one in our urge to seek happiness, even though that urge is seldom understood and therefore is channeled into unproductive aspirations, which are bound to ultimately bring unhappiness.

In the age-old Vedic tradition, we have the perennial philosophy in its most pristine form available today. The *Vedas* and *Upanishads*, which are anciently treated as sacred revelations, are indeed a tremendous treasure.

The Sacredness of the Individual

Acceptance of the need for diversity culminates in a recognition of the significance of the individual. According to the Vedic view, the living individual, as the bearer of the sacred flame of consciousness, is in essence one with the Divine. Truth is a matter of individual direct experience unmediated by any authority, dogma, or belief.

Therefore understanding the deep spirituality of the *Vedas* brings us back to understanding ourselves. According to the *Upanishads*, Self-knowledge (*atma-jnana*) is the highest form of knowledge. This implies that culture itself should be based upon such Self-knowledge. Even knowledge of God, or theology, does not have this importance. For, if we know God but do not know ourselves, the God we know is but a conceptual construct, a product of our imagination. If we truly know ourselves, we know the Divine (not merely the Creator God) as our innermost reality.

Yet Self-knowledge is not mere psychological understanding, or insight into our personal or emotional history. It is not merely an exercise of our memory but knowing the singular Being as it reveals itself in and through consciousness, which is eternal and transcends all outward and transient identities, including the I-am-the-body idea, which breeds only division and death. Authentic Self-knowledge is unmediated knowledge, or realization, of our true identity beyond the mind-body complex and its limitations in time and space.

The Homogeneity of Humanity and Its History

Our human species is both singular and plural. There is incredible ethnic and cultural variation, and yet we are one species with a shared history. But what is our human history? Is it a history of political struggles and wars, intellectual achievements and technological advances? This is what the modern, materialistic view of history paints for us: a history devoid of love, excluding the world of Nature, and not recognizing any contact with spiritual beings outside of the human sphere.

Or is ours a history of searching for the eternal, our transcendental identity? It is this second view that we find abundantly expressed in the perennial philosophy of the *Vedas*. Here humanity is portrayed not so much as progressing in time but as seeking to transcend time. Time, which is death, is the limit that we are all struggling to overcome.

The question is: Has our contemporary culture, which has not produced any legitimate way to directly know what is beyond death, succeeded in making adequate allowance for our innermost impulse and need? Is material happiness sufficient for the human individual who aspires to fulfill his or her greatest potential? Or does our soul, after tasting all that the modern world has to offer, still cry out for something more enduring and real?

These are the questions that force themselves upon us when we study the *Vedas* anew, without the bias of Western superiority. Our attachment to a purely mundane sense of history made in the image of our present materialistic culture; our ignorance of the deeper levels of consciousness; our sole reliance on the outer world for contacting reality; our tremendous isolation from Nature; our turning God into a ploy for political or economic exploitation, including genocide and terrorism; our utter disregard for the sacred presence—all oblige us to take another, more scrutinizing look at ourselves. By comparison with the sublime values and ideals of the primordial tradition ours is a civilization steeped in ignorance, trapped in misperceptions, clouded in arrogance and prejudice, and greatly in need of reformation, if not spiritual revolution.

The new view of the *Vedas* espoused in this book is that modern humanity possesses a spiritual heritage that goes back to the dawn of civilized history. That heritage has maintained a living tradition of Self-realization to the present generation. Clearly, we must honor such a tradition and seek to benefit from it, whatever our background may be. There have been great teachers in this Vedic-Hindu tradition, like Sri Aurobindo or Swami Vivekananda, who, in modern times, have shown us the way to a true civilization. Many, like Swami Vivekananda or Paramahansa Yogananda, have come personally to the West to sow the seeds for a new world order—a world order that reintegrates our scientific accomplishments with higher spiritual values.

There are other great spiritual traditions in which the highest principles of the perennial philosophy have been kept alive, such as the Tibetan tradition or Chinese Taoism, and to which we can look for significant guidance.

The time has come for humanity to return to a reverential view of life. No Westerner has seen this more clearly, and demonstrated its truthfulness more convincingly, than Albert Schweitzer, who stated:

> *Defined from outside and quite empirically, complete civilization consists in realizing all possible progress in discovery and invention and in the arrangements of human society, and seeing that they work together for the spiritual perfecting of individuals which is the real and final object of civilization. Reverence for life is in a position to complete this conception of civilization and to build its foundations on what lies at the core of our being. This it does by defining what is meant by the spiritual perfecting of man, and making it consist in reaching the spirituality of an ever deepening reverence for life.*[11]

We must grant reverence not only to the sacred presence in Nature but also in humanity. It is in this way that we may reconnect with the our spiritual forebears, who honored that presence and made it part of their daily lives and the basis of their cultures and traditions.

Such a return to reverence is not to be equated with an atavistic retreat into the past or a fall into superstition. It does not require that we become primitive or throw away the gains of science and technology. It is a matter of restoration and reintegration, of completing the circle. It means, above all, integrating the modern world into the eternal sacred Reality.

Let it be clear that this reappraisal of the past is not merely a spiritual issue. It is a matter of a more objective and rational examination as well, and one that allows us to establish a truer communication with ancient and traditional peoples. It also helps us see that there was more scientific knowledge, more literary greatness, and more philosophical depth in the ancient world than we have tended to assume.

We must now cast off such stereotypes as "primitives," "savages," or "heathens," by which we have dismissed ancient and traditional cultures. If we continue to take recourse to such labels, it is because there is much in our past that we are avoiding in order to blind ourselves to our present condition. Our political, economic, and sociological interpretations of history may all be part of a smoke screen whereby we fail to deal with the real issues of life, which is our connection with the universe as a whole, not as an outer reality, but as part of our own consciousness.

The fact that we have so deplorably misinterpreted a civilization as spiritually great as the Vedic shows how much we need to purge our vision. Such a reappraisal is just beginning. It will take some years to get established in the academic world, and perhaps even decades to gain wider acceptance. In the meantime we as individuals must ask the fundamental questions that are central to the primordial tradition. The quality of our lives and our common future depend on our answers.

NOTES

Preface

1 G. Bibby, *Looking for Dilmun* (New York: New American Library, 1974), p. 161.

Chapter 1

1 See T. S. Kuhn, *The Structure of Scientific Revolutions* (Chicago and London: University of Chicago Press, 2nd enlarged ed., 1970).

2 See J. A. West, *Serpent in the Sky: The High Wisdom of Ancient Egypt* (Wheaton, IL: Theosophical Publishing House, 1993).

3 See B. de Maillet, *Description of Egypt, Containing Many Strange Observations on the Ancient and Modern Geography of this Country, on Its Ancient Monuments, Its Morals, Customs, the Religion of Its Inhabitants, on Its Animals, Trees, Plants* . . . (Paris, 1735).

4 See M. Rice, *Egypt's Making: The Origins of Ancient Egypt 5000-2000 BC* (London and New York: Routledge, 1991).

5 P. W. Lapp, *Biblical Archaeology and History* (Cleveland, OH: World Publishing, 1969), p. 2.

6 Ibid., p. 32.

7 J. Soustelle, *The Olmecs: The Oldest Civilization in Mexico* (Norman, OK: University of Oklahoma Press, 1985), p. 7.

8 See P. Tompkins, *Mysteries of the Mexican Pyramids* (New York: Harper & Row, 1976).

9 J. A. West, *Serpent in the Sky*, p. 97.

10 See S. Kramrisch, *The Hindu Temple*, 2 vols. (Calcutta: University of Calcutta Press, 1946). See also G. Michell, *The Hindu Temple: An Introduction to its Meaning and Form* (New York: Harper & Row, 1978).

[11] See L. Schele and M. E. Miller, *The Blood of Kings: Dynasty and Ritual in Maya Art* (Forth Worth, TX: Kimbell Art Museum, 1986); L. Schele and D. Freidel, *A Forest of Kings: The Untold Story of the Ancient Maya* (New York: William Morrow, 1990); D. Freidel, L. Schele, and J. Parker, *Maya Cosmos: Three Thousand Years on the Shaman's Path* (New York: William Morrow, 1993).

[12] A. Toynbee, *Civilization on Trial and The World and the West* (New York: Meridian Books, 1958), p. 257.

Chapter 2

[1] M. Monier-Williams, *Hinduism* (London: Society for Promoting Christian Knowledge, 1894), p. 14.

[2] Hindus make a distinction between *shruti* ("heard" or revealed) literature and *smriti* ("remembered") literature. To the former category belong the *Vedas, Brahmanas, Aranyakas*, and *Upanishads*. Although the *Bhagavad-Gita* speaks of itself as an *Upanishad*, it belongs to the *smriti* category.

[3] A rare exception is Gordon Childe, who remarked about the *Rig-Veda*: "This priceless document also furnishes precious historical data." V. G. Childe, *The Aryans: A Study of Indo-European Origins* (New York: Barnes & Noble, 1993), p. 30.

[4] W. Keller, *The Bible As History*, rev. ed. (New York: William Morrow, 1981), p. 23.

[5] A. L. Basham, *The Origins and Development of Classical Hinduism*, ed. by K. G. Zysk (Boston, MA: Beacon Press, 1989), p. 7.

[6] T. Berry, *Religions of India: Hinduism, Yoga, Buddhism* (New York: Bruce Publ. Co., 1971), pp. 15-16.

[7] Ibid., pp. 18-19.

[8] R. Guénon, *Introduction to the Study of the Hindu Doctrines* (London: Luzac, 1945), p. 38.

[9] Ibid., p. 38.

[10] W. Doniger O'Flaherty, *The Rig Veda* (London: Penguin Books, 1981), p. 19.

[11] One of the authors of the present book (David Frawley) has taken up this task in his work *Wisdom of the Ancient Seers: Selected Mantras From the Rig Veda* (Salt Lake City, UT: Passage Press, 1992).

[12] J. Miller, *The Vedas: Harmony, Meditation, and Fulfilment* (London: Rider, 1974), p. xxxiv. We have altered the spelling of the word *rsis* to *rishis*.

[13] Ibid., p. 10.

[14] Sri Aurobindo, *On the Veda* (Pondicherry, India: Sri Aurobindo Ashram, 1956, repr. 1964), p. 1.

[15] Ibid., p. 7.

[16] R. N. Walsh and D. H. Shapiro, *Beyond Health and Normality* (New York: Van Nostrand Reinhold, 1983), p. 53.

[17] R. N. Walsh, *The Spirit of Shamanism* (Los Angeles: J. P. Tarcher, 1990), p. 5.

[18] Ibid., p. 5.

[19] J. Miller, *The Vision of Cosmic Order in the Vedas* (London: Routledge & Kegan Paul, 1985), p. 10.

[20] See, e.g., S. Radhakrishnan, *Indian Philosophy*, vol. 1 (London: Allen & Unwin, 1951), p. 72.

[21] W. Doniger O'Flaherty, *The Rig Veda*, p. 15.

[22] J. N. Farquhar, *An Outline of the Religious Literature of India* (Delhi: Banarsidass, 1984), p. 18. This is a straight reprint of the 1920 edition.

[23] V. A. Smith, *The Oxford History of India* (London: Oxford University Press, 1954), p. 52.

[24] S. Radhakrishnan, *Indian Philosophy*, vol. 1, p. 123.

[25] In the *Rig-Veda* (II.1), the eight principal priests are enumerated as being the *hotri*, *potri*, *ritvij*, *neshtri*, *prashastri*, *adhvaryu*, *brahmana*, and *grihapati*, with the *samaga* (*udgatri*) being mentioned separately in II.43.1.

[26] Cited in H. V. Glasenapp, *Die Literaturen Indiens* (Stuttgart: Alfred Kröner Verlag, 1951), p. 75.

[27] See J. Eggeling, *The Śatapatha Brahmana*, Part 1 (Delhi: Motilal Banarsidass, 1988), p. ix: "For wearisome prolixity of exposition, characterised by dogmatic assertion and a flimsy symbolism rather than by serious reasoning, these works [the *Brahmanas*] are perhaps not equalled anywhere; unless, indeed, it be by the speculative vapourings of the Gnostics."

[28] See, for instance, H. W. Tull, *The Vedic Origins of Karma: Cosmos as Man in Ancient Indian Myth and Ritual* (Albany, NY: SUNY Press, 1989) and Walter O. Kaelber, *Tapta Marga: Asceticism and Initiation in Vedic India* (Albany, NY: SUNY Press, 1989).

[29] Cited in German in A. Hillebrandt, *Upanishaden: Altindische Weisheit* (Düsseldorf-Köln, Germany: Diederichs Verlag, 1964), p. 8.

[30] A. Kaplan, *The New World of Philosophy* (New York: Vintage Books, 1961), p. 203.

[31] M. Müller, *The Six Systems of Indian Philosophy* (London: Longmans, Green & Co., 1916), p. xiv. First published in 1899, this work was reissued as a new edition in 1903 and was reprinted in 1912 and again in 1916.

[32] R. E. Hume, *The Thirteen Principal Upanishads* (London: Oxford University Press, 1921), p. vii.

[33] S. Radhakrishnan, *The Principal Upanisads* (London: Allen & Unwin/New York: Humanities Press, 1953), pp. 18-19.

[34] M. Müller, *The Six Systems of Indian Philosophy*, p. 34.

[35] Ibid., p. 35.

[36] See A. L. Basham, *Classical Hinduism*, p. 7.

Chapter 3

[1] See M. Howard, *The Occult Conspiracy* (Rochester, VT: Destiny Books, 1989).

[2] J. P. Mallory, *In Search of the Indo-Europeans: Language, Archaeology and Myth* (New York: Thames and Hudson, 1991), p. 125.

[3] M. Müller, "The Veda," *Chips from a German Workshop*, vol. I (New York: Charles Scribner's, 1900), p. 63. The essay was written in 1853.

[4] V. G. Childe, *The Aryans: A Study of Indo-European Origins* (New York: Barnes & Noble, 1993), p. 4.

[5] See M. Gimbutas, "The Indo-Europeans: Archaeological problems," *American Anthropologist*, vol. 65, pp. 815-836. Also by the same author: "The Three Waves of the Kurgan People into Old Europe," *Journal of Indo-European Studies*, vol. 5, pp. 277-338; "The Kurgan Wave Migration (c. 3400-3200 B.C.) into Europe and the Following Transformation of Culture," *Journal of Near Eastern Studies*, vol. 8, pp. 273-315; *The Goddesses and Gods of Old Europe—6500-3500 B.C.: Myths and Cult Images* (Berkeley and Los Angeles: University of California Press, 1982); *The Language of the Goddess* (San Francisco: HarperSanFrancisco, 1991).

[6] See C. Renfrew, *Archaeology & Language: The Puzzle of Indo-European Origins* (Cambridge: Cambridge University Press, 1987). Also by the same author: "Archaeology and Linguistics: Some Preliminary Issues," in *When Worlds Collide: Indo-Europeans and Pre-Indo-Europeans*, ed. by T. L. Markey and J. A. C. Greppin (Ann Arbor, MI: Karoma Publishers, 1990), pp. 15-24.

[7] The Russian scholar Igor M. Diakonoff has questioned the equation of U-ru-w-na-as-si-il with Varuna. According to him, *urwa-na* "is probably the Hurrian plural of the Indo-Iranian mythological term *urwan* 'soul' (preserved in Old Iranian)." He also notes that the treaty lists many deities, with the Aryan Gods appearing near the bottom of the list, which indicates their relative unimportance. See I. M. Diakonoff, "Language Contacts in the Caucasus and the Near East," in *When Worlds Collide*, p. 64.

[8] J. P. Mallory, *In Search of the Indo-Europeans*, p. 117.

[9] S. Piggott, *Prehistoric India* (Harmondsworth, England: Penguin Books, 1950), p. 246.

[10] See, e.g., D. Clarke, *Analytical Archaeology* (London: Methuen, 1968).

[11] See M. Zvelebil and K. V. Zvelebil, "Agricultural Transition, 'Indo-European Origins' and the Spread of Farming," in *When Worlds Collide*, pp. 237-266.

[12] M. Gimbutas, *The Goddesses and Gods of Old Europe*, p. 9.

[13] Ibid., p. 9.

[14] M. Gimbutas, *The Language of the Goddess*, p. xxi.

[15] C. Renfrew, "Archaeology and Linguistics" in *When Worlds Collide*, p. 23.

Chapter 4

[1] N. Marinatos, *Minoan Religion: Ritual, Image, and Symbol* (Columbia, SC: University of South Carolina Press, 1993), p. 39.

[2] Ibid., pp. 39-40.

[3] See S. R. Rao, *Dawn and Devolution of the Indus Civilization* (New Delhi: Aditya Prakashan, 1991), p. 162.

[4] See H. H. Hicks and R. N. Anderson, "Analysis of an Indo-European Vedic Aryan Head—4th Millennium B.C.," *Journal of Indo-European Studies*, vol. 18 (1990), pp. 425-446.

[5] V. G. Childe, *The Aryans: A Study of Indo-European Origins* (New York: Barnes & Noble, 1993), p. 30.

[6] S. Piggott, *Prehistoric India* (Harmondsworth, England: Penguin Books, 1950), pp. 200-201.

[7] J. M. Kenoyer, "The Indus Valley Tradition of Pakistan and Western India," *Journal of World Prehistory*, vol. 5, no. 4 (1991), p. 347.

[8] See S. Kak, "The Indus Tradition and the Indo-Aryans," *Mankind Quarterly*, vol. 32 (1992), pp. 195-213.

Chapter 5

[1] M. Wheeler, *The Indus Civilization*, 3rd ed. (Cambridge: Cambridge University Press, 1968), p. 131.

[2] B. Russell, *Mysticism and Logic* (Garden City, NY: Doubleday/Anchor Books, n.d.), p. 30.

[3] A. Toynbee, *Civilization on Trial, and The World and the West* (New York: Meridian Books, 1958), p. 1.

[4] This information was provided by Richard Heinberg, editor of *MuseLetter*.

[5] C. Pellegrino, *Unearthing Atlantis: An Archaeological Odyssey* (New York: Vintage Books, 1991), p. 246. See also the highly speculative book by I. Velikovsky, *Ages in Chaos* (London: Abacus Books, 1973).

[6] See C. L. Woolley, *The Sumerians* (New York: W. W. Norton, 1965), pp. 44-45.

[7] Various methods have been proposed for correlating the Mayan and the Gregorian calendars. The almost universally accepted method is that of Joseph T. Goodman, which was subsequently revised by Juan Martinez Hernández and J. Eric Thompson. The earlier method devised by Herbert J. Spinden yielded dates that were 260 years earlier than those arrived at by the Goodman-Martinez-Thompson (GMT) approach. The debate was settled by means of carbon-14 testing.

[8] See R. Heinberg, "Catastrophe, Collective Trauma, and the Origin of Civilization," *MuseLetter*, nos. 35 and 36 (November and December 1994).

[9] W. I. Thompson, *At the Edge of History* (New York: Harper Torchbooks, 1979), p. 175. In the original this sentence is in italics.

[10] Misplaced literalism in the interpretation of myths can be seen in the popular works of Immanuel Velikovsky and Zacharia Sitchkin. See, e.g., the former's *World's in Collision* (New York: Pocket Books, 1977) and the latter's *The Wars of Gods and Men* (New York: Avon Books, 1985).

[11] See V. N. Misra, "Research on the Indus Civilization: A Brief Review," *Eastern Anthropologist*, vol. 45 (1992), pp. 1-19. More than two-thirds of all the settlements have been found along the Sarasvati River and a majority of the remaining sites are in Uttar Pradesh and Gujarat; the Indus Valley proper has less than one hundred sites of a total of about 2,500.

[12] See H. P. Francfort, "Evidence for Harappan Irrigation System in Haryana and Rajasthan," *Eastern Anthropologist*, vol. 45 (1992), pp. 87-103.

[13] See R. N. Kak and S. Kak, "When was the Kashmir Valley Drained?" *Koshur Samachar*, vol. 39, no. 6 (1994), pp. 23-24.

[14] See J. M. Kenoyer, ed., *Old Problems and New Perspectives in the Archaeology of South Asia*, vol. 2 (Madison: Wisconsin Archaeological Reports, 1989).

[15] In the Madhyandina recension of the *Shatapatha-Brahmana*, translated by Julius Eggeling, the reference is I.4.1.14ff. In the Kanviya recension it is II.3.4.10ff.

Chapter 6

[1] J. Miller, *The Vedas: Harmony, Meditation and Fulfillment* (London: Rider, 1974), p. ix.

[2] The available oral traditions of the Australian aborigines may be much older than the Indic traditions, but they were not produced by a civilization in the strict sense of the word. Civilization, as understood here, involves cities and complex political and economic systems.

[3] M. Müller, *The Six Systems of Indian Philosophy* (New York: Longmans, Green & Co., 1916), pp. 34-35.

[4] Ibid., p. 34.

[5] See D. Frawley, *Gods, Sages and Kings: Vedic Secrets of Ancient Civilization*, Part III: Vedic Astronomy (Salt Lake City, UT: Passage Press, 1991).

[6] Ibid. pp. 180-184.

[7] H. Kulke and D. Rothermund, *A History of India* (London: Routledge, 1990), p. 34.

[8] See D. Frawley, *Gods, Sages and Kings*, pp. 185-191. Intriguingly, this date takes us back to the beginnings of the Indic civilization at the town of Mehrgarh.

[9] See ibid., pp. 45-67, where nearly a hundred references to the ocean and to maritime activities are listed from the *Rig-Veda* alone.

[10] See, e.g., *Rig-Veda* VII.3.7; 15.14; VI.48.8; I.166.8.

[11] See D. Frawley, *Gods, Sages and Kings*, pp. 327-330, for a discussion of Vedic cities.

[12] Ibid., pp. 104-113.

[13] Ibid., p. 251.

[14] Interestingly, in a hymn that probably belongs to a later portion of the *Rig-Veda* (I.133.3), reference is made to the ruined city of Vailasthanaka, home of many

sorceresses, whom God Indra is petitioned to strike down. We do not known whether the city was the victim of war in the precataclysm era or became derelict as a result of the great migration eastward after the cataclysm, or even whether we have here merely a metaphor. In late Vedic literature, such as the *Brahmanas*, a number of abandoned cities with Sanskrit names are mentioned, which could be Harappan. Several scholars have related Harappa to the city of Hari-Yupuya mentioned in the *Rig-Veda* (VI.27.5). However, already Sir Mortimer Wheeler noted that this identification "is not susceptible to proof and has therefore no serious value." M. Wheeler, *The Indus Civilization* (Cambridge, England: Cambridge University Press, 1968), p. 29.

[15] According to one hymn of the *Rig-Veda* (VII.18.25), Divodasa was the father of Sudas, but he is usually called Paijavana or "son of Pijavana." Divodasa appears to have been one of his ancestors.

[16] See I. W. Ardika and P. Bellwood, "Sembiran: The Beginnings of Indian Contact with Bali," *Antiquity*, no. 65 (1991), pp. 221-232.

[17] See, e.g., G. Ashe et al., eds., *The Quest for America* (New York: Praeger Publishers, 1971); B. Fell, *America B.C.: Ancient Settlers in the New World* (New York: Pocket Books/Wallaby Books, 1978); G. E. R. Deacon, *Seas, Maps and Men* (London: Crescent Press, 1962); and Z. Herman, *Peoples, Seas and Ships* (New York: Putnam, 1967).

[18] G. Bibby, *Looking for Dilmun* (New York: Mentor Books, 1974), p. 332.

[19] S. N. Kramer, *The Sumerians: Their History, Culture, and Character* (Chicago, IL: University of Chicago Press, 1963), p. 281.

[20] Ibid., p. 283.

[21] Bibby has suggested that the Mesopotamian name *Meluhha* could be a translation of the Sanskrit word *mleccha*, which in later times came to mean "foreigner" or someone speaking an unintelligible language, notably Greek. In the *Brahmanas* and the *Mahabharata* epic it was applied to the people of Western India, who were regarded as unorthodox in their religious practices. At any rate, this word made its first appearance at the time of the *Brahmanas* and is not pure Sanskrit, which feasibly could imply that the *Brahmanas* stem from the Harappan period.

[22] S. Piggott, *Prehistoric India* (Harmondsworth, England: Penguin Books, 1950), p. 201.

[23] S. Kramrisch, *The Presence of Śiva* (Princeton, NJ: Princeton University Press, 1981), p. 11.

[24] See I. Mahadevan, "The Cult Object on Unicorn Seals: A Sacred Filter," *Puratattva*, nos. 13-14 (1983).

[25] See M. K. Dhavalikar and S. Atre, "The Fire Cult and Virgin Sacrifice: Some Harappan Rituals," in J. M. Kenoyer, ed., *Old Problems and New Perspectives in the Archaeology of South Asia*, Wisconsin Archaeological Reports, vol. 2 (Madison: University of Wisconsin, 1989).

Chapter 7

[1] See, for example, *Rig-Veda* V.73.10.

[2] See C. W. Ceram, *Gods, Graves and Scholars* (New York: Alfred Knopf, 1952), p. 318.

[3] See F. Singh, *Sindhughati ki lipi mein brahmanon aur upanishadon ke pratik* (Jodhpur: Rajasthan Oriental Research Institute, 1969).

[4] Some researchers believe that the term *eka-pad* occurring in the *Rig-Veda* (II.31.6) is a reference to the unicorn. However, the word means "one-footed" rather than "one-horned" and here clearly refers to the sun.

[5] See P. V. Pathak, "The Indus Culture Seal of Three Forms and Seven Figures as Pictorial Representation of AV Hymn IV.37," *Puratattva*, no. 21 (1992), pp. 59-64.

[6] See G. R. Hunter, *Script of Harappa and Mohenjo-Daro and Its Connection with Other Scripts* (London: Kegan Paul, Trench, Trubner & Co., 1934).

[7] See J. E. Mitchiner, *Studies in the Indus Valley Inscriptions* (New Delhi: Oxford and IBH, 1978).

[8] See S. Kak, "Indus Writing," *Mankind Quarterly*, vol. 30 (1989), pp. 113-118. See also S. Kak, "A Frequency Analysis of the Indus Script," *Cryptologia*, vol. 12, no. 3 (1988), pp. 129-143.

[9] Agglutination signifies that all prepositions and modifiers are tacked on to a given noun to form a single word.

[10] See W. Hinz, *The Lost World of Elam: Re-Creation of a Vanished Civilization* (New York: New York University Press, 1973), pp. 21-22.

Chapter 8

[1] J. Jarrige and R. H. Meadow, "The Antecedents of Civilization in the Indus Valley, *Scientific American*, vol. 243 (1980), p. 131.

[2] An acre is 4,840 square yards or 0.405 hectares. There are 258.999 hectares in a square mile. Thus the area of 500 acres at Mehrgarh totals 0.78 square miles.

[3] J. Mellaart, "Çatal Hüyük—A Neolithic Town in Anatolia," in *New Aspects of Archaeology*, ed. by Mortimer Wheeler (New York: McGraw-Hill, 1976).

[4] On the evolution of human consciousness, see J. Gebser, *The Ever-Present Origin*, transl. by N. Barstad with A. Mickunas (Athens, OH: Ohio University Press, 1985). See also G. Feuerstein, *Structures of Consciousness* (Lower Lake, CA: Integral Publishing, 1987).

[5] R. Thapar, *A History of India* (Harmondsworth, England: Penguin Books, 1966), p. 34.

[6] Ibid., p. 34.

[7] J. Jarrige and R. H. Meadow, "The Antecedents of Civilization in the Indus Valley," *Scientific American*, p. 126.

[8] See S. P. Gupta, "Longer Chronology of the Indus-Sarasvati Civilization," *Puratattva: Bulletin of the Indian Archaeological Society*, no. 23 (1992-1993), pp. 21-29.

Chapter 9

[1] The past participle of the verbal root *vas* is *ushita* ("dwelled, existed"). In the *Atharva-Veda* (X.2.31), the word *purusha* is explained in a further metaphoric way. Here *pur* ("town") is said to be the human body with its nine orifices (two eyes, two ears, two nostrils, mouth, anus, and urethra) representing the "gates" to the outside world. The same verse also mentions eight wheels (*cakra*) associated with the town or citadel of the body, though does not explain what these are.

[2] Sri Aurobindo, *On the Veda* (Pondicherry, India: Sri Aurobindo Ashram, 1956), p. 4.

[3] C. Renfrew, *Archaeology and Language: The Puzzle of Indo-European Origins* (New York: Cambridge University Press, 1990), p. 287.

[4] See D. Anthony, D. Y. Telegin, and D. Brown, "The Origin of Horseback Riding," *Scientific American* (December 1991), pp. 94-100.

[5] See J. Shaffer, "Reurbanization: The Eastern Punjab and Beyond," *Urban Form and Meaning in South Asia: The Shaping of Cities from Prehistoric to Precolonial Times*, ed. by H. Spodek and D. M. Srinivasan (Washington, DC: National Gallery of Art, 1983).

Chapter 10

[1] J. Needham, "The Dialogue Between Asia and Europe," in *The Glass Curtain*

Between Asia and Europe, ed. by Raghavan Iyer (London: Oxford University Press, 1965), p. 296. This is the revised version of a presidential address to the Britain-China Friendship Association given in 1955.

2 See G. Feuerstein's forthcoming book *The Yoga Tradition: Its History, Literature, Philosophy, and Practice*. This is a thoroughly revised and expanded edition of *Yoga: The Technology of Ecstasy*, published in 1989.

3 A. Kaplan, *The New World of Philosophy* (New York: Vintage Books, 1961), pp. 227-228.

4 Paramahansa Yogananda, *Autobiography of a Yogi* (Los Angeles: Self-Realization Fellowship, 1987), p. 557.

5 See, e.g., D. Frawley, *Gods, Sages and Kings: Vedic Secrets of Ancient Civilization* (Salt Lake City, UT: Passage Press, 1991), pp. 203-236.

6 See, e.g., *Rig-Veda* I.5.3; I.30.11; X.114.9. The terms *yogya* and *yojana* apparently are used as synonyms of *yoga*.

7 Sri Aurobindo, *On the Veda* (Pondicherry: Sri Aurobindo Ashram, 1964), p. 38.

8 Ibid., p. 384.

9 See Paramahansa Yogananda, *Autobiography of a Yogi*, p. 96.

10 Regrettably, this criticism also applies in part to the earlier works on Yoga by one of the present writers (Georg Feuerstein), which espouse the Aryan invasion model. This error will be corrected in all revised editions of those publications. However, Feuerstein has always favored a spiritual interpretation of the *Vedas*, as is clear from the chapter "Some Notes on Rigvedic Interpretation" in *A Reappraisal of Yoga*, coauthored with the British Vedicist Jeanine Miller and originally published in 1971. This long out-of-print work included the following pertinent observation: "After a whole century of Vedic studies, Western interpretation and translations of the sacred scriptures of ancient India, and in particular of the *Rigveda*, their fountain source, still remain extremely far from satisfactory. Many prejudices, partly born of speculations about evolution, have militated against any deeper insight being directed into, or appreciation of, the philosophical thought underlying Vedic literature." (p. 48)

11 One of the few scholars to challenge the non-Aryan origin of Yoga was the German indologist and Yoga researcher J. W. Hauer. In his book *Der Yoga* (Stuttgart, Germany: Kohlhammer Verlag, 1958), he tried to show that Yoga has its roots in the Indo-Iranian world and that the Aryans brought yogic teachings with them to India around 2000-1500 B.C. He was half right. Yoga was an Aryan creation, but the Aryans, as we are arguing in the present work, were indigenous to India.

[12] No detailed study of the beginnings of Yoga exists. In addition to J. W. Hauer's work cited in note 11 and his out-of-print monograph *Vratya* (Stuttgart, Germany: Kohlhammer Verlag, 1927), both of which contain many interesting details, there are only a few general and often primarily speculative discussions. See, e.g., Thomas McEvilley, "An Archaeology of Yoga," *Res*, vol. 1 (Spring 1981), pp. 44-77; Jean Filliozat, "Les origines d'une technique mystique indienne," *Revue Philosophique*, no. 136 (1946), pp. 208-220; and Mircea Eliade, *Yoga: Immortality and Freedom* (Princeton, NJ: Princeton University Press, 1970), especially pp. 353-358.

[13] An original and empathetic treatment of the symbolic, figurative language of the *Rig-Veda* is Willard Johnson's *Poetry and Speculation in the Rg Veda* (Berkeley, CA: University of California Press, 1980).

[14] J. N. Powell, *Mandalas: The Dynamics of Vedic Symbolism* (Los Angeles: Wisdom Garden Books, 1980), p. 88.

[15] Sri Aurobindo, *On the Veda* (Pondicherry, India: Sri Aurobindo Ashram, 1964), p. 377.

[16] For an examination of these Vedic deities in this light see, e.g., David Frawley, *Wisdom of the Ancient Seers* (Salt Lake City, UT: Passage Press, 1992).

[17] See J. Miller, *The Vedas: Harmony, Meditation, and Fulfilment* (London: Rider, 1974).

[18] Ibid., p. 48.

[19] Ibid., p. 49.

[20] See D. Frawley, *Wisdom of the Ancient Seers*, Chapter 5, "Surya, Intelligence, the Solar Self."

[21] Sri Aurobindo, *On the Veda*, p. 323.

[22] See M. Eliade, *Yoga: Immortality and Freedom* (Princeton, NJ: Princeton University Press, 1973), p. 362.

Chapter 11

[1] See M. Polanyi, *Personal Knowledge: Toward a Post-Critical Philosophy* (London: Routledge & Kegan Paul, 1973); P. Feyerabend, *Against Method* (London: Verso Books, 1978) and *Farewell to Reason* (London: Verso Books, 1987).

[2] J. D. Bernal, *Science in History*, vol. 1 (*The Emergence of Science*) (Harmondsworth, England: Penguin, 1969), p. 3.

3 See A. Marshack, *The Roots of Civlization* (New York: McGraw-Hill, 1972).

4 See A. Seidenberg, "The Origin of Mathematics," *Archive for History of Exact Sciences*, vol. 18 (1978), pp. 301-342; S. Kak, *The Astronomical Code of the Rgveda* (New Delhi: Aditya, 1994).

5 See D. Bohm, *Wholeness and the Implicate Order* (London: Routledge & Kegan Paul, 1980).

6 Ibid., p. 209.

7 For a detailed study of the sexual symbolism of the *Vedas*, see S. A. Dange, *Sexual Symbolism from the Vedic Ritual* (Jawahar Nagar, India: Ajanta Publications, 1979).

8 J. Gonda, *Vedic Literature* (Wiesbaden, Germany: Otto Harrassowitz, 1975), pp. 362-363.

9 See D. Frawley, *Gods, Sages, and Kings* (Salt Lake City, UT: Passage Press, 1991).

10 See S. C. Kak, "Astronomy of the Vedic Altars and the Rigveda," *Mankind Quarterly*, vol. 33 (1992), pp. 43-55; "Astronomy of the Vedic Altars," *Vistas in Astronomy*, vol. 36 (1993), pp. 117-140; "Planetary Periods from the Rigvedic Code," *Mankind Quarterly*, vol. 33 (1993), pp. 433-442; "The Structure of the Rigveda," *Indian Journal of History of Science*, vol. 28 (1993), pp. 71-79.

11 See S. C. Kak and D. Frawley, "Further Observations on the Rigvedic Code," *Mankind Quarterly*, vol. 33 (1992), pp. 163-170.

12 See D. Frawley, "The Planets in Vedic Literature," *Indian Journal of the History of Science*, vol. 29 (1994).

13 See R. G. Bauval, *The Orion Mystery: Unlocking the Secrets of the Pyramids* (New York: Crown, 1994).

14 See J. B. Sellers, *The Death of Gods in Ancient Egypt* (Harmondsworth, England: Penguin Books, 1992) and R. A. Schwaller de Lubicz, *Sacred Science: The King of Pharaonic Theocracy* (New York: Inner Traditions International, 1982).

15 Pururavas was the son of Ila, who was the offspring of Manu, the progenitor of the human race in the present world cycle. The name is composed of the words *puru* (meaning "full" or "abundant") and *ravas* (meaning "roaring"), thus referring to someone who shouts or yells a great deal.

16 See A. Seidenberg, "The Origin of Mathematics," *Archive for History of Exact Sciences*, vol. 18 (1978), pp. 301-342.

[17] See E. Burgess, "Translation of Surya Siddhanta," *Journal of American Oriental Society*, vol. 6 (1860), pp. 141-498; reprinted as *The Surya Siddhanta*, edited by P. Gangooly (Delhi: Motilal Banarsidass, 1989).

[18] A. L. Basham, *The Wonder That Was India* (London: Fontana, 1971), p. 502.

[19] J. Filliozat, "The Expansion of Indian Medicine Abroad," in *India's Contribution to World Thought and Culture*, edited by Lokesh Chandra (Madras, 1970).

[20] However, the discovery of the importance of the left hemisphere in speech was made by Paul Broca as early as 1864.

[21] Sri Aurobindo, 1910, quoted in J. E. Bogen, "The Other Side of the Brain. VII: Some Educational Aspects of Hemispheric Specialization," *UCLA Educator*, no. 17 (1975), pp. 24-32.

[22] M. Eliade, *Patanjali and Yoga* (New York: Schocken Books, 1975), pp. 58-59.

[23] This Vedic *purusha* image has sometimes been used to justify the caste system. However, as one of the present authors (Subhash Kak) has noted elsewhere: "If man is made in the image of the cosmic person from different parts of whose body the various castes emerged, then clearly each human being has an element of each caste in him." Besides, the fourfold division of Vedic society represents an archetypal ideal rather than actual social reality. The four estates (rather than castes) should therefore not be thought of as a rigid structure immune to change or open to political exploitation. See S. Kak, *India at Century's End: Essays on History and Politics* (New Delhi: Voice of India, 1994), p. 15.

[24] M. Eliade, *Yoga: Immortality and Freedom* (Princeton, NJ: Princeton University Press, 1970), p. xx.

[25] See, e.g., *Rig-Veda* X.129, X.72, and X.81.

[26] Sri Aurobindo, *The Life Divine*, vol. 1 (Pondicherry: Sri Aurobindo Ashram, 1977), p. 3.

[27] A. L. Basham, *The Wonder That Was India*, p. 390.

Chapter 12

[1] See G. S. Hawkins, *Stonehenge Decoded* (London: Fontana Books, 1970).

[2] See W. L. Wittry, *Summary Report on 1978 Investigations of Circle No. 2 of the Woodhenge, Cahokia Mounds State Historic Site* (Chicago: Department of Anthropology, University of Illinois at Chicago, 1980).

[3] See S. Kak, "Astronomy of the Vedic Altars," *Vistas in Astronomy*, vol. 36 (1993), pp. 117-140. See also by the same author *The Astronomical Code of the Rigveda* (New Delhi: Aditya, 1994).

[4] A. Daniélou, *Shiva and Dionysus: The Religion of Nature and Eros* (New York: Inner Traditions, 1984), p.45.

[5] See T. Heyerdahl, *The Maldive Mystery* (Bethesda, MD: Adler & Adler, 1986).

[6] See B. G. Tilak, *The Orion, or Researches into the Antiquity of the Vedas* (Poona, India: Tilak Brothers, 1893).

[7] See G. de Santillana and H. von Dechend, *Hamlet's Mill: An Essay on Myth & the Frame of Time* (Boston, MA: Gambit, 1969).

[8] S. Kramrisch, *The Presence of Śiva* (Princeton, NJ: Princeton University Press, 1981), p. 44.

[9] S. Bhattacharya, *Indian Theogony* (Cambridge, England: Cambridge University Press, 1970), p. 300.

[10] See G. Michell, *The Hindu Temple* (Chicago, IL: University of Chicago Press, 1988), pp. 71-72.

[11] S. Kramrisch, *The Presence of Śiva*, p. 270.

[12] *Saptarshi* or "Seven Seers" is composed of *sapta* (seven) and *rishi* (seer). For euphonic reasons, the Sanskrit letter *ṛ* (rendered as *ri* in nonacademic transliteration) is changed to *r* when preceded by the vowel *a*.

[13] In his classic *Vorlesungen über die Philosophie der Geschichte* (Lectures on the Philosophy of History), Hegel displays both intellectual brilliance and overweening prejudice, particularly in regard to India and her citizens. However, Hegel's bias did not prevent him from regarding the Indian peninsula as the "starting-point for the whole Western world." G. W. F. Hegel, *Vorlesungen über die Philosophie der Geschichte* (Stuttgart, Germany: Reclam, 1961), p. 215.

[14] A notable exception is F. E. Pargiter, *The Purana Text of the Dynasties of the Kali Age* (London: Oxford University Press, 1913), p. 75. Pargiter made a strong case that the current editions of the early *Puranas* were translated into Sanskrit from an original Prakrit language. These translations, together with the unsettled form of the script used at that time, led to the well-known inconsistencies in the Puranic records.

[15] R. M. Smith, *Dates and Dynasties in Earliest India* (Delhi: Banarsidass, 1973), p. 1. Unfortunately, while Smith gives credit to the Indic chroniclers for reasonable accuracy in their genealogical compilations, he prefers more recent dates for everything, based in part on his calculating each generation at an

average of twenty years. According to Smith, the great war of the Bharatas occurred around 975 B.C., which seems far too recent.

[16] R. May, *The Cry for Myth* (New York: W. W. Norton, 1991), p. 20.

[17] In addition to Jung and Campbell, the Swiss cultural historian Jean Gebser argued the past's effectiveness in the present very persuasively in his magnum opus *The Ever-Present Origin* (Athens, OH: Ohio University Press, 1985).

[18] C. G. Jung, *On the Nature of the Psyche* (Princeton, NJ: Princeton University Press, 1969), p. 127.

Chapter 13

[1] H. Zimmer, *Philosophies of India*, ed. by Joseph Campbell (New York: Meridian Books, 1978), p. 1. First publ. in English in 1951.

[2] G. W. F. Hegel, *Vorlesungen über die Philosophie der Geschichte* (Stuttgart, Germany: Reclam Verlag, 1961), p. 216.

[3] Other renowned German scholars favoring an Indic influence upon Pythagorean thought include Richard Garbe, Moritz Winternitz, and Alfred Weber. While some of the claims made by these researchers are too far-fetched, there is enough substance to their overall argument to warrant the hypothesis that Pythagoras was to some degree exposed to Indic ideas.

[4] V. A. Smith, *The Oxford History of India* (Oxford, England: Clarendon Press, 1958), pp. 90-91.

[5] *The Meditations of Marcus Aurelius*, transl. by George Long (Mount Vernon, NY: Peter Pauper Press, n.d.), p. 60.

[6] See, e.g., R. Baine Harris, ed., *Neoplatonism and Indian Thought* (Albany, NY: SUNY Press, 1982).

[7] H. E. Barnes, *An Intellectual and Cultural History of the Western World*, vol. 1 (New York: Dover Publications, 1965), p. 401.

[8] A. A. Macdonell, *A History of Sanskrit Literature* (London: Heinemann, 1900), p. 1.

[9] L. S. S. O'Malley, "General Survey," in *Modern India & The West: A Study of the Interaction of their Civilizations*, ed. by L. S. S. O'Malley (London: Oxford University Press, 1968), p. 801.

[10] See the detailed academic study by Wilhelm Halbfass, *India and Europe: An Essay in Understanding* (Albany, NY: SUNY Press, 1988), p. 75. See also

Ram Swarup, "Indo-European Encounter: An Indian Perspective," *Journal of Indian Council of Philosophical Research*, vol. 8, no. 2 (1991), pp. 75-96.

11 Swami Vivekananda in a letter to the editor of *Brahmavadin*, published in *The Mahratta* (July 26, 1896).

12 M. Müller, *India—What Can It Teach Us?* (London: Longmans, Green and Co., 1883), p. 29ff. Cited after Halbfass, *India and Europe*, p. 82.

13 See R. Tarnas, *The Passion of the Western Mind* (New York: Harmony Books, 1991), p. 403.

14 E. Schrödinger, *What Is Life?* (New York: Macmillan, 1965).

15 C. G. Jung, *Modern Man in Search of a Soul* (New York: Harvest Books, 1933), p. 216.

16 See, e.g., the valuable discussion of Renfrew's model by M. Zvelebil and K. V. Zvelebil, "Agricultural Transition, 'Indo-European Origins' and the Spread of Farming," in *When Worlds Collide: Indo-Europeans and Pre-Indo-Europeans*, ed. by T. L. Markey and J. A. C. Greppin (Ann Arbor, MI: Karoma Publishers, 1990), pp. 237ff.

17 T. Taylor, "The Gundestrup Cauldron," *Scientific American*, vol. 266, no. 3 (March 1992), p. 84.

18 Ibid., p. 89.

19 C. G. Jung, *Modern Man in Search of a Soul*, pp. 215-216.

20 See H. Zimmer, *Myths and Symbols in Indian Art and Civilization* (Princeton, NJ: Princeton University Press, 1972), pp. 219-221.

Chapter 14

1 P. L. Berger et al., *The Homeless Mind* (Harmondsworth, England: Penguin Books, 1973), p. 11.

2 Ibid., p. 166.

3 C. G. Jung, *Modern Man in Search of a Soul* (New York: Harvest Books, 1933), p. 200.

4 Ibid., p. 241.

5 R. Panikkar, *The Vedic Experience: Mantramanjari* (London: Darton, Longman & Todd, 1979), p. 9.

6 Ibid., p. 9.

[7] S. Wolpert, *India* (Berkeley: University of California Press, 1991), p. 74.

[8] Cited in H. v. Glasenapp, *Die Literaturen Indiens von ihren Anfängen bis zur Gegenwart* (Stuttgart: Kröner Verlag, 1961), p. 38. Translated from the German by Georg Feuerstein.

[9] A. Huxley, *The Perennial Philosophy* (London: Fontana Books, 1958), p. 9.

[10] See H. Smith, *Forgotten Truth: The Primordial Tradition* (New York: Harper Torchbooks, 1985) and *Beyond the Post-Modern Mind* (Wheaton, IL: Quest Books, 1989), esp. Chapter 3.

[11] A. Schweitzer, *Civilization and Ethics* (London: Unwin Books, 1961), p. 233. We would like to state that, though we wholeheartedly endorse Schweitzer's emphasis on reverence, we do not concur with his assessment of Indic philosophy, which he characterized in summary fashion as life-denying. The ideal of renunciation in India has many forms, including inner renunciation that does not necessitate a cave-dwelling existence. Moreover, reverence for life need not be absent in those who choose to live in seclusion.

SELECT BIBLIOGRAPHY

This bibliography includes books only. References to specialist articles are given in the notes.

Anirvan. *Buddhiyoga of the Gita and Other Essays*. Madras, India: Samata Books, 1991.

Ashe, G. *Dawn Behind the Dawn: A Search for the Earthly Paradise*. New York: Henry Holt, 1992.

Aurobindo, Sri. *Hymns to the Mystic Fire*. Pondicherry, India: Sri Aurobindo Ashram, 1970.

_____. *On the Veda*. Pondicherry, India: Sri Aurobindo Ashram, 1956.

_____. *The Synthesis of Yoga*. Pondicherry, India: Sri Aurobindo Ashram, 1970.

_____. *The Life Divine*. Pondicherry, India: Sri Aurobindo Ashram, 1970.

Aveni, A. F., ed. *World Archaeoastronomy*. Cambridge, England: Cambridge University Press, 1989.

Barnes, H. E. *An Intellectual and Cultural History of the Western World*. New York: Dover Publications, 1965. 3 vols.

Basham, A. *The Wonder That Was India*. New York: Grove Press, 1959.

Bauval, R. and A. Gilbert. *The Orion Mystery: Unlocking the Secrets of the Pyramids*. New York: Crown Publishers, 1994.

Berger, P. L. *The Homeless Mind*. Harmondsworth, England: Penguin Books, 1973.

Bernal, J. D. *Science in History*. Harmondsworth, England: Penguin Books, 1969. 4 vols.

Berry, T. *Religions of India: Hinduism, Yoga, Buddhism*. New York: Bruce Publ. Co., 1971.

Bhattacharya, S. *Indian Theogony*. Cambridge, England: Cambridge University Press, 1970.

Bibby, G. *Looking for Dilmun*. New York: Mentor Books, 1974.

Burgess, E. *The Surya Siddhanta*. Edited by P. Gangooly. Delhi: Motilal Banarsidass, 1989.

Campbell, J. *The Hero with a Thousand Faces*. Princeton, NJ: Princeton University Press, 1949.

Chandra, L., ed. *India's Contribution to World Thought and Culture*. Madras: Vivekananda Rock Memorial Committee, 1970.

Childe, V. G. *The Aryans: A Study of Indo-European Origins*. New York: Barnes & Noble, 1993.

Clarke, D. *Analytical Archaeology*. London: Methuen, 1968.

Dange, S. A. *Sexual Symbolism from the Vedic Ritual*. Jawahar Nagar, India: Ajanta Publications, 1979.

_____. *Pastoral Symbolism from the Rgveda*. Poona: University of Poona, 1970.

Daniélou, A. *Shiva and Dionysus: The Religion of Nature and Eros*. New York: Inner Traditions International, 1984.

_____. *The Gods of India*. New York: Inner Traditions International, 1985.

Eisler, R. *The Chalice and the Blade: Our History, Our Future*. San Francisco: Harper & Row, 1987.

Eliade, M. *Patanjali and Yoga*. New York: Schocken Books, 1975.

_____. *Yoga: Immortality and Freedom*. Princeton, NJ: Princeton University Press, 1970.

_____. *Shamanism*. Boston, MA: Routledge & Kegan Paul, 1964.

_____. *Myths, Dreams and Mysteries: The Encounter Between Contemporary Faiths and Archaic Reality*. London: Collins, 1968.

Elst, K. *Indigenous Indians: Agastya to Ambedkar*. New Delhi: Voice of India, 1993.

Farquhar, J. N. *An Outline of the Religious Literature of India*. Delhi: Motilal Banarsidass, 1984.

Faulkner, R. O. *The Ancient Egyptian Pyramid Texts*. Warminster, England: Aris & Phillips, 1993.

Feuerstein, G. *Wholeness or Transcendence? Ancient Lessons for the Emerging Global Civilization*. Burdett, NY: Larson Publications, 1992.

_____. *Sacred Paths: Essays on Wisdom, Love, and Mystical Realization*. Burdett, NY: Larson Publications, 1991.

_____. *The Yoga-Sutra of Patanjali: A New Translation and Commentary*. Rochester, VT: Inner Traditions, 1989.

_____. *The Bhagavad-Gita: Its Philosophy and Cultural Setting*. Wheaton, IL: Quest Books, 1983.

_____. *Structures of Consciousness*. Lower Lake, CA: Integral Publishing, 1987.

Feyerabend, P. *Against Method*. London: Verso Books, 1978.

_____. *Farewell to Reason*. London: Verso Books, 1987.

Frankfort, H. *Kingship and the Gods*. Chicago, IL: University of Chicago Press, 1978.

Frawley, D. *Gods, Sages, and Kings: Vedic Secrets of Ancient Civilization*. Salt Lake City, UT: Passage Press, 1991.

_____. *Wisdom of the Ancient Seers: Mantras of the Rig Veda*. Salt Lake City, UT: Passage Press, 1993.

_____. *From the River of Heaven: Hindu and Vedic Knowledge for the Modern Age*. Salt Lake City, UT: Passage Press, 1990.

_____. *The Myth of the Aryan Invasion of India*. New Delhi: Voice of India, 1994.

_____. *Hinduism, the Eternal Tradition—Sanatana Dharma*. Salt Lake City, UT: Passage Press, 1995.

Ghosh, E. *Studies on Rigvedic Deities: Astronomical and Metereological*. New Delhi: Cosmo Publications, 1983.

Gimbutas, M. *The Goddesses and Gods of Old Europe—6500-3500 B.C.: Myths and Cult Images*. Berkeley/Los Angeles: University of California Press, 1982.

_____. *The Language of the Goddess*. San Francisco: HarperSanFrancisco, 1991.

Glasenapp, H. v. *Die Literaturen Indiens*. Stuttgart: Alfred Kröner Verlag, 1951.

Goel, S. R. *History of Hindu-Christian Encounters*. New Delhi: Voice of India, 1989.

Gonda, J. *Vedic Literature*. Wiesbaden, Germany: Otto Harrassowitz, 1975.

_____. *Notes on Brahman*. Utrecht, Netherlands: J. L. Beyer, 1950.

Guénon, R. *Introduction to the Study of the Hindu Doctrines*. London: Luzac, 1945.

_____. *Formes traditionelles et cycles cosmiques*. Paris: Gallimard, 1982.

Hadingham, E. *Secrets of the Ice Age: The World of the Cave Artists*. New York: Walker, 1979.

Halbfass, W. *India and Europe: An Essay in Understanding*. Albany, NY: SUNY Press, 1988.

Hapgood, C. H. *Maps of the Ancient Sea Kings: Evidence of Advanced Civilization in the Ice Age*. London: Turnstone Books, 1979.

Harris, R. B., ed. *Neoplatonism and Indian Thought*. Albany, NY: SUNY Press, 1982.

Hauer, J. W. *Der Yoga*. Stuttgart, Germany: Kohlhammer Verlag, 1958.

Hawkins, G. S. *Stonehenge Decoded*. London: Fontana Books, 1970.

Hegel, G. W. F. *Vorlesungen über die Philosophie der Geschichte*. Stuttgart: Reclam, 1961.

Heyerdahl, T. *The Maldive Mystery*. Bethesda, MD: Adler and Adler, 1986.

Hillebrandt, A. *Upanishaden: Altindische Weisheit*. Düsseldorf-Köln, Germany: Diederichs Verlag, 1964.

Hinz, W. *The Lost World of Elam: Re-Creation of a Vanished Civilization*. New York: New York University Press, 1973.

Hopkins, E. W. *Epic Mythology*. Delhi: Banarsidass, repr. 1974.

Howard, M. *The Occult Conspiracy*. Rochester, VT: Destiny Books, 1989.

Hume, R. E. *The Thirteen Principal Upanishads*. London: Oxford University Press, 1921.

Hunter, G. R. *Script of Harappa and Mohenjo-Daro and Its Connection with Other Scripts*. London: Kegan Paul, Trench, Trubner & Co., 1934.

Huxley, A. *The Perennial Philosophy*. London: Fontana Books, 1958.

Johnson, W. *Poetry and Speculation in The Rg Veda*. Berkeley, CA: University of California Press, 1980.

Jung, C. G. *Modern Mind in Search of a Soul*. New York: Harvest Books, 1933.

_____. *Psychological Types*. Princeton, NJ: Princeton University Press, 1971.

Kaelber, W. O. *Tapta Marga: Asceticism and Initiation in Vedic India*. Albany, NY: SUNY Press, 1989.

Kak, S. *India at Century's End*. New Delhi: Voice of India, 1994.

_____. *The Astronomical Code of the Rgveda*. New Delhi: Aditya, 1994.

Kaplan, A. *The New World of Philosophy*. New York: Vintage Books, 1961.

Kenoyer, J. M., ed. *Old Problems and New Perspectives in the Archaeology of South Asia*. Wisconsin Archaeological Reports, vol. 2. Madison, WI: University of Wisconsin, 1989.

Kirk, G. S. *Myth: Its Meaning and Function in Ancient and Other Cultures*. Cambridge, England: Cambridge University Press, 1970.

Kramer, N. S. *History Begins at Sumer*. New York: W. W. Norton, 1965.

Krupp, E. C. *Echoes of the Ancient Skies: The Astronomy of Lost Civilizations*. New York: Harper & Row, 1983.

_____. *Beyond the Blue Horizon: Myths and Legends of the Sun, Moon, Stars, and Planets*. New York: HarperCollins, 1991.

Kulke, H. and D. Rothermund. *A History of India*. London: Routledge, 1990.

Macdonell, A. A. *A History of Sanskrit Literature*. London: Heinemann, 1900.

_____. *Vedic Mythology*. Delhi: Banarsidass, 1981.

Mallory, J. P. *In Search of the Indo-Europeans: Language, Archaeology and Myth*. New York: Thames and Hudson, 1991.

Marshack, A. *The Roots of Civilization*. New York: McGraw-Hill, 1972.

Michell, G. *The Hindu Temple*. Chicago, IL: University of Chicago Press, 1988.

Miller, J. *The Vedas: Harmony, Meditation and Fulfillment*. London: Rider, 1974.

_____. *The Vision of Cosmic Order in the Vedas*. London: Routledge & Kegan Paul, 1985.

Mitchiner, J. E. *Studies in the Indus Valley Inscriptions*. New Delhi: Oxford and IBH, 1978.

Monier-Williams, M. *Hinduism*. London: SPCK, 1894.

Müller, M. *India—What Can It Teach Us?* London: Longmans, Green and Co., 1883.

_____. *The Six Systems of Indian Philosophy*. New York: Longmans, Green & Co., 1916.

Nayak, B. U. and N. C. Ghosh, eds. *New Trends in Indian Art and Archaeology*. New Delhi: Aditya Prakashan, 1992. 2 vols.

Neugebauer, O. *The Exact Sciences in Antiquity*. New York: Harper & Row, 1962.

_____. *A History of Ancient Mathematical Astronomy*. Part 2. New York: Springer Verlàg, 1975.

O'Flaherty, W. Doniger. *The Rig Veda: An Anthology*. Harmondsworth, England: Penguin Books, 1981.

O'Malley, L. S. S., ed. *Modern India & The West: A Study of the Interactions of their Civilizations*. London: Oxford University Press, 1968.

Panikkar, R. *The Vedic Experience: Mantramanjari*. London: Darton. Longman & Todd, 1979.

Pargiter, F. E. *The Purana Text of the Dynasties of the Kali Age*. London: Oxford University Press, 1913.

_____. *Ancient Indian Historical Tradition*. London: Oxford University Press, 1922.

Piggott, S. *Prehistoric India*. Harmondsworth, England: Penguin Books, 1950.

Polanyi, M. *Personal Knowledge: Toward a Post-Critical Philosophy*. London: Routledge & Kegan Paul, 1973.

Radhakrishnan, S. *Indian Philosophy*. London: Allen & Unwin, 1951.

_____. *The Principal Upanisads*. London: Allen & Unwin; New York: Humanities Press, 1953.

Rajram, N. S. and David Frawley. *Vedic Aryans and the Origins of Civilization: A Literary and Scientific Perspective*. St. Hyacinthe, Canada: World Heritage Press, 1994.

Rao, S. R. *Dawn and Devolution of the Indus Civilization*. New Delhi: Aditya Prakashan, 1991.

_____. *Lothal and the Indus Civilization*. Bombay: Asia Publishing House, 1972.

Renfrew, C. *Archaeology & Language: The Puzzle of Indo-European Origins*. Cambridge, England: Cambridge University Press, 1987.

_____. *Before Civilization: The Radiocarbon Revolution and Prehistoric Europe*. New York: Alfred A. Knopf, 1973.

Rice, M. *Egypt's Making: The Origins of Ancient Egypt 5000-2000 B.C.* London: Routledge, 1991.

Russell, B. *Mysticism and Logic*. Garden City, NY: Doubleday/Anchor Books, n.d.

Santillana, de G. and Hertha von Dechend. *Hamlet's Mill: An Essay on Myth and the Frame of Time*. Boston, MA: Gambit, 1969.

Schrödinger, E. *What is Life?* New York: Macmillan, 1965.

Schwaller de Lubicz, R. A. *The Egyptian Miracle: An Introduction to the Wisdom of the Temple*. Rochester, VT: Inner Traditions International, 1985.

Schweitzer, A. *Civilization and Ethics*. London: Unwin Books, 1961.

Sethna, K. D. *The Problem of Aryan Origins*. New Delhi: Aditya Prakashan, 1992.

Singh, Fateh. *Sindhughati ki lipi mein brahmanon aur upanishadon ke pratik*. Jodhpur, India: Rajasthan Oriental Research Institute, 1969.

Smith, H. *Forgotten Truth: The Primordial Tradition*. New York: Harper Torchbooks, 1985.

_____. *Beyond the Post-Modern Mind*. Wheaton, IL: Quest Books, 1989.

Smith, V. A. *The Oxford History of India*. London: Oxford University Press, 1954.

Stutley, M. *Ancient Indian Magic and Folklore: An Introduction*. Boulder, CO: Great Eastern Book Co., 1980.

Swarup, G., A. K. Bag, and K. S. Shukla. *History of Oriental Astronomy*. Cambridge, England: Cambridge University Press, 1987.

Swarup, R. *The Word As Revelation: Names of Gods*. New Delhi: Impex India, 1980.

Talageri, S. G. *The Aryan Invasion Theory: A Reappraisal*. New Delhi: Aditya Prakshan, 1993.

Tarnas, R. *The Passion of the Western Mind*. New York: Harmony Books, 1991.

Thompson, W. I. *At the Edge of History*. New York: Harper Torchbooks, 1979.

Tilak, B. G. *The Orion, or Researches into the Antiquity of the Vedas*. Poona: Tilak Brothers, 1893.

Toynbee, A. *Civilization on Trial, and The World and the West*. New York: Meridian Books, 1958.

Tull, H. W. *The Vedic Origins of Karma: Cosmos as Man in Ancient Indian Myth and Ritual*. Albany, NY: SUNY Press, 1989.

Walsh, R. and D. H. Shapiro, ed. *Beyond Health and Normality*. New York: Van Nostrand Reinhold, 1983.

West, J. A. *Serpent in the Sky: The High Wisdom of Ancient Egypt*. Wheaton, IL: Quest Books, 1993.

Wolpert, S. *India*. Berkeley: University of California Press, 1991.

Woolley, C. L. *The Sumerians*. New York: W. W. Norton, 1965.

Yogananda, Paramahansa. *Autobiography of a Yogi*. Los Angeles: Self-Realization Fellowship, 1987.

Zimmer, H. *Philosophies of India*. Princeton, NJ: Princeton University Press, 1959.

_____. *Myths and Symbols in Indian Art and Civilization*. Princeton, NJ: Princeton University Press, 1972.

INDEX

D

E

F

H

J

K

Q

R

S

T

Z